Time to Write

A Powerful Writing Practice for Your Classroom

Beth Cregan

amba press

© 2023 Beth Cregan

All rights reserved. No part of this book may be reproduced or transmitted in any form or by any means, electronic or mechanical, including photocopying, recording or by any information storage and retrieval system, without prior permission in writing from the publisher.

Access the resources, templates and reproducibles from the book at www.writeawaywithme.com or www.ambapress.com.au/products/time-to-write

Published in 2023 by Amba Press, Melbourne, Australia.
www.ambapress.com.au

Previously published in 2022 by Hawker Brownlow Education.
This edition replaces all previous editions.

Editor: Lauren Mitchell
Designer: Matthew Harrod

ISBN: 9781923116214 (pbk)
ISBN: 9781923116221 (ebk)

A catalogue record for this book is available from the National Library of Australia.

This book is dedicated to my mother, Mary Cregan (1926–2003) – a passionate teacher, a lifelong learner and a generous supporter of all my plans and dreams.

Acknowledgements

Many of the ideas in this book were developed from my work at The Writer's Club. I am forever grateful to the many young writers who have shared their creativity and writing with me over the years. Your love of words and storytelling has inspired and encouraged me to find my voice and share my story. Thank you to Kara Saks, Ruby Hall, Choetso Cohen, Hudson Tarasiuk and Tate Spencer who kindly shared samples of their work in this book. I want to thank the many wonderful teachers and parents who trust and support my work at Write Away with Me. You have enabled me to follow my passion and chase my dreams and for that I am truly grateful.

Thank you to my partner Patrick Roseman and my daughters Molly and Neve who wholeheartedly share my belief in the power of creativity. Special thanks to Jeanene Booth, Noelene Bowen, Christine Paruit, Linnet Hunter, Emmanuelle Emile, Caroline Giles, Sandra Radja, Roseanne Cregan, Veronica Moran, Alicia Cohen, Mark Hamilton and Kath Walters, who read drafts of the book at various stages, provided feedback and gave me the courage to keep writing. Thank you also to my writing buddy Terri Connellan. Our dawn writing sessions kept me steady and accountable in uncertain times. Thank you to friends and family near and far who have expressed a real interest in my work and cheered me on during the years it has taken to complete this book. Thank you too to Lauren Mitchell, my editor at Hawker Brownlow Education, who worked diligently to transform my manuscript into this book.

I also want thank Dr Don Carter for taking the time to speak with me and generously sharing his research and knowledge of the Australian education system. And finally, thank you to author Natalie Goldberg, whose writings enriched and inspired both my writing and teaching practice.

Table of contents

Acknowledgements v

List of classroom activities ix

About the author xi

Introduction 1

Chapter 1: Reimagining creativity 15

Chapter 2: The power of a writing practice 39

Chapter 3: Writing routines and rituals 55

Chapter 4: A new way of workshopping 75

Chapter 5: The feedback loop 91

Chapter 6: Individualising your writing practice 109

Chapter 7: A community of writers 129

Classroom activities 153

Conclusion 289

References 293

Index 299

List of classroom activities

Personal writing: Mine your life for writing inspiration
1. List poetry 159
2. I remember 163
3. Wonderings.. 166
4. Mind maps 170
5. What do I need to know about you? 174
6. The story of my name 176
7. Journal writing 179
8. What if? 182
9. True, true, false... 186
10. Make up your mind... 189

Imaginative writing: Just imagine
1. Ink-blot writing... 195
2. Musical moods 198
3. Random words 202
4. It's all in the name 205
5. Object writing... 209

6. Flip the switch 214
7. Show, don't tell 217
8. Playing with poetry 220
9. Shape a story 223
10. What a place! 225

Reflective writing: Hello writer
1. Untangling the creative process 231
2. Working with images 238
3. Writing spaces 244
4. Writing symbols 248
5. Choosing a writing mentor 253
6. Letter-writing 257
7. Planning styles 260
8. Mind freeze 266
9. Creative flow 269
10. Writing inspiration 273

Editing games
1. Dumper 278
2. Scale up 281
3. The writer's hot seat 284
4. Turn on your senses 286

About the author

In 2010, Beth Cregan combined her passion for creativity with her love of writing and storytelling to launch her business Write Away with Me. Since then, her high-energy workshops have inspired hundreds of students to find their voice and discover their unique power as writers and storytellers. With her keen sense of fun and her passion for words and communication, Beth sees writing as a springboard for exploring self-expression and human connection. She presents her original writing workshops for schools and organisations in Australia and overseas, as well as professional development workshops for teachers. Beth lives in Melbourne and when she is not writing or teaching you'll find her rummaging in her permaculture garden, painting, reading or in a forest, hugging trees. You can read more at www.writeawaywithme.com.

Introduction

At the end of 2016, I was asked to present to a leadership team at a primary school in Melbourne. The school's curriculum focus was writing and I was to outline a strategy for supporting and extending both teachers and students. When briefing me over the phone, one of the school leaders listed a wide range of impressive writing programs and resources that staff had used over the previous five years. The school's National Assessment Program for Literacy and Numeracy (NAPLAN) results were solid.

'But here's the thing,' the principal said, 'we have kids who can write and we have good teachers, but our writing program still feels like this … slow burn. It's missing that …' He paused and searched for the right word. 'Energy!'

In that moment, the principal articulated what I see in the teaching of writing in our schools.

Every week, teachers share similar observations and stories with me. We have more knowledge and tools at our disposal than ever before, but our programs lack that spark, that creative energy. Schools have invested so much time and money into programs that develop essential writing skills, but many young writers – and teachers – feel disconnected, nervous or, worse, ambivalent about writing. So much emphasis is placed on collecting data and measuring students against a set of assessment criteria, only to discover that this information doesn't actually bring us any closer to understanding who our students are, what motivates them to write or how we can maximise their creative potential. No wonder teachers are frustrated.

Do you long to close your classroom doors, dial down the focus on assessment and just teach? Do you wonder if it's possible to slow the race to the finish line and nurture a lifelong love of language and writing? If you feel like you are part of an education system that's racing ahead without you, take heart and keep reading. Even in the face of our system's limitations, it's possible to offer your students an authentic writing experience. In the pages that follow, I'll share a practical framework and give you the tools you need to develop a daily writing practice in your classroom. This book is dedicated to educators of writers in Years 3–6. Your students stand at an exciting educational crossroad. A daily writing practice empowers them to step into their authority, find their voice and stride confidently towards writing independence. But this book also has a life beyond these primary years. The philosophy, teachings, writing exercises and call to harness your creative potential connects with writers of all ages.

Finding true north

In our eagerness to control the process (and the outcomes) we have lost our sense of direction, our true north. We have forgotten that writing is first and foremost, a creative act of self-expression. And if we're totally honest, that's the part that makes us nervous, isn't it? Creativity is tricky to capture, let alone define and evaluate. It has a reputation for being unpredictable, unreliable, mysterious and downright messy. To complicate matters further, each of us enters the teaching profession tangled up in a net of stories (both real and imagined) about our own creative potential.

Rather than sit with the uncomfortable notion that creativity is subjective and open to personal experience, our education systems attempt to control the process in the best way they know how: rules. Spelling, grammar, punctuation, vocabulary and formulaic structures all help teachers tame the writing process. Even our language has changed. *Stories* are *narratives*. *Personal writing* is a now a *recount*. *Genres* have become *text types*, each with their own set of rules and requirements. We focus less on creative self-expression and more on assessment criteria and student performance. But when we split creativity and writing skills down the middle, writing quickly becomes a linear process.

We often expect our students to knuckle down and produce a piece of writing in a single sitting. Donald H Graves (1985), commonly known as the father of process writing, refers to this as the *one-shot approach*. It is possible to produce a good piece of writing under these conditions, but it doesn't set writers (or teachers) up for long-term success in the real world.

Distilling writing down to a list of learning objectives, skills, tasks and assessment criteria may enable schools to wield control, but it deprives writers of this one simple truth: writing touches the wild, uncensored voice inside each of us. Writing nails down feelings and wrestles thoughts to the ground. It's an active, energetic exchange. When we split creativity and writing skills down the middle, we risk missing the very reason we write: to communicate, to connect, to belong, to find language that helps us make sense of ourselves and our world. We risk bypassing the heart and soul of writing – and our students miss the chance to discover their unique expression of creativity.

Your writing practice is a doorway, a portal to creative thinking and self-expression. It is an active training ground where each day students harness their creativity and put it to work, mastering skills and developing their creative processes in their own way. This not only improves writing skills in the here and now; it also gives your students an opportunity to develop kinship with writing that lasts a lifetime. In *The Element: How Finding Your Passion Changes Everything*,

Ken Robinson (2009) says, 'The fact is that given the challenges we face, education doesn't need to be reformed – it needs to be transformed' (p. 238). Your classroom writing practice is part of that transformation.

If only I had time

If only I had time is a phrase I often hear when teachers talk about their writing programs. We begin our teaching careers motivated by the impact we want to have on the lives of our students, but too often the battle against time leaves us feeling overwhelmed and disillusioned.

Having presented writing workshops in schools for more than a decade now, I'm familiar with the sight of teachers warding off their fierce to-do lists. But just as one task is brought under control, another rears its ugly head. It's a hopeless quest and one most teachers understand only too well. As administrative and curriculum demands increase, teachers struggle to stay ahead of the game.

Do you remember the media hype of the eighties (and regularly since) that predicted computers and robots would replace teachers? Advances in technology have certainly changed the face of education, but they haven't lightened the load of the average teacher. Quite the opposite, in fact. School curriculums are more sophisticated than ever before. So too are pedagogy and teaching practices. Standardised testing tightens the pressure valve even further. And now, thanks to the internet, teachers never officially log off – they are readily accessible to students, parents and colleagues around the clock. We live in a culture that demands increasing levels of productivity and it's hard not to fall into the trap of speeding up our days. We're so accustomed to having our time over-scheduled and tightly managed that we feel guilty – or worse, substandard – if we grant ourselves permission to slow down. Sadly, our writing programs have fallen victim to this same frantic pace. This collective lack of time impacts not only the way we teach writing, but also the way our students experience the writing process.

Teaching to the test

When it comes to understanding why teachers and students feel disconnected or plain ambivalent about writing, let's deal with the elephant in the room.

NAPLAN is an annual assessment of Australian students in Years 3, 5, 7 and 9. Students are assessed in numeracy, reading, writing, language and literacy every May and school results are publicly available on the My School website in September of the same year. Introduced in 2008, NAPLAN heralded the first national set of literacy and numeracy benchmarks in Australia, but its arrival on the educational landscape was not without considerable controversy. Australian educators and school communities raised valid concerns about how NAPLAN data would be used and the impact this would have on students and teaching practices. Some of these fears have now been realised.

Both primary and secondary teachers speak candidly about the way NAPLAN testing has changed the way they teach writing, and this sentiment has been supported by a report commissioned by the Australian Primary Principals Association (APPA) in 2013. This independently conducted survey of primary school principals found the following:

> *Teachers, despite knowing that they should not be teaching to the tests, do alter the regular curriculum delivery to 'train' the students in the peculiarities of the tests. Much time is given over even in the previous year to NAPLAN, to enable the students to have the best opportunity to demonstrate their skills and knowledge.*
> (APPA, 2013, p. 15)

It's easy to appreciate why teachers feel a growing pressure to teach to the test. NAPLAN data plays a broad role in assisting governments and school communities to understand trends and allocate resources, but in the real world, NAPLAN results and rankings secure school enrolments and funding, both of which determine a school's future.

This means teachers are under more pressure than ever before to get results – and this can come at the expense of child-centred learning.

Teaching to the test dials down both student engagement and the joy of writing, but it undoubtedly amps up stress levels. The same report cited many examples of the negative impact NAPLAN testing has on students' self-esteem and levels of anxiety in our classrooms (APPA, 2013). Consequently, teachers find themselves juggling anxious parents, overwhelmed students and the high expectations of school leadership teams, all of which drain their precious time and energy.

The five-month delay in receiving test results is another criticism. One teacher I've worked with summed it up perfectly when she said, 'I wouldn't mind spending all this time on assessment if it actually helped me teach my students to write.' Educators agree that standardised testing has a place in education, just not in the driver's seat, not steering the course.

Untangling the writing process from test results

I'm cognisant too of the insidious way NAPLAN colours our feelings and beliefs about writing and the residue it leaves in its wake. Our life experiences trigger specific conscious and unconscious responses in our minds and bodies. We naturally pair experiences with specific beliefs, feelings and physical responses. I leave my yin yoga class feeling calm and relaxed. Now, because this experience has been reinforced many times over, my body starts to relax as soon as I enter the room. In the same way, our experience of NAPLAN triggers a range of conscious and unconscious responses. It's not uncommon for teachers to fuse their personal and professional credibility with the teaching of writing and test results. I've seen teachers cheer with relief on the day test results hit schools. I've also supported teachers who are disappointed or in tears.

If NAPLAN incites feelings of anxiety, frustration, resentment or anger, it's natural to pair these responses with the teaching of writing. Your students likely experience a similar emotional progression.

Thankfully, the pairing of thoughts and beliefs also works in the opposite direction. Stop for a minute and think about how you want to feel about teaching writing. How do you want the students in your class to feel about writing? What sorts of experiences and activities will lead you in this direction? Instead of feeling powerless in the face of standardised testing, it's time to take control. It's time to make space for a new conversation.

You may not have full control over the available time in each day, but you *can* make decisions about how you invest your time and energy to get maximum results. Let's review what we have on the table so far:

- Creativity is a messy concept to untangle and understand, both in the classroom and in our heads.
- Our curriculum is sophisticated and complex. We're juggling more moving parts than ever before and it can feel like there are simply not enough hours in a day to meet our professional responsibilities and obligations.
- Our current education system places a strong emphasis on assessment and standardised testing which directly impacts the time we have available and way we teach writing.
- Teachers are under pressure to get results often at the expense of individualised creative teaching practices.

Our daily schedules aren't always negotiable. As much as we would like to, we can't simply close the doors and do it our way. To stay sane, most teachers I know have learnt to split how they would like to teach (their ideal) with what's realistically possible in the time they have available. But what if you didn't have to make a choice? What if you could bridge the gap between your real and your ideal worlds? Developing a daily writing practice with your students is that bridge.

A daily writing practice

A daily writing practice is an opportunity for your students to meet writing face to face, without all the unnecessary noise and baggage. In the pages that follow I'll share a powerful framework designed to maximise the creative potential of students in the middle to upper primary years. Imagine setting aside as little as fifteen minutes a day for your students to write, workshop, collaborate and explore the craft of writing. No rankings. No formal testing. Instead of marking students against set criteria, I will teach you how to observe and analyse what's happening in your classroom while your students are writing. You'll gather valuable data about the whole child, not just data relating to their literacy or cognitive skills. The creative thinking and writing skills you develop during this time have a wider application beyond your literacy program. I have developed a collection of quick writing prompts, activities and resources to get you started. These open-ended exercises invite your young writers to explore their natural storytelling ability in their own way. When you allow your students to take ownership of their writing and creativity, engagement levels soar. Better still, when it comes to developing a daily writing practice, time constraints are your biggest ally. Short, frequent writing sprints provide a condensed experience of the writing process. You don't always need wide expanses of time for creativity to flourish. The truth is that creativity likes a leash. Creativity craves structure and boundaries.

A daily writing practice works seamlessly alongside whatever literacy program you are currently using in your school. You don't need to throw out what you have and start again. And you don't need any fancy resources or hours of training to introduce a writing practice to your classroom. Your students are by far your most valuable resource. A class set of notebooks, pencils and this book are all you'll need to get started. Take the practical strategies presented in this book and shape them to suit your students. One of the unexpected benefits of a writing practice is the opportunity it provides to develop a deep trust and rapport with your students. As you loosen the reins and explore the creative process together, you'll start to teach writing from a place of intuition and confidence.

Using this book

It has become my personal quest to show both teachers and students that our education system sells writing short. Words and writing are powerful beyond measure. This book is a work of action research. I call on my own experiences as a writer and teacher, underpinned by current research in the fields of creativity, writing and education, and include personal stories and examples to ground concepts in the practical world of the classroom. In reading this book you will come to understand the essential elements of a daily writing practice and gain a clear action plan for implementation as well as a wealth of tried-and-true activities to put into action.

In the pages that follow I'll guide you through the process of developing a writing practice that you can tailor to your students, and at the end of each chapter you'll find:

- 'Power points' – a brief, bulleted summary of the main points of the chapter
- 'Pause and reflect' – thinking points for journalling and collegial discussion
- 'Your action plan' – a sequential task designed to move you through the process of implementing a writing practice.

Now let's take a helicopter view of what each chapter has in store for you.

Chapter 1: Reimagining creativity

While we experience creativity differently, research shows us that the creative process isn't quite as mysterious or as unpredictable as we might imagine. In Chapter 1 we'll untangle our beliefs and bust some commonly held myths about creativity. We'll also explore the factors that influence the development of creativity in your classroom.

Chapter 2: The power of a writing practice

In Chapter 2 you'll discover that a classroom writing practice combines three processes – discovery writing, workshopping and response – underpinned by three essential principals. I'll step you through the overarching framework for developing a writing practice in your classroom.

Chapter 3: Writing routines and rituals

You can't get more hours in a day, but armed with the right strategies you can use the time you have to maximise the creative potential of your students. In this chapter I'll offer practical ways to organise your writing practice as well as show you how writers use routines and rituals to develop the habit of writing and assist creative flow.

Chapter 4: A new way of workshopping

All three streams of your literacy program – reading, writing and oral language – combine in the magic of workshopping. Workshopping connects writers to their audience, which is often the missing link in our writing programs. In Chapter 4 I'll break down the basics of workshopping and show you how to amplify the potential of this powerful teaching tool.

Chapter 5: The feedback loop

Feedback is critical to the development of writing skills. In this chapter I'll share three feedback loops to keep your writing practice in balance: program planning and evaluation, teacher–student observational records and self-regulated assessment. This chapter also showcases a range of assessment tools teachers can use to monitor and support their writers and their writing practice.

Chapter 6: Individualising your writing practice

In Chapter 6 we explore the factors that affect writing achievement. I'll introduce a reflective goal-setting process that teachers can use to support all students – be they talented writers, reluctant participants, English language learners or students with special needs. Combined with formal assessment, this is a powerful tool for understanding the skills, mindsets, behaviours and motivations of your writers.

Chapter 7: A community of writers

Your classroom writing community is a dynamic force that enhances relationships and connects writers to wider networks to support their skill development. Chapter 7 guides you through the process of developing an active and engaged community of writers across three complementary channels: classroom, school and wider writing communities.

Classroom activities

This is where the magic begins. In this section, you'll find a wide range of writing activities and prompts divided into three categories: personal, imaginative and reflective writing. These exercises support students to use writing to clarify thinking, tell stories and reflect on their understanding and experience of the creative process. I've developed these activities over the last twenty years in real classrooms with real students, and each features an instructional plan as well as tips and opportunities for extension. I've also included some writing samples to inspire you and give you a taste of what to expect.

Let's begin

You may have already developed a writing practice in your classroom and be looking for inspiration, or the concepts in this book may be totally new to you. You may feel perfectly comfortable teaching writing, or you may be overwhelmed and confused. You may enjoy writing, or it may be your least favourite activity. Whatever the case, this book can be used successfully to support both you and your students. All you need is an open mind and a willingness to follow your curiosity.

Power points

- A writing practice is a framework underpinned by research and harnesses creative energy in a time-efficient way to complement any existing writing program.
- Though we tend to think of creativity as difficult to manage, particularly in an education system that emphasises assessment and standardised testing, a daily writing practice kickstarts imaginative thinking and provides your students with tools and strategies for generating creative ideas. This practice has far-reaching impacts for your students.
- Built into your writing practice, the systems for collecting meaningful data allow you to maximise the creative potential of the students in your classroom and track their growth as writers.
- You don't need hours of time or any special resources to introduce a writing practice – just the practical strategies, prompts and activities in this book, a class set of notebooks and pencils, and your own curiosity.

Pause and reflect

- What inspired you to become a teacher? All of us have one poignant memory of a childhood teacher we loved. A teacher who believed in us and took time to nurture our interests and talents. A teacher who changed the way we saw the world. Write about your childhood teachers. Describe your favourite teacher and the way this teacher made you feel.

- Can you recognise any feeling or beliefs that you have unconsciously paired with the writing process? What stories are circling in your head? Do they help or hinder the way you teach writing?
- How would you plan your day and interact with your students in an ideal teaching world? Is there a way of bringing some of your ideals to life in the real world?
- Make a list of the many ways time or other constraints impact the way you teach writing. Suspend judgement. Get curious instead. What would you like to do differently?

Your action plan

Set up your action research journal

Through journalling I've come to know the benefits of committing ideas to paper. Your action research journal is a place to collect your questions and ideas as you progress through this book and begin to introduce a writing practice in your classroom.

Take a moment now to find an empty notebook to use for this purpose. Any notebook will do. When I present writing workshops for teachers, I give them the same advice I give my students: don't worry about buying a fancy notebook. A fancy notebook carries the expectation that its pages will be filled with perfect ideas and impeccable handwriting. Before you know it, you're censoring your writing. You don't want that! You want your journal to be a space where you can write without constraint. There is no right or wrong method. Feel free to write, sketch, build mind maps, use colour – collect your ideas in whatever way makes sense to you. You can also use a digital method if you prefer.

At the time of writing, I'm teaching an after-school class with a group of students at a school in Melbourne. At the end of each session the supervising teacher and I excitedly swap our insights about the students, their shared writing and the exciting learning that is taking place. This collegiate collaborative approach is a breath of fresh air. Consider pairing up with other teachers and read this book together; you can workshop your findings, share your questions and troubleshoot any issues. It makes the journey much sweeter, especially as I know that once your students start daily writing you'll want to talk about the changes you see happening around you. Whether you're working with a partner or going it alone, this journal gives you the chance to reflect and find language to cement your new understandings.

This action research journal also becomes your own writing practice – a safe space to record your experience of teaching and writing. It will also serve as a road map for those times when you lose your way. At the end of each chapter you will find a series of prompts that you can use as a starting point. Remember to jot down your own questions too. Questions have an uncanny knack of hunting down answers.

Access the resources, templates and reproducibles from the book at www.writeawaywithme.com

Chapter 1
Reimagining creativity

5B has invited me to present a writing workshop. The students have their notebooks and pens ready. A line of faces stare at me, waiting for their first writing prompt. I hold up a bright-pink, plastic lunchbox.

'Let's play "The perhaps game",' I say. 'Perhaps this lunchbox …' I stop and do that thing teachers do with their eyes and hands to invite students to complete the sentence.

'Perhaps this lunchbox … could come to life?' a boy at the front says, his voice rising up into a question, just in case he's missed the mark entirely.

I smile and nod.

'Perhaps there's something weird inside it, moving around,' another boy offers.

'Perhaps the lunchbox has been stolen,' a girl at the back calls out.

'Perhaps someone lost it.'

'Or found it!'

'Perhaps it belongs to someone famous.'

'Perhaps this lunchbox is Instagram famous!'

There's a ripple of laughter.

'Perhaps the lunchbox is a portal into another dimension.'

'Perhaps it is another dimension.'

'You mean, like another world? Planet Lunchbox? That's cool!' his classmate laughs.

There's a distinct shift of energy in the room. We're warming up and creative ideas flow thick and fast. Instead of a sea of faces, now all I see are hands waving madly before my eyes. One student who had his head on the table when we started is now sitting up and paying attention. Building ideas is captivating. It focuses our physical, mental and sensory channels all at once. Humans are hardwired to think like this. Our minds and imaginations separate us from every other species on earth.

I tell the class that I'm going to set a timer for five minutes.

'There is no right or wrong,' I say. 'You are still playing with ideas, but this time you are capturing an idea on paper. There's no pressure to wrangle this idea into a complete story. Just start with one scene and see what happens. You can start anywhere. You can write anything.'

Then we write. When the timer goes off, some students volunteer to read their writing to the class. Their scenes are alive with imagery and characters and interesting plots.

'Can we keep going with our stories?' the students ask.

Creative flow is mesmerising. There's nothing more exciting than a group of students who want to keep writing. Their class teacher is excited too. One of her reluctant writers (the boy with his head down on the table at the beginning of the workshop) is writing furiously. This alone feels like a miracle. Over the course of the next hour, students write for short bursts of time and stop at intervals to share their writing.

'I wish we could do this sort of thing in our classrooms,' the teacher says as we pack up afterwards.

'What's stopping you?' I ask.

'Time,' she sighs. 'We just never have enough time.'

And just like that, the spell is broken.

Creativity needs a new story

The word *create*, the root of which comes from the Latin *creare* – meaning to 'bring into being' (Macquarie Dictionary Publishers, n.d.) – feels full of inspiring possibilities, doesn't it? A lump of clay. A blank page. A problem to solve. But for the average classroom teacher grappling with the complexities of creativity, the question usually isn't 'What will we make today?' Rather, it's 'How on earth will we make time for this?'

I recently had the opportunity to speak with Don Carter, education writer, researcher and senior lecturer (teacher education) at the University of Technology Sydney, about the place of creativity in our literacy programs. Carter said,

> *The problem is that there are currently two systems of education in place in Australia. There is the implementation of the authorised curriculum which teachers are trained and paid to do but at the same time there is a system of standardised testing which sucks time and resources and diverts attention away from the key aims of education. (personal communication, July 31, 2020)*

No wonder teachers are exhausted at the end of the day! It's demanding enough, meeting the diverse needs of your students, without juggling two conflicting systems: one designed to develop and nurture your students' love of reading and writing, and the other founded on competitive academic achievement, rankings and benchmarks.

This duel between the opposing forces of creativity and conformity is not limited to schools or literacy programs. It reverberates across all sectors of our community. We face a daily storm of unprecedented global challenges. (As I write this chapter, the world is confronting a pandemic.) Now more than ever, the world is relying on creatives and creative industries to lead us forward, to equip us for a world that is changing faster than we can reimagine it. A world that constantly requires new services, products, concepts, ideas, understandings and technological advancements.

There was a time in the nineties when this narrative made teachers stand up and pay attention. Many of our students would work in industries that had not yet been developed, but some skills, we were told, would stand the test of time. In order to embrace this brave new world, our students needed to be effective communicators, risk-takers, innovators, and imaginative and original thinkers. This reality held great promise for educational reform. Now, like many teachers, when I hear governments talk about the value of creativity I know that, by and large, they are talking about creativity as an economic commodity with productive, measurable outcomes.

The problem with this definition of creativity is that it's just so limiting. Creativity isn't only an economic currency in the hands of a band of innovators, inventors and technological geniuses. Creativity is a dynamic, life-enhancing force available to each and every one of us. Giving your students the opportunity to understand and harness their creativity will not only make them better writers; it also has the power to change the trajectory of both your and your students' lives.

Busting some myths about creativity

Is it only the constraints of our current system that keep creativity out of reach in our classrooms? If standardised testing was abolished today, would the pressure teachers feel to choose between creativity and academic achievement simply vanish? Or, instead of butting up against the system, would we find ourselves wrestling instead with our own internal dialogue about the true value of creativity?

Early in my secondary education it became clear that school subjects were sorted into two major camps (humanities and maths/science) and I was expected to swear allegiance to one group or another. I am not quite sure when the deal was struck, but as time went on, maths and science became distant landscapes on my educational horizon. Each of us holds beliefs, stories and very real experiences that have shaped (and continue to shape) our creativity. These same beliefs, stories and experiences also impact our teaching practice.

Pause for a minute and think about the questions that rise to the surface when you hold creativity up to the light. Is everyone creative? Can creativity even be taught? Managed? Measured? Is creativity essential to learning? Is it worth my time and effort? These are valid (and often uncomfortable) questions and even teachers who fly the creativity flag will experience frustration, doubt and uncertainty. But what if I told you that your questions and doubts are no longer a liability?

In 2019 I was privileged to attend a retreat in Ireland with world-renowned poet David Whyte. On a page of my notebook I captured his words: 'The marvellous thing about a good question is that it shapes our identity as much by the asking as it does by the answering.' Developing a daily writing practice sets you on a journey of discovery where your bank of questions are your most valuable resource. So instead of rolling up your tangled and messy beliefs about creativity and hiding them in a junk drawer, let's lay them on the table and unravel some of the myths and misconceptions that trip us up.

Myth #1: Not everyone is creative

Creativity is often viewed through the narrow lens of artistic talent or as cognitive intelligence linked to science, technology and innovation. For many of us who don't identify with either camp, the space between these two extremes is an undiscovered wasteland where creativity becomes a passive spectator sport: we cheer on the creative talents of others, but fail to ever realise our own underlying creative potential. And simply stating that everyone is creative isn't enough to inspire the non-believers to rethink their position.

Let's start by broadening our understanding of creativity to make it more inclusive. British speaker, author and educationalist Ken Robinson (2011) defines creativity as a basic process made of three interconnected ideas:

> ... imagination, *which is the process of bringing things to mind that are not present to our senses;* creativity, *which is the process of developing original ideas that have value; and* innovation, *which is the process of putting new ideas into practice.* (emphasis in original, pp. 2–3)

Every time we solve a problem, test a theory or make something new, we engage our imagination, connect ideas and create something that wasn't there before. Creativity isn't limited to certain fields either, according to the National Advisory Committee on Creative and Cultural Education (NACCCE; 1999):

> *Creativity is possible in all areas of human activity, including the arts, sciences, at work [sic] at play and in all other areas of daily life. All people have creative abilities, and we all have them differently.* (p. 6)

This realisation takes time to settle. After all, when we compare ourselves to colleagues, friends, family and students, it's clear that some of us are more 'creative' than others. Let's tackle that next.

In 'Beyond big and little', Kaufman and Beghetto (2009) articulate four different levels – mini-c, little-c, Pro-c and Big-C – in their Four C Model of Creativity. Mini-c creativity encompasses ideas and outcomes that may not be original but are new and personally meaningful to the creator. A good example of mini-c creativity is found in my current online class. We are exploring poetry, so each week I introduce new poems and poetic structures. We then innovate on these given structures to play with imagery, rhythm and pace. The poems aren't totally original, because we have 'borrowed' the structure, but they are new and meaningful to the author. This mini-c process reduces the creative load and allows students time to analyse techniques and develop concepts, voice and style. It builds the writing skills they need to fly solo. Little-c steps creativity up a notch because here the creator is developing original ideas that are considered useful and valuable to others. If we continue with our poetry example, after we have a knowledge of classic poetic structures, writers can use what they have learnt to write original poems that reflect their unique experience of the world. The next level is Pro-c creativity, which is the result of rigorous practice and training where the creator has accumulated some level of expertise and skills that support a body of knowledge. They have mastered a range of creative thinking tools and techniques. Pro-c creatives often make a living from their creative thinking skills. Finally, Big-C creativity results in a body of work that makes a significant ongoing contribution to the growth of our society. Interestingly, creativity at any level relies on individuals practising their creative thinking skills (Kaufman & Beghetto, 2009).

When we think about creativity, many of us focus on only one end of this continuum: the the Pro-c and Big-C masters. However, Kaufman and Beghetto's (2009) model gives voice to the everyday nature of creative thinking. It recognises all those useful insights and decisions we make along the way.

We can all locate ourselves somewhere on this creative thinking continuum. You may not be another Da Vinci or Picasso (yet), but every day, thanks to the complex workings of your human brain, you are accessing your imagination and practising a range of creative thinking skills that impact your life and the lives of those around you.

Myth #2: Creativity is an unpredictable, random process that is difficult to control

For all its whimsy and magic, creativity is firmly rooted in science. In 1926, psychologist and educationalist Graham Wallas outlined his theory of creativity, positing that creativity passes through four distinct and sequential stages: preparation, incubation, illumination and verification. During the preparation stage we activate our imagination and sensory perception and visualise the way forward. This helps us plan and gather the materials and information we need to get started. During the incubation stage our unconscious mind blends our knowledge and personal experience. We soak up sensory and intuitive information, recognise patterns and connect ideas. Much of the action at this stage is flying under the radar of conscious thought and often takes place while we are completing other tasks, but this critical time allows our brain to synthesise the data we have collected so far and make vital links. A lightbulb is often used to symbolise the illumination stage because during this stage we are metaphorically 'switched on', actively organising and structuring ideas into a cohesive whole. If the project is going to plan, we feel a thrust of momentum compelling us forward. We may become so absorbed in the process that we lose sense of time and space. And finally, as the process is coming to an end, we move into the verification stage. This is where we experience a sense of letting go, either literally by sharing the work with an audience or by achieving another form of closure that ends the cycle.

We often limit creativity to the confines of right-brain thinking, but the creative process has been shown to be 'a dynamic interplay of many different brain regions, emotions, and our unconscious and conscious processing systems' (Gregoire & Kaufman, 2016, par. 11). To fully access your creativity, you need both imagination and a heightened sensory perception (right brain) as well as a range of executive functioning skills (left brain).

While Wallas's (1926) theory of creativity mirrors the experience of artists and innovators alike, it's also evident in the regular tasks we complete each day – from solving a problem at work to preparing a meal. Although the creative process isn't always orderly or linear, each of us cycles through the stages of creativity many times over the course of an ordinary day. Armed with this knowledge, teachers and students can come to understand their strengths and weaknesses across the entire creative process. It's also possible for teachers to provide feedback and support students along the journey, rather than only assessing the finished product. This is particularly pertinent because feedback that informs and guides students through the writing process inspires them to keep writing (Brookfield, 2015).

Our individual experience of creativity is unique. However, if we consider Wallas's (1926) work, the creative process isn't as mysterious or unpredictable as we might imagine. Wallas's theory is a portal into the human mind and a guide for understanding and maximising our creative potential. Instead of resigning ourselves to being held captive by an unknowable, unmanageable creative muse, this gives us an expansive language for navigating and regulating the process from start to finish.

Myth #3: Only creative teachers can teach creativity

This misconception stops many teachers in their tracks, especially those who harbour limiting beliefs about their own inherent creativity. But we can call on Bob Jeffrey and Anna Craft (2004) to help clarify and reframe this myth. Citing the important distinction made in the 1999 NACCCE Report between teaching creatively and teaching for creativity, they note that teaching creatively is about 'using imaginative approaches that make learning more interesting and effective' (NACCCE, 1999, p.89, as cited in Jeffrey & Craft, 2004, p. 77). In contrast, Jeffrey and Craft (2004) continue, teaching for creativity represents 'forms of teaching that are intended to develop young peoples [sic] own creative thinking or behaviour' (p. 77).

Although it is widely accepted that creative teaching practices are more likely to engage learners and foster creativity in students, a teacher's natural creative quotient is not the determining factor when it comes to their ability to develop creativity in their classrooms (Fryer, 1996). Jeffrey and Craft (2004) found that teachers who only see creativity as centring on divergent thinking or coming up with original ideas are less likely to nurture their students' creative capabilities in the classroom than teachers who hold a more comprehensive understanding of creative thought and its broader traits and benefits. Those teachers who understand and believe that creativity is a dynamic skill that can be developed in all students will work towards that intention.

A deep understanding of pedagogy and a strong belief in the inherent value of creativity is critical when it comes to developing creativity in our classrooms. Moreover, students model themselves on their teacher's approach (Jeffrey & Craft, 2004). If we want our students to take risks and experiment, which is essential for creativity, we need to model this same behaviour in our actions and language. We need to be prepared to make mistakes and share our experience of creativity – our fears, vulnerabilities and breakthroughs.

In *Living With a Creative Mind*, Jeff Crabtree and Julie Crabtree (2011) share a modified version of Wallas's (1926) theory of creativity. Their model centres on the stages of perception, discovery and production and lists the factors that both enhance and block creativity at each stage (Crabtree & Crabtree, 2011). In considering my own experience and both approaches to understanding the creative process, I have established three conditions that consistently promote creativity in our classrooms:

1. An open and accepting environment that is free of judgement and encourages exploration, experimentation and risk-taking.
2. Structured time and space (both physical and mental) to flow through the creative stages.
3. A classroom environment that fosters a growth mindset and supports students' ownership and agency over their learning.

The ability to replicate these conditions in your classroom is not dependent on your level of creative talent but rather your values, beliefs and knowledge of creativity.

To teachers who may feel unsure of their next step, let Eric Maisel's (2000) advice to creatives be your new manifesto:

> *What's required are certain changes: that you begin to think of yourself as creative, that you use your imagination and your mind more, that you become freer*

*but also more disciplined, that you approach the world
with greater passion and more curiosity. (p. 1)*

Teachers don't need to be natural designers or writers or artists to foster creativity in their classrooms. They do, however, need to be curious, open to new ideas and practices, eager to learn and willing to adapt their teaching practice to support their students. A teacher's understanding of creativity, their attitudes and their commitment to a growth mindset are deciding factors when it comes to developing creativity in their classroom.

Myth #4: Differentiation and creative freedom are not possible in the time I have available

Teachers are under pressure to get results. They need time-saving ways to teach a wide range of complex skills and knowledge. Enter: tools such as writing templates, formulas and graphic organisers which prune and shape creativity into an orderly measurable process. But often these tools are counterproductive and provide a false sense of security in terms of time management. When we provide the same style of graphic organiser every time, we inadvertently model the idea that there is one correct path through the writing process. This approach doesn't consider that your students have different personality types, traits and natural tendencies. Creativity isn't one size fits all. Not all templates and formulas match every student.

Brave teachers embrace the ambiguities of creativity and acknowledge that there are many ways to approach creative tasks. They introduce a range of tools and methods over time and encourage their students to try them on for size and analyse which tools and systems work best for them. When students have some ownership, they are more likely to achieve higher levels of independence and engagement, both of which significantly improve productivity and time management.

Another assumption lurking here is that creativity needs hours of uninterrupted time. Allowing time for your students to experience high levels of focus and flow is important, but ironically the opposite is also true. Creativity loves a leash and, as we'll explore in the coming chapters, thrives in tight spaces; time constraints can be your greatest ally when it comes to developing creative thinking skills in your classroom. This is confirmed by the work of Theresa Dirndorfer Anderson (2014), who created the 4P model – consisting of plan, play, pressure and pause – to represent four factors that encourage creative ideas to take flight. Creative pressure in the form of soft deadlines can 'compel us to stop thinking too much and to just go with our heart, gut feeling or an intuitive judgement of what is good enough' (Anderson, 2014, p. 6). I particularly like Anderson's use of the words *good enough*. It challenges the perfectionist in me. It reminds us that creativity is a process of developing ideas and that good enough ideas serve as a valuable starting point. Time and time again in my teaching I have seen how soft deadlines, such as short writing sprints, focus the mind and force ideas to collide. In Chapter 2 I'll unpack the elements of a daily writing practice, but rest assured, in as little as fifteen minutes a day, you can use the 4P principles to develop your students' creativity.

A manifesto for creativity

When two distinct systems are, as Don Carter suggests (see page 17), pitted against each other, teachers get caught in the crossfire. The constant demands of the school day make it increasingly hard for them to keep the faith, let alone advocate on creativity's behalf. Who has the time or energy to consider a radical change in direction anyway? But the thing is, we don't need a new manifesto or a radical change of policy to move creativity into position at the head of our classrooms and literacy programs. Sometimes, to move forward, history first takes you back.

If we want to trace the Australian Curriculum back to its original aims and rediscover its essential spirit, we only need to return to the 2008 Melbourne Declaration on Educational Goals for Young Australians (Ministerial Council on Education, Employment, Training and Youth Affairs). This visionary document, signed by every Australian minister for education, chartered the key aims and ideals of Australian education. It was to become the foundation stone for the Australian Curriculum, which followed in 2010.

The Melbourne Declaration was updated to become the Alice Springs (Mparntwe) Education Declaration in 2019 (Education Services Australia). The preamble sets out one of the fundamental beliefs that motivates teachers to keep the faith despite the many challenges they face: 'Education has the power to transform lives. It supports young people to realise their potential' (Education Services Australia, 2019 p. 2).

Goals of Australian education

The Alice Springs (Mparntwe) Education Declaration sets out two interconnected goals for Australian education:

> *Goal 1: The Australian education system promotes excellence and equity*
>
> *Goal 2: All young Australians become:*
> - *confident and creative individuals*
> - *successful lifelong learners*
> - *active and informed members of the community.*
> *(Education Services Australia, 2019, p. 4)*

These two foundational goals underpin the three-dimensional structure of the Australian Curriculum, which comprises of eight key learning areas, seven general capabilities and three cross-curriculum priorities. The seven general capabilities develop the skills, knowledge and behaviours students need to be successful confident and creative learners. These general capabilities are not isolated skills or subjects; they are woven into the fabric of the key learning areas.

Surprisingly, many teachers have never heard of the Alice Springs (Mparntwe) Education Declaration; however, it deserves a place on every teacher's desk because it clearly maps out the founding principles that underpin our national curriculum and provides teachers with both the confirmation and the conviction they need to reinstate creativity to its rightful place in our classrooms.

If we consider a daily writing practice alongside the goals of the Alice Springs (Mparntwe) Education Declaration, it becomes clear that this classroom practice wholeheartedly supports your students on their journey to become successful lifelong learners, confident and creative individuals, and active and informed citizens.

Confident and creative

The Alice Springs (Mparntwe) Education Declaration recognises the individual needs of young Australians and strongly promotes personal learning: 'Schools need to provide opportunities to enable students to explore and build on their individual abilities, interests, and experiences' (Education Services Australia, 2019, p. 5). This goal is also central to your writing practice. The daily writing opportunities and related experiences encourage your students to understand and develop their creative processes. Their writing confidence develops from actively engaging with words and writing over and over again, all the while learning to understand their individual traits, tendencies and learning preferences.

Successful lifelong learners

Both your writing practice and the Alice Springs (Mparntwe) Education Declaration highlight the importance of fostering relationships and promoting a strong sense of belonging within schools. Comparison and competition break down the connective tissue of relationships, while high-quality, positive relationships nurture a sense of connection and create optimal conditions for learning. Writing in community not only builds literacy skills, but also promotes personal values such as strength of character, initiative, intuition, self-awareness, empathy, active listening and responsibility. These important skills prepare your students for life in and out of the classroom, now and into the future.

Active and informed

In the Alice Springs (Mparntwe) Education Declaration, the Australian government has made a public commitment to actively pursue and maintain strong partnerships between families, schools and the wider community (Education Services Australia, 2019). Your writing practice is a practical vehicle for taking the authentic craft of writing into family homes and the wider school community, as well as seeking out the wisdom and experience of the industry leaders by tapping into the global literary community (more about this in Chapter 7). Your writing practice is an active interface where the craft of writing can be processed, shared and consumed by all stakeholders, teachers, students, parents, authors and professional writers. Once writing bursts out of textbooks and assessment, it takes on new meaning in our students' lives.

A definition of creativity

In the Australian Curriculum's general capabilities, creative thinking is defined as:

> *... learning to generate and apply new ideas in specific contexts, seeing existing situations in a new way, identifying alternative explanations, and seeing or making new links that generate a positive outcome. This includes combining parts to form something original, sifting and refining ideas to discover possibilities, constructing theories and objects, and acting on intuition. (Australian Curriculum, Assessment and Reporting Authority, n.d., par. 6)*

This definition of creative thinking feels expansive and process-driven. Generating new ideas, sifting, refining, discovering, combining and acting on intuition are not skills you learn with worksheets or formulas. These creative thinking skills require practical, on-the-job experience. Writers learn them by writing. Skills and knowledge are essential tools for every writer, but when your students engage openly with the writing process, they learn to trust their creative intuition. They develop their writing style and voice. They play with words and imagery. They refine and make links between their ideas. Rather than wait for inspiration to strike (or wait for their teacher to patiently feed them ideas), these students know they have access to a wide variety of strategies to stoke their creative fire.

What locks creativity out of your literacy program?

What happens when we take an inherently energetic and creative process, and package it up into basic skills, rigid rules and prescriptive formulas? What gets lost along the way? Of course, it's necessary to break down a complex process into learning objectives, but when we focus solely on skill development, we twist and warp the writing experience. We downsize writing into a purely cognitive activity and lead writers away from developing an intuitive, sensory understanding of storytelling. When we water down the strength of our students' voices, their writing can become prescriptive and artificial.

Let's see how this might play out in our classrooms.

Slow storytelling

During her primary years, my daughter Neve encountered a teacher who focused heavily on spelling. Despite finding spelling challenging, Neve wrote imaginative stories at home, full of interesting characters and plots. In comparison, the stories in her writing book at school had a simple, Dr Seuss-like quality about them. When I asked her about this, she explained, matter-of-factly, that her class wrote in the mornings and had to correct their spelling before heading out to recess. When she wrote freely, she spent part of her recess correcting her spelling mistakes. This of course wreaked havoc with her social life and self-esteem, so she'd devised a very practical way around it. At home she did as she pleased, but at school she wrote simple stories using only words she could spell. Neve was happy. Her teacher seemed happy enough. But her ability to tell a good story had taken a hit.

It's human nature to try to control variables and measure outcomes – and that's especially true for teachers who are time-poor and under pressure to achieve results. Narrative structure, grammar, spelling and punctuation all rely on a broad set of universally accepted rules. They move writing out of the murky grey and into the definitive territory of black and white, wrong and right, where mistakes of any kind are to be avoided at all costs (as Neve accurately surmised). But this denies writers the one great truth that ultimately defines their creative potential: to make or create anything, you must be prepared to fail and make mistakes, repeatedly. Writing is an adventure, a creative process of trial and error. Our students deserve an educational system that values risk-taking, one where making creative mistakes doesn't carry the public shame of missing out on recess.

In the same way that focusing on skills helps us control and measure outcomes, introducing formulas provides a possible template, a structural starting point. But when the use of formulas and templates become too rigid, our students miss the opportunity to embrace their agency as writers. Recently a student in one of my workshops was developing a detailed quest story. He had designed his setting and had a clear idea of his main character and plot, but as soon as he picked up his pencil to start writing, his shoulders slumped.

'Am I writing the introduction?' he asked. 'Is it only meant to be a paragraph? What if I don't want to introduce the character in the first paragraph? Do I have to?'

Young writers need to see and hear and play with a range of writing structures, trying them all on for size. Over time, story by story, young writers develop an intuitive understanding of how storytelling works.

Fast writing

Ironically, while we put roadblocks and tight controls on the storytelling process, we speed up the writing process. There isn't time to explore a range of ideas or build imagery or develop characters, let alone workshop scenes or test out ideas on an audience. With more time, it would be possible to stop and admire the view, or even allow writers to travel at their own pace, but often we see writing as having a linear trajectory with set outcomes. Our students board the writing train, pass through the necessary checkpoints and get off at destination 'Finished story'. But professional writers rarely experience writing as a linear process. Rather, they expect to draft, write, revise and constantly circle back to check whether their words say what they want them to say. And although some writing skills can be distilled down to a set of firm rules, skills like plotting, character development and voice are more subjective. If a piece of writing works well, we know these skills are in the house. We might not always be confident about how to invite them in, particularly when just starting out, but these are the skills that can transform a piece of writing. Writers need vigorous on-the-job training to learn how to use them effectively.

When we speed through the writing process to get to the finished product we limit the scope of our young writers' ambition and the strategies they have at their disposal. We cut them off from the magic of writing. Anxious, overwhelmed and unmotivated students drain their teachers' energy and waste truckloads of time. After teaching writing for many years, I know that a strong desire to write is equally as important as a writer's ability to use a range of writing skills (Kirmizi, 2009).

Inviting creativity in

You may not be able to teach creativity in the same way that you teach mathematics, but allowing your students to experiment with writing builds their growth mindset skills.

Confident decision-making

This is particularly true of their decision-making skills. In his book *The Path of Least Resistance*, Robert Fritz (1989) brings our attention to an essential but often overlooked element in the creative process: our ability to make choices. He explains, 'Creativity is all about choice. In every stage of the creative process, we are making decisions that move us forward' (Fritz, 1989, p. 83).

Decision-making is central to Wallas's (1926) understanding of creativity too: ultimately, it's our decisions that determine how we move through the stages, from generating that first idea to completing the cycle. In the preparation stage we choose our focus and materials. We actively visualise a direction. Next comes the process of incubating ideas. Although much of this stage may fly under the radar of conscious thought, we can (and do) make decisions about where we will place our attention and whether or not we will open up the time and space for ideas to play with each other. During the illumination stage, we choose how to construct and organise our creative project and then finally we decide how we will share our creative work with others.

Fritz (1989) says, 'when faced with a choice, we naturally veer towards the one that takes the least effort' (p. 84). This might help explain why some reluctant writers, when faced with a writing prompt, feel so paralysed that they do nothing. One-shot writing doesn't give writers enough opportunities to practise making choices, but a daily writing practice does. A daily writing practice gives your students plenty of opportunities to write (and make choices), which soon demystifies the decision-making process. They discover it's possible to pivot, iterate and even start again with no dire consequences. They begin to see experimentation as a valuable part of the process. Flexible, nimble thinkers are more likely to find solutions to problems and adapt more easily to their environment (Puccio, 2017). Learning to harness their creativity increases your students' ability to achieve in all core subjects, including personal development.

Engagement

In a recent storytelling workshop, I guided a group of eight- to ten-year-old boys through the creative process to develop an adventure-fantasy story. We spent time generating ideas, writing short scenes, collaborating and workshopping. The writers were fully absorbed in the process of creation. Afterwards, when I was heading to my car, I saw one of the writers crouching on the footpath with his mum. He was using an illustration of his character as a puppet to tell his story. 'I've never seen him like this about writing,' she said, looking up at me. That's the power of creative process in action.

In her book, *The Writer's Process*, Anne H Janzer (2016) says, 'The state of flow connects you to the joy of writing' (p. 31). Flow is exhilarating and exciting. When we sweep broad classifications and student rankings to one side and clear space for creativity in our classrooms, we give students an opportunity to experience the magic and freedom of creating. It's not just students who experience this high either. Tired teachers benefit from it too. The creative process has energy to burn. Exploit it and watch your students' levels of engagement soar.

Open outcomes

Inviting creativity into your writing program can be as simple as making space for more than one outcome. Like many teachers, I have planned activities with a goal in mind, only to see students take off in a much more interesting direction. If the outcome is not predetermined, students learn to step into their authority and think their way through the process.

We learnt earlier in the chapter that students model themselves on their teacher's approach. Open activities confirm the simple truth that creativity is not static or rigid. It's a continuing process of experimentation, of trial and error. In this terrain, mistakes are not shameful errors of misjudgement; they are stepping stones along the pathway of discovery and self-awareness.

Summary

Creativity is not a wild phenomenon in the hands of colourful artists and inventors. It's an organic, dynamic, living and breathing system available to every one of us. We don't have to sit patiently waiting for our creative muse to turn up, either. In this chapter, we have discussed a variety of theories and models that show creativity can be operationalised and managed in our classrooms.

Though creativity is often disregarded in the face of the pressing demands of the key learning areas, creativity is a cornerstone of the

Australian Curriculum. The Alice Springs (Mparntwe) Education Declaration gives teachers the courage they need to find their voice and implement simple practices that reinstate creativity at the head of their literacy program. Developing creative thinking skills directly increases the likelihood of your students experiencing success across all curriculum areas. That's why it's essential for teachers to challenge and update the stories they hold about creativity. Our tightly held beliefs and assumptions have the power to colour all aspects of our teaching practice and life. Inviting creativity into your classroom is as much about spring cleaning your mindset as it is about rearranging your timetable. Our goal as teachers is to develop independent, motivated and switched-on writers. Your students need a teacher who is curious about the writing process and willing to help each of them to find their voice.

Creativity is writing's true north. Point your compass towards creativity and your students will have the chance to see how writing enhances their lives. Just like that boy on the footpath, they will have something to say.

Power points

- While we each access our creativity differently, the creative process is not as mysterious or unpredictable as we might imagine. Rather, it cycles through a series of distinct and recognisable stages.
- Simple mindset changes and teaching practices can have a significant impact on our students' creative potential and their motivation to write.
- Our experiences, beliefs and personal stories shape our creative potential and our teaching practice.
- Creativity is multidimensional. Developing creative thinking skills as part of your writing program can result in adaptable, more engaged learners across all subject areas.

Pause and reflect

- Which part of the creative process (perception, discovery or production – or perhaps another stage) do you find most enjoyable? Which stage is most challenging? Why do you think that is?
- How do you respond to the statement 'Everyone is creative'? How would your students respond to this statement?
- Do you believe you are creative? How and when? What inspires your creativity? What dampens the fire?
- Look at the four factors that promote creativity. How does your writing program stack up? Which condition do you think you cater for best?
- List some changes you would like to make in your writing program to nurture your students' creativity. Don't edit your list based on time constraints – list anything that comes to mind. You don't need to tackle every item on this list, but the simple act of getting your ideas down on paper will help to clarify your thinking. Then choose the smallest item on your list or the task that lights you up most and get started.

Your action plan

Practise decision-making with your class

This high-energy creative thinking game puts the fun back into decision-making and gives you the opportunity to practise some of the principals that enable creative ideas to flourish. It's the perfect way to activate creative thinking skills and set the stage before writing.

Your aim is to encourage writers to make choices in a fun, low-stakes atmosphere. This game is an open, judgement-free zone. Talk afterwards about how it feels to make choices across the board from ice cream flavours to character names. Making a wrong choice is the number one fear when it comes to decision-making. Share your feelings and experiences with your students. This game will provide plenty of information about the writers in your classroom and how they approach writing tasks.

What could happen?

1. Start with some generic character possibilities, such as frog, caterpillar, girl, chef and so on. Ask students to create options with you.
2. Choose a character, such as a frog.
3. Ask the group to offer three possible names for the frog. Hands will shoot up.
4. Choose three students to share an answer. For example, Croak, Mr Green and Freddie.
5. Choose another student to choose one of the three answers. Now your character has a name: Freddie.
6. Now do the same with the setting.
7. Ask three students to share a possible setting for Freddie. You may have a lily pond, a castle and a classroom.
8. Nominate another student to choose one of the three answers as the setting. So now we know Freddie the frog lives in a castle. But what kind of castle?
9. Ask for words to describe the mood or atmosphere of this castle.
10. Choose three students to offer suggestions and ask another student to choose one of the options. The trick is to move the game along quickly, so students offer ideas and make fast decisions. So now we know Freddie lives in a spooky castle.
11. Then ask, 'What might happen to Freddie in this spooky castle?'
12. Again, ask for three possible ideas and select another student to choose.

So now we have Freddie the frog lost in a spooky castle. You can go ahead and build the story or start again with a new character.

Chapter 2
The power of a writing practice

A writing practice has the power to do so much more than develop writing skills alone. Grounded in daily routines and actions, a practice of any kind offers us a tangible, concrete way to engage with a particular philosophy or teaching and to connect with others who share our values and desires. But a daily practice also has an introspective quality. It turns your gaze inward and grants you access to your inner world, your thoughts, feelings, fears and joys. It unlocks the door to self-awareness and welcomes you home.

Your classroom writing practice offers you the same pathways of connection. With this particular practice, you and your students have an opportunity to engage with the authentic craft of writing: the nuts and bolts of how words work and play together to communicate ideas. When writers read aloud – as they do in the workshopping portion of your writing practice – they engage in the age-old tradition of telling stories, connecting words and experiences, all the while making sense of their world. It's there, in their classroom community, that writers experience a powerful sense of belonging. But writing is also a solo affair. As we write and reflect, we understand – and learn to accept –

the delicate workings of our hearts and minds. We experience clarity of thought. We discover our unique voice and style. We wrestle ideas to the ground and write ourselves into meaning.

These pathways of connection run through every practice I can think of – from a concert pianist investing countless hours in their craft to my friend gently tending to her indoor plants every day. And in a world where everything changes so quickly, these points of connection become guiding stars. But if you're a teacher worn down by standards and benchmarks, creativity and connection seem more like distant galaxies than guiding stars. Thankfully, this couldn't be further from the truth.

Creativity and a deep desire for connection and relationships are instinctive human qualities. After attending one of my workshops and taking back a host of activities to try with her class, one primary school teacher returned for the second workshop in the series carrying a pile of her students' notebooks. Dropping them on the table, she addressed the group: 'In two weeks, I've learned more about my students than I have all year!' Daily writing gave this teacher access to how her students experience the world.

Start now with practical partial solutions

The principles and processes I'll show you how to implement as part of your writing practice blend seamlessly with any literacy program you currently use in your school. You don't need any special materials or talents beyond a natural curiosity and willingness to actively engage with the creative process.

As a young graduate teacher I felt constrained by the obvious flaws in the education system and the realities of classroom teaching. I spent hours dreaming about creating the perfect school from scratch. But rather than inspiring action, an all-or-nothing approach to problem-solving creates the sort of overwhelm that stops us dead in our tracks. Over the years I've learnt that change is best achieved through a series of small intentional iterations rather than a 'clear the block and start again' approach. That's why I have come to love partial solutions. There's no need to swing dangerously across the deep ravine between where you are and where you would like to be. Your daily writing practice is your partial solution, the bridge between creativity and conformity. You can't overhaul your school's literacy program, but scheduling as little as fifteen minutes a day for a classroom writing practice moves you towards the goal of creating independent, engaged writers.

In this chapter I'll take a helicopter view of a classroom writing practice. This overview helps you see how the working parts of a writing practice fit together. I'll lay down the guiding principles that invite creativity into your classroom as well as show you a simple, sequential process to get you started. Then, in the chapters that follow, I'll address practical ways to incorporate these principles into your literacy program.

Every classroom, every group of students and every teacher is different. With this in mind, I'll walk you through a set of principles and a process I have developed and used successfully with hundreds of young writers across varying ages and stages. Once you understand the underlying principles and how to implement the process, use this as your guide for creating a writing practice that works for your students.

Don't wait for perfect conditions. That day will never come. Focus on practical partial solutions.

Your guiding principles

Three guiding principles, captured in a single sentence, set the foundation for building your writing practice: *regular writing* in a *carefully managed environment* where students are free to explore language *without the pressure and scrutiny of formal assessment*.

Your writing practice has many working parts, but these three guiding principles set down the foundational beliefs and clarify your sense of purpose. When you find yourself in unfamiliar territory, these three principles point true north. Be prepared to come back to them again and again. Let's explore each principle now.

Principle 1: A regular commitment to write

Regular scheduled writing time is fundamental to any writing practice. Think about the people who are important in your life; you invest time, energy and resources into building relationships with them. A writer needs to experience this same energetic exchange with the process of writing. There will be times when the words fly onto the page and others when the writer and their writing sit together in stony silence. An ongoing commitment to turn up to the page regardless develops grit and the capacity to persist.

Donald H Graves's (1985) groundbreaking article 'All children can write' championed a process approach to writing, sparking a movement known as *real-world literacy*. Reflecting on the conditions that best support young learners' writing, Graves (1985) notes:

> *Our data show that children need to write a minimum of four days a week to see any appreciable change in the quality of their writing. It takes that amount of writing to contribute to their personal development as learners.* (pp. 174–175)

Daily writing results in a substantial body of work and a layering of experience. This is important if we want to move students away from comparative thinking and towards a greater understanding of their strengths and attributes as writers.

Regular writing facilitates incubation

As we explored in Chapter 1, writing doesn't always start when we pick up a pen. Sometimes an idea is silently planted in our imaginations and sends out hopeful shoots while we are busy doing other things. Incubation is an essential part of the creative process.

When writers know they have a regular scheduled time to offload their thoughts and ideas they are more likely to think about writing between these sessions. They subconsciously start to collect ideas, images and feelings to bring to the page and writing becomes a natural extension to their lives. After one of my regular after-school workshops, a father reported that his son had set up a writing space at home and was even tracking his writing habits. He smiled, saying, 'He calls himself a writer these days.'

Principle 2: A structured environment

Many of us believe that absolute freedom is a prerequisite for creativity and self-expression, but I've found the opposite is also true: creativity craves boundaries. In fact, applying constraints – such as limited time – often forces ideas to connect in interesting and unusual ways.

Creativity also responds well to predictable habits and routines. If you want your students' creativity to roam free, structure your environment in such a way to minimise distractions and improve focus. Constant distractions require your students to refocus their attention and this slows momentum (Uncapher & Wagner, 2018). I have found setting clear expectations around behaviour, as well as limiting noise and movement during writing practice, is most effective.

In the chapters that follow I'll show you how to design routines and codes of behaviour to promote creative flow. When your students understand how setting boundaries makes writing easier, they not only jump on board – they will also be motivated to track their responses.

Principle 3: The suspension of judgement

In his book *Writing Without Teachers*, Peter Elbow (1998) explores the impact on students of high- and low-stakes writing. High-stakes writing is results-orientated; the structure and content are specifically designed to test writers' knowledge and skills. The outcome of a piece of high-stakes writing directly impacts the writer in some way. This pressure alone affects the writer's response; some writers swing into action while others are paralysed by their fear of failure (Elbow, 1998).

In contrast, your writing practice balances this equation by setting aside time each day for your students to play with language and experiment without penalty. This low-stakes approach to writing swings the emphasis from product to process. With time, your students will learn to make peace with the fact that writing rarely pours out onto the page perfectly. Rather, we write, we read and we revise, each time getting a little closer to the essence of what we are trying to say.

Removing set outcomes and formal assessment from your writing practice also acknowledges that classifying and ranking students only paints part of the picture. A writing practice helps teachers fill in the dots and develop a deeper understanding of their writers.

Facing down the inner critic

Simply removing set outcomes doesn't necessarily silence the most powerful judge and jury we encounter: our inner critic. However, your writing practice teaches students strategies to dial down the noise and learn to listen to their own voice. Removing the limitations of formal assessment also helps writers develop a range of interpersonal skills. The development of skills such as collaboration, confidence, empathy, observation and initiative, also known as 'soft' skills, not only improve writing outcomes, but also assist students across all curriculum subjects and, as such, have been highlighted in the Alice Springs (Mparntwe) Education Declaration.

The three steps of a writing practice at work

Now you have the essential principles that form the foundation of your writing practice, let's explore the three, sequential steps that bring this process to life. A writing practice uses a simple model of discovery writing, workshopping and response (which includes modelled teaching) – in that order. Working with as little as fifteen minutes a day, I recommend teachers choose one prompt and plan for five minutes of discovery writing, five minutes of workshopping (with up to three writers sharing their work) and five minutes of response. If you have more than fifteen minutes available to you, simply divide your time into approximate thirds to cycle through the three elements. Once you develop your practice and start to experience the positive benefits, you may want to extend the time dedicated to each component to suit your requirements.

Step 1: Discovery writing

You may be aware of stream-of-consciousness writing or free writing, but I suggest opening your writing practice with a slight variation: discovery writing. Fans of true free writing don't typically advocate for the use of prompts, but I've found prompts (as we use in discovery writing) give writers a concrete starting point, much like a mantra in meditation. Because discovery writing isn't weighed down with expectation and set outcomes, once writers get started they are free to head off in all sorts of interesting directions. The prompt is used to get them started.

The goal of discovery writing is fluency and flow. *Flow* is the exhilaration of being in the moment and unaware of time and space. *Fluency*, on the other hand, enables ideas to flow easily, one after another. This is your students' authentic on-the-job training. Discovery writing helps writers discover their voice and style. The word *voice* implies the act of speaking – and discovery writing is an active conversation with your muse. You can't develop your writer's voice by completing worksheets. You must write regularly. There is no way around this.

Discovery writing allows writers to see the process in action. They can trace how their sparks of inspiration combine with their knowledge of writing to create narratives. Like stretching before you exercise, discovery writing loosens up the imagination. Another benefit is that your students will accumulate many short pieces of writing with which to practise editing skills, set writing goals and observe the progress they are making. (You will read more about all of this in the coming chapters.)

Three styles of discovery writing prompts

If we want our students to meet writing face to face, they need a balanced diet of writing opportunities. They need to use writing to communicate what they know as well as express their feelings, tell stories, imagine and reflect on the writing process. Over the last ten years I have developed a range of prompts and exercises so that, in the course of a week, your students can use discovery writing across three broad categories:

Personal writing: Mine your life for writing inspiration

These personal writing prompts and exercises (from page 157) ignite your students' curiosity in the small details of everyday life as they actively mine their lives for writing inspiration. Personal writing also invites self-awareness and encourages students to look for patterns and connections between their inner world (feelings and memories) and their concrete experiences. For example, in 'The story of my name' (on page 176) students explore their personal identity through writing about how they got their name. They see how their name connects them to their family and personal history. This then becomes the perfect springboard for a discussion about naming fictional characters.

Imaginative writing: Just imagine

This is a set of prompts and exercises to help writers generate original ideas for works of fiction (from page 193). The imagination is the powerhouse of creative thinking, visualisation and problem-solving. 'Just imagine' encourages students to build a collection of imagery, prose, characters and plots. Creating a stockpile of ideas like these helps your students be creative at a moment's notice – they never need to start from scratch. In this section, we use images, music, random words, shapes and more to inspire fresh ideas for storytelling.

Reflective writing: Hello writer

In your writing practice, students are active shareholders in the creative process and are accountable for their habits and behaviour. Encouraging your students to work with their natural tendencies is the key to harnessing their creative potential. 'Hello writer' (from page 229) is a set of reflective writing prompts and exercises that invite writers to share their experience of the craft of writing and explore their writing identity. For example, in 'Planning styles' (on page 260) students have an opportunity to reflect on the positives and negatives of various planning styles so they can explore and refine their own processes.

Step 2: Workshopping

Workshopping generally refers to the practice of sharing writing through reading aloud to an audience; however, workshopping in your writing practice fulfils a much more exciting brief than that. Combining the spoken and written word is a powerful way to teach writing skills and techniques in context. In Chapter 4 I'll guide you through the workshopping process in detail, but for now let's focus on the important role workshopping plays within your writing program.

Creativity takes courage

The mantra 'creativity takes courage', often attributed to Henri Matisse, resonates with anyone who has read a piece of writing aloud to an audience, but putting your writing on the line is exactly why workshopping develops skills and builds relationships so successfully. Reading aloud cuts to the chase. The audience hears the emotion beneath the writer's words. Writers, too, hear their words in a new light. As they read, they self-correct, add punctuation, clarify meaning. Despite the fact that your class will not formally critique each other during this time, immediate feedback is available in the form of laughter, sighs, gasps, confused expressions and, sometimes, heartfelt silence.

In *Wild Mind: Living the Writer's Life*, Natalie Goldberg (1990) shares this insight: 'The simple act of reading aloud allows you to let go. By reading your writing, you become less attached to whether it is good or bad' (p. 81). Short writing sprints aren't designed to produce a perfect piece of prose. That is the point; we're aiming for progress rather than perfection. The goal is for writers to claim their voice and step into their authority.

Enriching writers

Workshopping combines a strong spoken component with active and focused listening. We're accustomed to moving and writing and thinking and doing. How often are you formulating a response before a person has even finished speaking? But when we stop and hold space for another person's ideas to sit beside our own, we validate and affirm the speaker. We build connection and community.

The workshopping process also gives students an invaluable opportunity to hear a variety of different voices and styles in their own classroom. Not only does this enrich our understanding of writing, but it allows like-minded students to recognise each other. Once, while workshopping with a group of my regular students, two writers introduced different characters who naturally seemed to fit together. After the session, these two writers paired up to create a hilarious script that neither of them could have created alone. Workshopping moves your writers from a competitive space, where ideas are guarded and protected, to a collaborative environment where teamwork and learning from one another is highly valued.

Step 3: Response

Your classroom writing practice provides the perfect opportunity for teachers to model their understanding and experience of the creative process while also developing skills in context. When responding to writers, teachers obviously draw on their knowledge of writing, but their central role is to stop and pay attention, to bear witness to the writer and the writing. For this short block of time each day, your students need your undivided attention. When your students are writing and sharing, your role is to practise what I call *deep listening* – combining your intuitive observation and active listening skills.

Deep listening

When students are writing and sharing, teachers are 'switched on' and operating intuitively. Resist the urge to complete tasks when your students are writing. Instead, observe body language, look for pencils moving quickly across pages and listen for frustrated sighs. Note which students jump in first and which ones sit and watch. Be prepared to unmask the beliefs and stories you have about your writers. Pay attention to the present moment.

When working in class groups, I limit workshopping to two or three students per writing prompt. Waiting for everyone in your class to share their writing waters down the experience. I cover how deep listening plays into feedback and classroom practice in more detail on page 82, but for now remember: until you really know your students, you can't fully cater for their unique needs and talents.

The feedback loop

Students write and share; teachers observe and facilitate the process. What happens next? How do you respond to your students? If you want to suspend judgement and move beyond the currency of right and wrong, what options are available to you? Our current system trains us to focus on what our students can't do and where they fail to meet particular standards. We focus on the shortfall. We are forever pruning and shaping students towards a desired outcome. Now instead of pruning, teachers become the trellis supporting and shaping creative growth. Instead of applying judgements, ask open questions. What skills has the writer used? Is there an evocative image that stays with the audience? What makes that piece of writing work so well? This 'just in time' teaching provides feedback that writers can immediately use. We'll explore using three types of feedback loop in detail in Chapter 5.

In *The Skillful Teacher*, Stephen D Brookfield (2015) suggests that students need feedback that sparks their desire to engage in further inquiry. If you want to move writers, especially reluctant writers, through the process, use feedback to build confidence, self-esteem and writing skills in an authentic way. This style of feedback plays to your writers' strengths and encourages them to grow towards the sun.

Summary

Storytelling is at the heart of your writing practice. Each component of this model – discovery writing, workshopping and response – is built on the imaginative possibilities of storytelling. Telling, listening and identifying with our story is how we learn to belong in the world.

The degree to which you experience a sense of freedom and openness in your relationships relies on the strength and quality of your communication. Your relationship with writing is no different. The goal of your writing practice is to open the channels of communication and free up your students to engage with their creativity as well as build meaningful relationships with their peers. A supportive classroom environment built on a foundation of honest, open relationships accelerates the development of writing skills. Starting a writing practice in your classroom sends a powerful message to your writers. It says: 'I believe in your capacity to be creative. Rely on your intuition. Understand your natural tendencies. Take risks with your writing. Be vulnerable. Trust in each other.'

Power points

- A writing practice offers your students three invaluable points of connection: a relationship with the craft of writing, an opportunity to belong to a community of writers and a strengthened sense of self.

- Based on a simple model of discovery writing, workshopping and response (in that order) a writing practice blends seamlessly with any literacy program you are currently using.

- The success of your classroom writing practice rests on three guiding principles: regular writing, an environment structured to assist creative flow and a culture of non-judgement.

- Time is no longer an obstacle to creativity or improvement. You can spend as little as fifteen minutes a day developing your writing practice.

Pause and reflect

- Essentially a practice is a series of habits that form a simple, consistent routine. The term *practice* means different things to each of us. What does it mean to you? What practices sustain you in some way?
- What are the repeated actions, beliefs and values that underpin your teaching practice?
- Reflect on high- and low-stakes writing experiences in your literacy program. How do these writing opportunities stack up in your classroom?

Time to Write

Your action plan
Create student notebooks

Your students will each need a lined A4 exercise book for their writing practice. Use this process to set up your class notebooks with your students.

1. Paste a blank sheet of paper on the front and back covers of the exercise book.

2. Encourage students to label and design a front cover that's instantly recognisable to them with artwork, images, colour, stickers and so on. Make sure students' names are clear and easy to read, too.

3. Create an index with the first three pages. I divide these index pages into four columns: date, page number, title and notes. After each writing session, ask students to write the date, the page number they started their work on, a short title that captures the piece of writing and any note they might want to add in the relevant columns. This provides a simple log of pieces of writing and makes it easy for writers to go back and locate their previous work and ideas.

4. Allocate the next five pages for your writing lists. These lists can be used to collect and condense information related to discovery writing. Your students can decide what lists will work for them and they can always add more list pages to their notebook as they go. Here are some lists I've seen in action:

    - 'Interesting character names'

    - 'Stories I want to write'

    - 'Books I want to read' (If you are using literature to demonstrate writing techniques, no doubt your writers will be inspired to hunt down some of these books for themselves. Having a place to collect these titles is valuable.)

- 'My favourite words'
- 'My best writing tips'.

5. Number the remaining pages of the notebook in the bottom outside corner of each page. This is what students will refer to when adding page numbers to index entries.

6. When their notebooks are all set up, students can begin recording their discovery writing from the front of the book, while I suggest collecting their reflective 'Hello writer' responses from the back.

7. Having initially left it blank, after a few weeks of getting to know the 'Hello writer' process ask students to decorate and label the back cover in a way that reflects what they now understand about what they do in this section of their exercise book. Though you can ask students to label and decorate the back cover right away, this delayed approach can be interesting because the writer's choice of title tends to reflect something about how they view this new process of writing about writing. I've seen titles like:

    - 'My think tank'
    - 'My "reflecty" book'
    - 'Jacqueline's thoughts about writing'
    - 'The story of me becoming a writer'
    - 'My writing reflections'.

Chapter 3
Writing routines and rituals

In *Hare Brain, Tortoise Mind: Why Intelligence Increases When You Think Less* cognitive scientist Guy Claxton (1998) makes a case for slowing down our conscious, results-orientated thinking to allow our intuitive, unconscious mind to come to the fore. Aesop's fables were my first foray into the world of human behaviour, so Claxton's imagery immediately appeals to me.

Writer and actor John Cleese (2020) credits Claxton's hare–tortoise analogy as the inspiration behind his own theory of creativity, which centres on establishing the right conditions to coax creativity (a tortoise, in this metaphor) from its shell. Building on this, Cleese advocates that creatives need to build themselves a tortoise enclosure, a safe space, for their creativity to thrive by creating boundaries of time and space. It's a sweet metaphor that's easily accessible to both adults and children, but it packs a punch. It reminds us that unless creativity feels safe and secure, it won't poke its head out and explore the world.

In this chapter we'll explore how habits, routines and rituals give your students access to their full creative capacity. This is a grassroots approach to nurturing and supporting creativity, but I am confident that you will see the positive effects across the curriculum when you use specific routines and rituals to monitor your environment in this way.

Creative routines

When I started my own business in 2010 I was finally free to choose how I would spend my days. I relished the freedom of working at different times and anywhere that took my fancy: cafes, beautiful old libraries, outdoors and occasionally my home office. Some days my muse turned up on cue and entertained me for hours on end, but some days (and weeks) she played a frustrating game of hide-and-seek. I felt like an adorable, unpredictable toddler was in charge of my creativity. I started to approach writing with an unsettling mix of excitement and dread. My haphazard approach to writing obviously wasn't working for me. Then I discovered the power of designing daily habits, routines and personal rituals to support my writing. My productivity soared, but more importantly I learned to befriend my muse. I started bringing these processes to my teaching and, like me, my students experienced the same sense of ease and flow. Predictable patterns and routines worked for them too; they were able to access their creativity and settle into writing more easily.

Habits, routines and rituals are all repeated behaviours; we often use the words interchangeably, but there are subtle differences in meaning between each of them. A *routine* describes a set of regular, intentional behaviours that builds a system or pattern. *Habits* are automated actions and require less conscious thought (which is why they can be hard to break). A *writing ritual*, on the other hand, has a symbolic quality, ripe with personal meaning, such as lighting a candle or using a specific object on your desk to inspire confidence and self-belief.

Train the brain

Writing routines and rituals essentially train the brain into linking certain events with particular responses. In his bestselling book

The Power of Habit, Charles Duhigg (2012) explains why these sets of repeated behaviours are so powerful. A habit forms a strong neurological loop consisting of a cue, a routine and a reward. The cue triggers a set of behaviours resulting in a positive reward. In terms of your writing program, cues are repeated actions that trigger a writing response. I have found that linking and overlaying a series of sensory cues reinforces the writing response even further, allowing students to quickly move into a creative state.

Teachers have long known the effectiveness of using routines to help organise the school day, but here we're shifting gears and exploring which cues and actions increase your students' creative capacity. This isn't a short-term solution either. The time you invest into developing effective writing routines pays substantial ongoing dividends to your students. Neurological pathways are stored in the brain and can be reactivated, even after the original routine has been forgotten (Barnes et al., 2005).

In his bestselling book *Atomic Habits*, James Clear (2018) pinpoints four conditions that cement habits in place. For best results, he argues, cues need to be obvious, attractive, easy and satisfying. Your creative routines need to be easy to follow and fun to do so they support your writing practice. The last thing teachers need is yet another set of complex tasks to add to their day.

Routines and rituals not only provide the necessary structure that creativity craves; they also carry a sense of predictability and safety. This is especially important for reluctant writers, for perfectionists and for highly sensitive students who feel especially vulnerable. Your writing practice is that safe tortoise enclosure; it protects and nurtures young writers to allow them to roam independently.

The three-act play

It is helpful to think of your writing practice as a three-act play. In Act 1 your class organises props and sets the stage for writing and creativity. In Act 2 the plot thickens as discovery writing begins. In Act 3 workshopping and discussion give rise to an active exchange of ideas.

Using this familiar three-act structure to plan lessons and improve classroom management is certainly not unique to your writing practice. But the routines, habits and rituals that underpin your practice play a much deeper role than improving productivity and classroom management. These simple yet powerful systems can be used intentionally to foster a sense of security, enhance focus and trigger a state of flow – all essential for a successful writing experience.

Act 1: Getting ready to write

Writing classes usually begin with an exciting prewriting activity, a lesson hook designed to spark creative thinking and get your class buzzing with ideas. In contrast, the energy in the initial stage of your writing practice is more subdued. Instead of raising the collective energy in the room, your routines and rituals encourage your students to look inward and mentally prepare for the task of writing. Rather than active discussion, you begin with a set of predictable and intentional actions to calm and settle your group.

Take out the guesswork

One of the best ways to maximise the impact of your writing practice is to develop a predictable structure that takes the mental guesswork out of preparing to write so your students can quickly access their creativity. You can achieve this goal by:

- scheduling a consistent time slot
- working in a familiar setting each time
- following a predictable sequence of events for the duration of your practice.

Regularity and predictability are essential elements when it comes to building your tortoise enclosure. Working in a predictable setting at a regular time develops a deep sense of safety, an important backdrop to taking risks and experimenting with language. Teachers are not required to come up with a new anticipatory event every day to get the ball rolling; all you have to do is flow from one familiar action to the next.

I know that developing a new routine in a crowded timetable can feel almost impossible for some teachers, but don't let this be a reason for not beginning at all. Remember, this isn't an all-or-nothing approach. Take the essence of this ideal and work towards a partial solution. If your writing practice needs to happen at different times every day, try to keep the room and the sequence of actions predictable. Play with these three elements. By far, the most important question to ask is this: what routines will create a sense of safety and coax creativity out to play?

Use sensory cues

We experience the world through our senses. Layering sensory details, auditory and visual, can be incredibly useful when it comes to developing triggers to assist creative flow. If these particular sensory cues are used only for your writing practice, they are even more effective.

For example, if you plan to start the day with your writing practice, take a few minutes at the end of the day to set writing notebooks and materials out on tables. Seeing their writing materials waiting for them serves as an important visual cue when your students enter the room in the morning. They will also come to link the sound of the first school bell with the act of writing. One teacher I know built upon this routine for her class's writing practice. She displays her class's five guidelines for writing practice (more on these in Act 2) on her smartboard and plays the same piece of music as students enter the room at the start of the school day. They move into writing before completing admin tasks and their usual meet and greet. This soft start to the day works well for them. Another class I've worked with schedules their writing practice after recess. They organise their materials before they leave the room so it's ready for their return, and their teacher diffuses mandarin essential oil during the break (as another sensory cue) to prepare the room for writing.

Organise the physical space

For some of us a clear workspace helps settle a busy mind, but the jury is out on whether a clear desk actually assists creative flow. I have run workshops in classrooms across the broad spectrum of tidiness and found no direct correlation between the state of the room and how students respond to writing.

Classroom organisation is a matter of personal preference, but for me the key is to set up your space in such a way that students can easily access their writing materials. Hunting down notebooks, pens and a clear surface to work tends to halt momentum and drain motivation. I ask my students to use a calico bag to keep their writing materials together. These bags are cheap, mobile and easy to personalise.

Take Clear's (2018) advice and keep your cues obvious, attractive, easy and satisfying. I was in a class recently when the students came back after their lunchbreak and moved into their writing time. The teacher simply said, 'One, two, three.' Suddenly, his Year 1 class was a hive of activity. They knew what this simple auditory cue meant:

1. Clear your table (remove all paper and put away books).
2. Clear the floor space around your table.
3. Organise your drink bottle for the afternoon.

I watched in amazement as this class of six- and seven-year-olds worked like a well-oiled machine. Each table area had all the materials they needed (dustpan, brush and small bin) to make this task efficient and fun. There was no time-wasting. The focus was on action and team-work, and in next to no time the room was clean and the class was ready to write. This simple, regular routine, layered with sensory cues, not only reset the room, but also enabled students to mentally prepare for the task of writing together.

Acknowledge the symbolic importance of ritual

Once we have organised our physical environment, rituals, which are more personal in nature, prepare our mental space. Rituals are symbolic acts that, in this context, might be intended to invoke the muse and invite writers to recognise the mystery of the creative process. Some professional writers are highly superstitious about their writing rituals. For example, Steven Pressfield (2003) recites Hamer's invocation before he begins to write for the day. Other writers read poetry, rich in imagery to stir their imagination.

Introducing symbolism and metaphor in your writing practice rituals invites students to tune in to their relationship with writing. Symbols transcend literal meaning. They carry the subtle nuances of sensory perception, intuition, emotion and personal experience. In 'Writing symbols' (page 248) in the activities section, I lead you through a process to help writers choose a symbol that means something to them and their writing. My own writing symbol is two gold pens given to me by my father and they serve as a visual reminder of my writing philosophy. Because physical objects can get lost in classrooms, writers could include pictures of their precious symbols in their writing notebooks or bags. This is a great way to personalise the writing experience and introduce the concept of creating meaningful writing rituals to slide into the creative process. Your class could also develop a ritual together, such as playing a piece of music, lighting a candle or reading a short poem before you begin.

Act 2: Discovery writing

If in Act 1 our goal was to create predictable, regular routines to coax creativity out to play, now we want her to taste the freedom and exhilaration that comes with exploring new ground and making discoveries. The second act of our writing practice is the discovery writing phase, when students put pencil to paper and start to create. It's essential we build strong boundaries and sturdy support structures in Act 2 so this creativity can roam free.

Minimise distractions

Cleese sums up reams of research on distractions with a single pithy remark: 'the enemy of incubation is interruption' (as told to Wagner, 2016, par. 15). Strong boundaries minimise distractions and maximise your students' focus.

The first disruption you need to head off at the pass is other students and teachers knocking on your classroom door. Ideally your writing practice is an interruption-free zone. Communication is key here. If your colleagues know of your desire to establish this routine, they are in a better place to support you or, better still, join in. I often see signs on doors to indicate a class is reading silently; this same approach might do the trick. Of course, sometimes disruptions are inevitable, but working to protect your tortoise enclosure sends a powerful message to your school community: your writing practice is sacred.

When you're writing, your imagination is creating a series of visual images and then capturing these images in words on the page. This cognitive process requires focus and concentration. Multitasking – that is, talking and writing – means your students are constantly refocusing on the task at hand and beginning again. Out of respect for the energy this process demands, I ask students not to speak to each other during the discovery writing phase. Using a timer (more about that soon) helps reinforce this rule; once the timer is set, talking ceases.

Some writers enjoy silence, while others like to write with music or ambient noise. Currently my ambient noise of choice is the sound of rain and thunder. In my workshops I often use the same piece of instrumental music as ambient noise that doubles as a familiar auditory clue. I encourage you to try a range of options with your class so your students have an opportunity to explore their personal preferences. I've also seen students in classrooms wearing noise-reducing headphones and choosing their own ambient sound options to improve their levels of concentration. As a homework task for members of The Writer's Club, I sent home a playlist with a range of auditory cues and a tracking sheet. The task was to track which options improved clarity, concentration and creativity. Writers came back the following week with many ideas to discuss. There is power in understanding and working with your personal preferences and processes. There is no single right answer. It's a process of iteration, of trial and error.

Our minds are continually fighting distractions. We've become so accustomed to responding to spontaneous impulses that it's easy to ignore the impact this has on our clarity of thought. We're either too cold or too hot, or itchy, or uncomfortable. We need to sharpen a pencil or get this or go there. The need to keep moving is more heightened when we are anxious or agitated so to help students learn to regulate these impulses, I ask them to stay seated during discovery writing. Learning to bypass distraction helps control that part of the mind that wants to keep us jumping from one idea to the next. Talk about this with your students. Once your students get on board, they'll be interested in tracking the improvements they make in this area.

Articulate supportive guidelines

In her bestselling book *Writing Down the Bones: Freeing the Writer Within*, Natalie Goldberg (2005) outlines a disarmingly simple approach to writing practice and shares some important ideas that we can use to frame the discovery writing process. I share these five guidelines, adapted from Goldberg's (2005) approach, with all of my students before we write:

1. Keep your hand moving. Don't censor your ideas or content. Let go.
2. Don't cross out. That's editing. Even if you write something you didn't mean to write, leave it.
3. Don't worry about grammar, spelling or structure during this phase – just write.
4. Lose control. Write what you want to write, rather than what you think you should write.
5. Be specific in your language. What sort of tree was it? How did the child move?

These guidelines function as supportive structures for your writers' creativity, designed to offer the balance of freedom and safety they need.

The first guideline is critical. Challenge your writers to keep moving their pencil across the page until the end of the writing time. 'Just keep writing' is a good mantra to use. It's important to emphasise that the focus is on making creative connections rather than handwriting or grammar. If writers are stuck, I suggest they tune in to their surroundings and tap into their senses to get them started. They could describe the room or explore what it feels like to have no ideas when everyone around them is writing. What sensations are they experiencing? Sweaty palms? Racing thoughts? I once heard Melbourne writer, Adam Wallace, give young writers permission to write 'I have no ideas' over and over until something finally rises to the surface. These strategies mean students always have a starting point.

Create soft deadlines

Another supportive boundary I suggest installing in your tortoise enclosure is timed writing, which was also introduced to me by Goldberg (2005). Before using timed writing I was a self-confessed binge writer. I'd write for hours on end, for weeks at a time and then not write again for months. But at Goldberg's suggestion, I started to add ten minutes of timed writing to my daily routine. While it sounds counterintuitive, timed writing sprints focused my attention and allowed me to push pass my inner critic. Before long, I started to experiment with this approach in my workshops with great success.

My process has evolved over time, but I've found between four to six minutes allows students to develop a short piece of writing. I don't emphasise the length of time. Instead, I say, 'I'll mind the time and let you know when to finish the sentence you are working on.' Though I often use the timer on my phone, I use a singing bowl chime rather than a jarring alarm to signal the end of writing time.

Some writers in your class will take to timed sprints easily and immediately experience a sense of release, but I've also worked with highly sensitive and anxious students who may find this approach unnerving. In many cases, clarifying your purpose is the key. The aim of timed writing is not to race students against each other or the clock and finish in record time. It's not about finishing first or finishing at all. Keeping time is an intentional strategy, a soft deadline, which helps 'force' creative connections between ideas. Talk to your students about this strategy, allow them to discuss their reactions and encourage them to remain open minded and give it a try first. Encourage them to experiment with timed writing outside of their practice. This style of self-study is an integral part of developing your writing identity.

We have all experienced how a deadline inspires action, so I use timed writing for my own writing projects and my writing workshops. Here's what I've discovered:

- A short time frame encourages playfulness and experimentation and writers often find that ideas collide in interesting and original ways.
- Without time to mull over or censor a piece of writing, writers learn to turn up and trust their intuition.
- In many cases, fear of failure proves to be more of a hurdle for young writers than writing proficiency. There is an expectation that writers will complete a piece of writing, just not a polished final draft. There is no set outcome and no expectation to complete a perfect piece of writing in the short time frame.
- Shorter time frames allow writers to practise making lots of quick decisions. They discover that creative decisions (in this context) are not set in concrete. The stakes are low. Writers can choose to run with an idea and if it doesn't pan out for them they can leave it or even rework it another time.

Timed writing is a wonderful paradox. Exercising control and placing limitations on the time frame often allows writers to crash through roadblocks and experience a creative release.

Act 3: Workshopping and responding

Act 3 signals the end of writing independently and the start of coming together as a community to share pieces of writing and focus on skill development. Here, your classroom routines need to facilitate an active exchange of ideas by clearing the pathways of communication. Because of the vulnerable nature of reading writing aloud, this is when our tortoise – our creativity – may threaten to curl up into its shell. Once again, predictable routines and boundaries encourage students to take risks and step into their authority as writers.

Connecting writers to an audience and teaching skills in context is a critical part of your writing practice. We will break down the workshopping process in Chapter 4, but for now it's helpful to consider a range of routines that enable students to tune in to each other.

Pause first

Firstly, make sure you have scheduled enough time for workshopping to take place without a sense of urgency. After writing, ask students to put down their pens. Give them a moment to compose themselves. This mindful pause allows everyone to take a collective breath and prepare to share their writing and give each other their undivided attention.

If you find you are running against the clock, scale back the number of students sharing. Giving one student your full attention is better than rushing through three readings. As a speaker there is nothing worse than finally deciding to take the plunge and suddenly hearing the bell ring, prompting everyone to get up and move around the room mid-sentence.

Conclude with ceremony

We develop creative rituals to set the wheels in motion, but we often don't allow time or space at the end of the writing practice for emotions and ideas to settle before students move on to the next task. What short ritual could you use to end your writing practice? Your closing ceremony could be as simple as packing writing materials away while listening to a familiar piece of music, blowing out your candle or sharing a short poem together as a class.

Staging notes

Developing a set of creative routines doesn't happen in isolation. Nor do routines come fully packaged and ready to roll out in your class. Developing creative routines is a work in progress. It's a way of keeping your finger on the creative pulse of your classroom and playing with how you can best manage your learning environment to meet the changing needs of your writers. Here are some suggestions for you to consider as you introduce a writing practice in your classroom.

A change is as good as a holiday

Routines are designed to adapt to your circumstances so if you find your creative routines are not having the same impact they once did, experiment with alternatives. Rather than starting again from scratch, try to vary one aspect of your routine at a time. Perhaps keep the time of day and the time frame consistent but change where your class writes. Or dim the lights a little or vary one of your auditory cues. Just one small change in your routine at the right time can invigorate your writers' sensory perception and shift the energy in your practice.

Collaboration

If you want to motivate your students to write, your classroom writing practice needs to speak their language. It has to be relevant to your students so they see the direct benefit.

In my experience, managing routines is much easier when your writers wholeheartedly participate in the process. Rather than planning routines and rituals on behalf of your class, draw them into this process. Writers need some skin in the game, they deserve real decision-making power and a level of personal responsibility. The routines your students develop now have the potential to steer them through many creative projects in the future. Consider sharing current research relating to creativity and exploring how other writers incorporate routines and rituals into their writing lives.

Some thoughts on handwriting

Rather than debate the merits of handwriting and keyboards, I'd prefer to share my experience of teaching writing and some of the benefits of putting pen to paper. When students first experience timed writing as a part of their writing practice they have a tendency to grip their pencils and write furiously, shaking out their cramped hands at regular intervals. Just keep reminding them there is no hurry, no pressure to finish a piece of writing during this time. Once they settle into the process, they usually discover that handwriting has a slower, steadier rhythm that gives ideas and words a chance to find each other.

Handwriting also provides a valuable record of the writer's thinking process. My handwriting gets loopy and loose when I am making connections or experiencing those much loved *aha* moments. But for me, the real advantages of choosing handwriting over keyboards are about accessibility and boundaries. A notebook and pencil are available to most people in most environments – no special equipment necessary here. Devices also display a constant stream of notifications and distractions, but handwriting is a solo affair. I've also witnessed pieces of writing and whole stories lost in an instant because they were not saved properly or a battery died unexpectedly. This can be devastating. With a hard copy, handwritten record of their work, writers can also view the development of their skills and learnings. Even if they go back and edit a piece, they will retain a record of their first attempt. Finally, handwriting is portable. Grab a notebook and head outdoors! No charge, no worries. That said, there are students who for a variety of reasons find handwriting so challenging that it drains the joy out of writing. This calls for a change of plan, so adapt to meet their specific needs.

Summary

Routines, habits and rituals are the secret to creating a predictable and safe space that entices creativity out to play. Use the suggestions and ideas in this chapter as a springboard for active discussion with your class about the importance of setting yourself up for success. Let your creative routines develop organically, building them together one step at a time. Once you and your students see the value of using routines to assist creative flow and fluency, you will be hooked. Then as your students become more comfortable with their writing practice they'll naturally experiment with what works for them.

Writing isn't just about the words that end up on your page. Approaching your creative life with curiosity and a sense of discovery develops more than writing skills. This time is an opportunity to develop essential growth mindset skills and attitudes that shape our students' identities. When we celebrate our differences and our strengths, we begin to hold space for ourselves, as creatives. This is a powerful shift for young writers. They learn to trust themselves and their creativity.

Power points

- Routines, habits and rituals are developed through repetition.
- Certain behaviours and environmental conditions can be used to trigger a writing response and enable your students to slide into the creative process.
- Layering sensory cues strengthens your writing routine.
- Routines, habits and rituals need to be obvious, easy, attractive and satisfying to complete.
- Build your routines organically, habit by habit.
- Collaborate with your students to develop your writing practice together. Use this as an opportunity to develop a growth mindset.

Pause and reflect

- Think about your experience of writing. (This could be report writing, personal writing projects and so on.) Do you use any particular strategies for staying focused and motivated?
- What routines do you currently use to provide structure in your day? Can you spot the neurological loop consisting of a cue, a routine and a reward?
- Every class is different. What kind of routines do you think will be most beneficial for getting your class ready to write? How might your class organise their writing practice materials to minimise disruption?
- Developing a writing routine with your class encourages both teachers and students to think about their personal writing preferences. Using binary opposites to pose questions can help us clarify our thinking. Which do you prefer?
  - messy or clean workspace
  - ambient noise or silence
  - movement or stillness
  - solitude or community.
- I love Claxton's (1998) and Cleese's (2020) ideas of the tortoise mind. It helps me practise self-compassion and reminds me to be gentle with myself and my students. What makes your creativity feel safe and protected? What environmental conditions coax your creative spirit out to play?

Your action plan

Staging the three-act play

Daily habits and routines provide a useful container to enable you to prioritise your classroom writing practice in your literacy program. Predictable routines and patterns invite your students to make positive associations with writing and creative thinking. Your action step in this chapter is to use the three-act play metaphor to build rituals and routines into your writing practice. As you think through the processes and guidance offered here, make note of what you think might work in your classroom, things you'd like to try, tips you'd like to remember and so on in your action research journal (see page 13).

At each stage of the process, call on routines and rituals to help your students access their focus and flow. Remember too to build your writing routines step by step. Start with one or two cues to see what works for your class and then add to and refine routines. Talk through this process with your writers and give them some ownership in the decision-making process.

Act 1: Getting ready to write

In Act 1, the beginning of your writing practice, the focus is on developing regular and predictable routines to trigger a writing response. This first act is especially important because a smooth transition will ensure your students move through their writing practice with ease. Here are some ideas for you to work through to ensure your writing practice runs smoothly:

- Let's focus first on your timetable. Your goal is to make your writing practice a consistent, regular event in your timetable rather than a spontaneous occurrence. You can do this by scheduling a regular timeslot for your writing practice. If you can't choose the same time (for example, 9.15 am, Monday–Thursday) then try to work at consistent times and days each week (Wednesday at 1.30 pm and then Thursday at 9.15 am, for example).
- When your timetable is sorted, let's consider how your classroom environment can be used to create powerful visual writing cues. This could be as simple as setting out writing books and materials ready on the table or projecting a particular image on the smartboard as students move into their writing practice. Visual cues that hold meaning for your

students deepen the connection. What do you think would best indicate to your students that it's time to write?

- Consider what additional sensory cues could become part of setting the stage to write. Layering sensory cues can be effective for creating strong associations. Could you use an auditory cue to signal writing time such as a familiar piece of music or the vibrating chime of a singing bowl? Would you like to add a scent or a texture such as laying a silk cloth across a table? Could this add a sense of ritual that sets your writing practice apart from other classroom activities?

- Once you've set the stage for writing by establishing regular and predictable practice times and sequence of events, it's time to turn your attention to how your students will organise their writing materials. Keep organisational systems simple. Students need to be able to access materials easily and independently and have everything they need in one place. A calico bag or sturdy document wallet is useful here.

- Finally, a writing ritual holds a sense of evoking the muse. It's a call to recognise the mystery and magic of creativity. Remember: rituals evolve over time. Allow room for students to develop routines and rituals naturally and see what arises. Would you like to light a candle to represent the igniting of imaginations? Or help students choose a personal writing symbol?

Act 2: Discovery writing

The second act of your writing practice is the discovery writing phase. This is when students put pencil to paper and move into creation mode. It's essential at this stage that your routines build strong boundaries and sturdy support structures so your students' creativity can roam free. Here are some things to think about when working through the second act for your writing practice:

- It's important at this stage to limit distractions to maximise your students' focus, so consider how you will place limitations on noise and movement in your classroom during this time. I use a simple rule of saying that when the timer is set, students stay in their seat and work independently for the complete duration. In Chapter 7 I will guide you through the process of developing a code of conduct for your writing practice. This code of conduct reflects the beliefs and expectations held by you and your students, and will help shape the routines you choose here.

- In collaboration with your students, you may also want to trial whether ambient noise or familiar pieces of music are conducive to writing. On the opposite side of the scale, perhaps some students would benefit from dimming environmental stimuli and working with noise-cancelling headphones. In the activity 'Creative flow' (see page 269) you will find prompts encouraging students to experiment with a range of environmental conditions. This will help them find what works for them and inform what options you may offer at this stage.

- While there needs to be some flexibility so students can experiment and trial new ways of working, it is essential to be consistent in your approach so that students respect the boundaries. Likewise, be sure to communicate what is happening and why so students can get a handle on the rules and understand why they are important.

Act 3: Workshopping and responding

Act 3 is when we come together in community to share pieces of writing and focus on skill development. Here your writing routines need to facilitate active listening and allow for the vital exchange of ideas by clearing the pathways of communication and encouraging a flow of ideas. Consider how these suggestions might work in your classroom:

- As noted on page 66, it can be helpful to pause when discovery writing comes to an end before moving into workshopping. A simple auditory cue, such as 'Pencils down, pause,' can be effective in asking students to stop writing, pause for a minute and prepare for the next important stage of the process. In time, this simple auditory cue will trigger an automatic response from your class and allow them to regroup, take a breath and move from creative to receptive mode. Use the pause to remind students to make eye contact and to be physically and mentally present for the next stage of the process.

- Think ahead about how many workshopping opportunities you can offer in each session. Unless an activity demands it, I tend to limit workshopping to two or three students per prompt to avoid rushing. You want to spark a range of ideas so you can find those teachable moments, but keeping this stage dynamic and energetic is key.

- Reading our writing aloud is a vulnerable thing to do, and this is when our tortoise – our creativity – may threaten to curl back into its shell. Once again, predictable routines and consistent boundaries encourage students to take risks and step into their authority as writers. I would encourage you to take some time to discuss the vulnerable nature of workshopping when introducing this practice. This conversation can also be useful when developing your code of conduct with your class, as noted in our discussion of Act 2. Prompt students to reflect on what will make them feel safe and respected during this time. Sometimes it is worth reflecting on what would not feel safe and work back from there.

- We spend much time thinking about setting up and preparing for activities, but choosing a ritual to end your session is also important. It doesn't need to be time-consuming or complicated. It could be as simple as asking your students to gather their materials and pack them away so they are ready for the next session, or inviting them to turn to the writer on their left and thank them for their work.

Chapter 4
A new way of workshopping

Writing skills, like stones carefully placed across a river, help students and teachers step their way through the writing process. But sometimes it's hard to know where to place your foot, especially if you're under pressure to keep moving forward. The workshopping process gives your class a rare opportunity to slow down and take stock of the terrain. This is often the missing link.

All three streams of your literacy program – reading, writing and oral language – combine to create the magic of workshopping. Your writers have a chance to hear language patterns, work with imagery, activate their senses and explore fresh ways to express their ideas. Reading aloud immediately connects writers to a powerful but often overlooked energy source: their audience. It's here too that they learn the value of community, of belonging to a group of peers invested in challenging their creativity (more on that in Chapter 7).

Workshopping gives your writers the best possible chance to develop an understanding of writing that goes beyond following a set path across the river. Workshopping invites writers and teachers to step into their power and forge their own path. How do I know this?

The process of observing, listening and responding to pieces of writing is my ongoing writing apprenticeship. This dynamic process has taught me more about creativity and the teaching of writing than I ever thought possible.

In this chapter, I'm going to share what I have learnt over many years of workshopping and step you through the logistics of sharing and responding to your students' writing. Then in Chapter 5 we'll explore systems for collecting and using your observations and anecdotal records to support the young writers in your class.

A field guide to workshopping

When I first introduced workshopping into my writing programs I encountered many of the same reservations I'm sure teachers reading this book will face. My greatest fear wasn't that students wouldn't share their writing in a public forum, but whether my knowledge of writing would hold up to this type of scrutiny. Did I know enough about writing to do justice to the workshopping process? Would I be able to teach 'off the plan'? Would throwing the workshop open to the class derail my ability to keep everyone engaged and on task? I underestimated the power of storytelling.

Instead of manufacturing connections and forcing writing skills to the surface, I learned that workshopping allowed me to respond to language naturally through the context of story. Instead of feeling intimidated and under pressure to perform, I discovered the roles of teacher and student were more fluid and collaborative. Each piece of shared writing was a reflection of the writer's skills and their experience of the world. I quickly discovered that the success of workshopping didn't hinge on my ability to critique pieces of writing. Rather, I learnt that my goal was to stay present and hold space for the writer. I wasn't expected to have all the answers – and that was strangely liberating.

Drowning in a sense of overwhelm puts teachers (and students too) in survival mode. So let workshopping become your version of creative play. Placing creativity at the centre of your teaching practice is a revolutionary act. This short daily reprieve from standards and set outcomes allows you to crawl out from under the never-ending list of demands and let the day surprise you. More than a chance to build writing and literacy skills, this is also your opportunity to reconnect with your students and build strong relationships based on mutual trust, respect and creativity. Keep in mind that there is an art to making the process of workshopping safe, inclusive and collaborative. I'll share a practical framework for you to follow with useful strategies designed to open the channels of communication so your class can maximise the workshopping experience.

A framework for workshopping in the classroom

Teachers are familiar with students sharing their work and ideas in class, but workshopping adds an important dimension to this style of interaction. Workshopping is a springboard for teaching writing skills and developing relationships. Your routines and rituals play an essential role in setting the stage and encouraging students to participate, both as readers and as writers. As well as modelling writing skills, workshopping allows teachers to model active listening, curiosity and a growth mindset. Your students will follow your lead.

Let me walk you through a workshopping session with students from one of my after-school classes at The Writer's Club. At each step I will detail the course of action to be taken and then share how that often looks in my sessions. Your classroom will likely be different, but this will help you visualise the process within your own context.

1. Prompt

Start with your prompt. You might begin by playing 'The perhaps game' detailed in Chapter 1 (page 15), but you can also check out the activities section for more prompts and ideas. Remind your students that they can respond in whatever genre they choose, from writing a poem to starting a story. Then set your writing time (I suggest starting with five minutes) and get going.

> *I'm using a set of random words as writing prompts (see 'Random words', page 202) and I reach in and pull out the word* statue. *I set the timer for five minutes.*

> *Some of these writers have worked with me for many years so they know there is no pressure to complete a full piece of writing in five minutes. They also know they are free to respond to the prompt in any way they wish: write a poem, develop a fictional scene or start a reflection. They can write about not having any ideas. They can write about running out of ideas. They can even write about not wanting to write, but their challenge is to keep writing for the set time. Sometimes the most interesting ideas surface after we think we have finished.*

2. Observe

While your students are writing, simply observe. What do you notice? Focus on body language.

> *While my students are writing, I observe them in action. I tune in to their body language. I look for writers who jump right into the task without hesitation. I look for writers who ponder or who chew on the end of their pencil. I might see the excitement of an idea taking flight, witness that look of frustration or even clock a blank stare. Sometimes I catch a smile.*

> *The more I observe my students writing, the sharper my tools of observation become. I'm looking for patterns, too. Is this student always stuck, or are they just stuck today? Five minutes of focused observation delivers many insights.*

3. Listen

When your students are finished writing, ask then to place pens down and pause, then ask for a volunteer to share. As they read their work, practise deep listening. Listen to the words as well as the energy, images and ideas beneath them.

> When the timer goes off, one student, Liam, volunteers to read his piece of writing. His story is about a scientist who brings a statue to life, but something has gone wrong. The statue is threatening to destroy the world. In this scene, the scientist and the statue meet each other face to face in the laboratory. It's a short piece of writing, only a couple of paragraphs, but it's enough to provide some real insight into how Liam approached this piece of writing.
>
> Straight away, I can see that Liam can use a random word to inspire and connect a series sequential images and ideas. He includes lots of detail about the laboratory, so his ability to visualise the scene in his imagination is strong. I know Liam is a lover of science fiction. I can see how his combination of fact and fiction makes the scene feel real and believable. I can also see the influence of Liam's love of reading in this piece of writing. His writing has a natural rhythm and voice, a familiarity with how words fit together. He is also mastering the basics of writing dialogue. The dialogue between the characters is emotive and realistic. I'm tuning into the energy and expression in his voice when he reads the dialogue. Liam is invested in this piece of writing.

4. Respond

Suspend judgement and approach this part of the workshopping process with a sense of curiosity. Choose an open response. What did you notice about this piece of writing? What can this piece of writing teach us?

Further on in this chapter, I have included some suggestions for what teachers might look for in a piece of shared writing (page 85). Be guided by this list of writing skills until you build your knowledge and confidence.

> *'When I listen to you read your story, Liam, I can see your setting, the laboratory, so clearly.' Looking around at the group, I ask, 'How did you experience the setting? Could you see it in your mind's eye?' Some students nod. 'What do you think made this possible?' I ask them.*
>
> *One student recalls certain details of the setting that made it feel real.*
>
> *'What other details can we remember?' I ask.*
>
> *As a group we start to list the details in the setting – from the white walls to the way the door clicked shut, which made us think it might be locked. We see that details, especially sensory details, hook us into the story and are important when it comes to developing a sense of place.*

Thank your reader for allowing the group to work with their writing. If time allows, listen to another piece of writing. If another student shares their writing, look for any natural connections between the pieces of shared writing. This makes it possible for you to reinforce what you have discussed. In this case that might be the importance of sensory details, or you may find another teaching point naturally arises.

Teachers often use mentor texts to highlight skills and now your students have an opportunity to mentor each other. Teaching writing skills in context makes them more accessible to all writers in your class.

Practical ways to get the most out of workshopping

Because teachers are working against the clock, it might feel more productive to critique or edit a piece of shared writing together so that the writer in question, and the class as a whole, can see what didn't work and learn how to fix it. Although there is a time and place for editing pieces of writing together with your class, workshopping in the context of your writing practice invites you to accept the inherent value in a piece of writing and work out from there. Our aim is to develop writing skills without the familiar currency of right or wrong. This calls for a different mindset and a new approach for both teachers and students.

Fine-tune your observation skills

Fine-tuning your powers of observation starts while your class are discovery writing. As hard as it can be, resist the urge to complete important admin tasks while your students are writing. This is your time to tune in to the energy of the room and hone your powers of observation.

We can get locked into particular stories and beliefs about the writers in our class, but what if you didn't know each students' backstory? What if you were seeing them for the first time? Observe your students' body language. See pencils moving swiftly across pages. Listen for frustrated sighs. Note who jumps into writing quickly and who takes time to get started. Who anxiously watches their peers or stares out the window? You might catch a smile floating across a writer's face, or a frown.

Much of a teacher's life is spent actively measuring, evaluating and solving problems. Observation feels passive in comparison, but don't misjudge its potential; focused observation gathers valuable information about both your students' mindset and their writing skills. We'll explore this more in Chapter 5.

Offer a sliding scale of participation

Rather than trying to include every class member as a reader in workshopping, which would result in speeding through the process and making few if any connections to the writing under consideration, I find focusing on two or three students per prompt gives your class plenty of scope and keeps the process active and alive.

Let's be mindful, too, of how we can support all class members to participate in the workshopping process. What practical steps can teachers take to encourage everyone to get involved? The aim of workshopping is not for your talented writers to model their skills while their classmates sit in awe (or drown in self-doubt). Although this sounds counterintuitive, one of the best ways to encourage your students to join in is to make sharing voluntary. This simple shift loosens the balance of power. Set the expectation that all members of the class will benefit from workshopping but then ask students to join in as they are ready. Giving them agency and responsibility for their involvement is key. Sometimes I might sense a writer needs a gentle, encouraging nudge forward, but the writer makes the final call; 'I'll pass on sharing today' is a valid response.

For introverts and reluctant writers, reading a piece of their writing aloud may be beyond their comfort zone so it's important to consider ways to offer a steadying arm to support them. You can scaffold this process by building in a sliding scale of participation. Before you ask for a workshopping volunteer, ask your class to silently read through their writing and underline their favourite sentence or even a single word. Then ask students to share their sentence or single word. Or ask writers to reflect on how they felt while they were writing and to share their response. Once again, all answers are acceptable. Providing opportunities to share a word, a sentence or a personal response is a necessary first step for some writers.

Employ deep listening

As your writers read aloud, train yourself to listen to more than their words. Listen for rhythm, inflection, trepidation, hesitation. Listen for vulnerability, for the writer who says, 'This isn't very good' before they start to read but keeps going anyway. Listen for the space between words. Be aware of the hand that always shoots up first as well as the hand that half lifts and is then pulled down again. Listen for stories that match or challenge what you know about the writer's experience of the world, like the child whose mother has passed and is writing about the death of her character's mother. Tune in to the emotions buried deep beneath the words. It's hard to sustain this intense level of listening throughout the day, but for this short period of time, be fully present.

Deep listening gives you access to the conscious and subconscious thinking that sometimes cloud our vision and perception. It helps develop an intuitive understanding of writing and writers. By simply paying attention you open a portal into the writer's inner world and begin to understand your students' writing skills from the inside out. There's a synergy here, too, because the data you collect (through observation and anecdotal records, as we'll discuss in Chapter 5) hones another vital teaching skill: your intuition. This adds a new dimension to the teaching of writing.

Give feedback that focuses on strengths

Our educational system is powered by a deficit model that trains teachers to focus on the shortfall – that is, what their students can't do and where they fail to meet curriculum standards. Workshopping is almost the opposite incarnation; you are focusing on the strengths and qualities of a piece of writing. I always thank writers for sharing their writing because I know how vulnerable I feel when I share, then I highlight the skills and techniques the writer has used. It's not until we start to suspend judgement that we realise how entrenched we are in the black-and-white economy of good or bad. When you're not under pressure to form judgements, you're free to accept the piece of writing as it stands. Once students realise that their writing will be accepted, less confident writers are often more willing to share their work.

Ask open questions

Instead of applying judgements, ask open questions and model open responses. What skills has the writer used? Is there an evocative image that stays with the audience? Often this will be a colour or a sensory detail. What is your instinctive physical response to the piece of writing?

What message is your body giving you? This tells you about the mood and energy of a piece of writing.

Modelling this style of response encourages your students to notice the details, the essential elements that build a piece of writing. This sort of feedback also provides the writer with information they can immediately use. In *The Skillful Teacher*, Stephen D Brookfield (2015) suggests that students need feedback that sparks the desire to engage in further inquiry. If we want to move writers (especially reluctant writers) through the process, they need feedback that builds confidence, self-esteem and writing skills in an authentic way.

Here are some examples of open responses to pieces of writing:

- What I feel when I listen to your writing is …
- What I see in my mind's eye …
- What I hear …
- What I imagine …
- When I listen to your words …
- This detail stayed in my mind. Tell us more about that?

Build your knowledge

The workshopping process may be unfamiliar and perhaps even uncomfortable territory for some teachers, but your knowledge of writing skills and curriculum guidelines are still your landmarks and points of reference. Just like your writers, who need a sliding scale of participation, teachers need strategies to assist their transition to workshopping.

When I first presented writing workshops in schools I'd prepare for a workshop by mapping out one or two possible focus skills to guide the workshopping experience. For example, if we were working with an imaginative prompt, I might choose sensory details as a possible springboard for discussion. Then, as writers shared, I would listen out for sensory details such as colour, sound, smells and textures. Mapping out possible focus skills in advance gave me the structure I needed to approach workshopping with more confidence. Interestingly enough, planning focus skills in this way also helped me build my own writers toolkit. As soon as I chose a set of focus skills I'd naturally start looking for examples in my own reading. I'd start listening to what other writers said about sensory detail, description or pace.

Your literacy program and curriculum guidelines provide many leads regarding focus skills. Any skill can be introduced through the workshopping process. Here is a list of skills that I'm always on the lookout for ways to highlight when I'm teaching because I know they can transform a piece of writing:

- sensory imagery (words and phrases that engage a reader's senses)
- active verbs
- pace
- mood and atmosphere
- word choice
- fresh metaphors and similes
- engaging story hooks
- strong writer's voice
- character development
- active dialogue (dialogue that provides valuable information or moves the narrative forward)
- perspective (zooming in on significant and specific details).

Workshopping requires a different mindset and approach to developing writing skills, but it's also the very place where the magic and science of writing come together. Writing is full of surprises; there are always new discoveries to make along the way.

Develop and maintain a code of conduct

I use this same framework when I work with teachers; we write, share and respond to pieces of writing. One teacher who attended a professional development seminar later told me how anxious she felt when she finally shared her writing with the group. This prompted her to open up a discussion with her class and together they developed a series of guidelines for workshopping to ensure everyone felt supported and comfortable to participate.

Developing a workshopping code of conduct with your students is essentially creating a set of shared expectations to guide and shape behaviour. It is there to help you navigate your way around any obstacles you encounter along the way. For help with collaboratively developing a code of conduct for workshopping, see 'Your action plan' in Chapter 7 (page 150).

Summary

All three streams of your literacy program – writing, reading and oral language – collide in workshopping. First, discovery writing gives shape and form to abstract thoughts, ideas and feelings; then workshopping steps in and allows your students to engage with writing in new ways. Whether we are journalling for an audience of one or writing to share with others, the simple combination of reading and speaking gives writers time to fully digest the imagery, language and skills they have set down on their page. The opportunity to teach writing skills in context is motivation enough to add this vital stage to your writing practice, but workshopping is also a powerful way to build relationships and develop community (as we'll see in Chapter 7).

At its core, workshopping acknowledges that we all have something valuable to say. It gives writing and writers an opportunity to show up and be seen and heard. It invites teachers and students to lean into their intuition, trust their gut instincts. Workshopping requires an intense focus which is impossible to sustain throughout the school day, but for a short period of time, this is your active training ground.

Power points

- All three streams of your literacy program – reading, writing and oral language – combine in workshopping, which features reading aloud and responding to peers' writing.
- Workshopping connects writers to their audience, which is one of the missing links in our writing programs, and encourages students to learn with and from each other.
- Instead of forcing connection and writing skills, workshopping allows class groups to respond to language through the context of story.
- Approach workshopping from a place of non-judgement and encourage open responses.
- Your main goal is to open the channels of communication, allowing opportunities to arise for teachers and students to learn together.

Pause and reflect

- It's challenging to observe your students without judgement, to see them as a stranger might see them. What did you notice when you stopped and observed your class writing?
- Did any of your observations provide new insights about your writers?
- When it comes to workshopping, how comfortable or challenging is it for you to respond to writing without making value judgements?
- Workshopping involves a loosening of the reins of control, allowing the roles of teacher and learner to be more fluid. How do you feel about this? How did it impact your teaching style?

- What writing skills are you most familiar with? Which skills trip you up a little?
- What strategies could you use to build your working knowledge of writing skills?

Your action plan

Try workshopping

In this chapter, I'm asking you to try workshopping with your students and then take some time to reflect on your experience. Possibly the biggest stumbling block you will encounter is moving from actively critiquing pieces of writing to suspending judgement and exploring this new mindset. Let's get started!

1. Start with your prompt. If you haven't tried this activity before, get yourself an empty lunchbox or any other object of your choice and play 'The perhaps game' as detailed at the start of Chapter 1 (page 15).
2. Set your writing time. I suggest starting with five minutes.
3. While your students are writing, simply observe. What do you notice? Focus in on their body language and jot down any details you notice.
4. When the time is up and your class has finished writing, ask for a volunteer to share their work.
5. Practise deep listening. Engage your senses. Listen to the words as well as the energy and imagery beneath them.
6. Choose your response. Stay open and curious. What did you immediately notice about this piece of writing? What physical sensations did you have? This might tell you about the mood or tone of the writing. Use the list of skills provided to guide your questions. What can this piece of writing teach you? Even

A new way of workshopping

the most basic piece of writing will offer a starting point for discussion. Has the writer introduced a character? Ask them to tell you a little more about this character. Not everything that comes up in workshopping will necessarily be written on the page.

7. Thank your reader for allowing the group to work with their writing.

8. If time allows, listen to another piece of writing and see if you can make a connection with the first piece. Is there an opportunity to reinforce skills or will you explore something new?

Chapter 5
The feedback loop

Teachers welcome the vital role assessment plays in guiding and monitoring their teaching practice, but the swing towards standardised testing means that they often experience assessment as a powerful adversary, swooping in to control what they teach and how they teach it. Debra Dirksen (2013) captures the collective frustration felt by teachers the world over:

> *Too often we teach a unit of instruction, give a test, look at the results and move on to the next unit, regardless of the outcome. Sometimes it feels that the only measures of student learning we value are the tests we use to assign a grade in a course. (p. 15)*

The one-shot approach to assessment doesn't value the individual experience of writers or measure achievement in a meaningful or ongoing way. It doesn't come close to representing the genuine teaching and learning that takes place in our classrooms. Your writing practice, however, provides a unique opportunity to redress this shortfall. Rather than measuring and ranking your students' skills against static curriculum standards, your writing practice is student focused and collaborative. It celebrates your students' abilities and effort regardless of where they fall on the continuum.

In this chapter I'll explore three practical feedback loops and a range of simple record-keeping systems teachers and students can use to monitor writing skills in a meaningful, purposeful way. Your writing practice may not follow a fixed course towards a set destination, but teachers are not flying blind. In fact, the opposite is true. The data you gather during your writing practice tells an ongoing comprehensive narrative that authentically represents each student's writing abilities and efforts in real time.

Using feedback loops

Testing and formal assessment weigh heavily on most teachers. Despite the fact that it is impossible to control all the variables, teachers often feel they shoulder full responsibility for their students' results. The pressure to 'get your students over the line' doesn't always build positive relationships or foster a love of writing.

Formal assessment is not the best fit for monitoring your writing practice, but to maximise the efficiency of this short period of time each day, teachers do need a method of capturing the important learning that is taking place and feeding this back into their planning and teaching. We will now delve into three vital feedback loops which allow teachers to:

1. plan, track and assess their writing practice as a whole
2. monitor their students' skill development, interests and learning needs
3. empower students to take responsibility for their learning through the use of self-assessment practices.

Using these circular feedback loops ensures your writing practice is responsive to the needs of your specific group of students and recognises the adaptive nature of your writing practice. It's circular, rather than linear; it's student centred, conversational and collaborative.

While there is a place for formal assessment as part of your overall literacy program, your writing practice relies on systemising a range of formative assessment tools that I'm confident teachers already use, such as observation, anecdotal records, logbook style planning and class meetings.

Before you launch into your classroom practice, you'll need to gather the necessary materials and set up a simple record-keeping system. Once you have your system in place, you can use this 'Writing practice action plan' (figure 1, page 94, available for download) to map out the week ahead. Observations, anecdotal records and even your class discussions are absorbed into the time frame of your writing practice. I want to ensure that the time and energy you invest in collecting data directly benefits you and your students. The minute you start accumulating information that doesn't feed back into your writing practice and inspire your next step, it's time to take stock.

Feedback loop 1: Program planning and evaluation

All teachers know the value of good planning and preparation. This first feedback loop provides a structure and a methodology for both mapping the direction of your writing practice over the week and recording the learning that surfaces during your sessions. Once recorded, these important discoveries inform the direction your practice will take the following week.

While teachers take responsibility for the weekly planning process, evaluating your writing practice as a whole is a collaborative experience. Regular class reviews allow students to give valuable feedback and troubleshoot any issues that arise.

Start with a plan. When you're steering a course towards a fixed outcome, your program planning has a jumbo-jet quality to it: you select your route and fly steadily towards your destination. Any changes in the weather or unforeseen circumstances need to be managed quickly so you can get back on course. Your writing practice on the other hand has the same light quality of hot air ballooning. You can't plot the

Time to Write

Writing practice action plan	Focus students	1	2	
Date		3	4	
				Focus skills
Monday	Notes			
Tuesday	Notes			
Wednesday	Notes			
Thursday	Notes			
Friday	Notes			

Future directions/week in review

Figure 1: Writing practice action plan
A free reproducible version of this figure is available

exact course in advance. You're relying on wind currents and making judgements based on your instinct, knowledge and observations. Your planning needs to reflect this fundamental difference.

The 'Writing practice action plan' (figure 1) invites you to chart the course of your writing practice in advance and keep brief records of your daily writing adventures in logbook style. This simple A4 planner captures prompts, records focus students for the week and provides space to note any discussion topics that arise during workshopping so you can reinforce and expand learning. Your workshopping discussions and teaching points inform not only your writing practice, but also spill into your greater literacy program. Your planner also offers space to note which students shared their writing so you have a way of tracking student interactions. These logbook details are designed to be collected quickly after your session and give teachers a sense of control over the process.

Let's walk through the planning process.

1. Create your timetable

The first task is to allocate days and times for your writing practice to take place. Daily writing is your ideal goal, but if this isn't possible then aim for a minimum of three fifteen-minute blocks during the week. As discussed in Chapter 3, a regular time frame improves creative flow, but aim for progress rather than perfection. Work with the time you have and adapt where necessary.

2. Map your prompts

In the activity section I have included three styles of prompts: 'Mine you life for writing inspiration', personal writing prompts; 'Imagine this', prompts designed to spark works of fiction; and 'Hello writer', prompts to help writers reflect on their writing identity. Young writers need a balanced writing diet. They need opportunities to use writing to demonstrate what they know as well as opportunities to tell stories, to imagine, to express feelings, to reflect and to make sense of the world. Choose one prompt to work with for each session. Writing at least three times a week gives your students a chance to work with prompts across all three categories.

3. Record focus students

At the top of the planner you will see a space for recording the names of your focus students for the week. In previous chapters I've referenced the importance of limiting readings to two or three students per session to allow both the writers and the writing to shine. Now I am going to take this one step further and recommend you choose a small group of focus students each week. This ensures that over the course of your school term, every student comes under your observational gaze. The number of students you choose to focus on each week is not prescriptive, but, depending on the size of your group, four focus students per week should allow you to cycle through your class with some regularity. Your goal each week should be to write one detailed observation for each of your focus students. Your observations are designed to add depth and clarity to the assessment data you already have as part of your literacy program. This system of choosing focus students is ultimately more useful than scribbling down general, vague notes about many students each week. In the next feedback loop we'll zoom in on writing effective observational records and how to organise your notes.

4. Record focus skills

If you are planning to focus on any particular skill for the session, note this under your prompt. (See the short discussion of focus skills on page 85 for inspiration.)

5. Note discussion topics (after writing)

I always have a whiteboard ready for workshopping sessions. This allows me to capture the conversation as I go. I write the date on the board as students are setting up. After your writing session, when your students are packing up their materials, jot down the main topic or theme that emerged during workshopping and take a photo of the whiteboard for your reference. Although you are not collecting and correcting each piece of writing, it's important to track these conversations because they feed into your literacy program and help you adapt your teaching.

6. Record observations

Depending on your available time, record your observations or simply write the student's name on a sticky note, index card or digital file with a word or two to jog your memory so you can return to this task as soon as possible. We will cover observational records in more detail shortly.

7. Consider future directions

This space at the bottom of your planner invites you to reflect on your next steps. What came up during the week that could be valuable to consider in your future planning? What skills could you expand or reinforce in the following week?

Class evaluation: Writing practice review

While program planning and record keeping is the teacher's domain, conducting a regular review of your writing practice gives your students the opportunity to play a vital role in this feedback loop. The length and frequency of your meetings is flexible, but checking in at least once a term is favourable and gives students an opportunity to develop their critical thinking skills. Taking ownership for the smooth running of your practice also develops teamwork, cooperation and interpersonal skills that benefit students across all curriculum areas. If time is particularly short, you could schedule a writing practice review in place of one of your writing sessions. At the end of this chapter, 'Your action plan' (page 106) suggests some questions you can use to conduct your first writing practice review.

Feedback loop 2: Teacher–student observational records

Our first feedback loop centred on preparing for and then evaluating the learning taking place in your writing practice – a wide-angle view of your class and their collective engagement with writing. With that foundation firmly in place, you are now ready to note and appreciate the unique interests and strengths of each member of your class with teacher–student observational records.

Your observational records reveal how your students engage with their creativity and make use of their writing skills. As students write, share work and build community, you will also bear witness to a range of academic and personal development skills, including leadership, empathy, risk-taking and teamwork. Collect these insights. They breathe life and energy into your assessment practices.

Observational records

Your observational records offer a clear snapshot of your students' skills, strengths and relationship with writing. This can be more valuable than a test result. While observational records are brief and to the point, there is a skill to writing them well. Be guided by the information that feels most useful to you. Because your observational notes record your students' skills and strengths, it's possible to share this with your students to assist them in setting goals and tracking their progress.

Here are my top tips for making observational records:

- An observational record is brief. You are trying to catch the essence of an observation, not give a detailed response.
- Always record the student's name and the date.
- Record what the student is doing and any supporting evidence.

    Max is exploring writer's voice through developing his tree character. He captures the character's stream of consciousness and shows the reader exactly what his character is thinking and feeling. He also uses dialogue effectively to reveal character details such as accent, personality traits and physical characteristics.

- Make your observations student centred and provide concrete examples of behaviour and experiences. I've written notes like

'Emma is engaged and on-task today!', but when I come back to it, I have no real idea what prompt caught Emma's attention or what 'on-task' actually meant. The following entry would be more helpful.

Using a single object (a golden key) to inspire her piece of writing helped Emma settle into her flow. She wrote for five minutes without distraction and was first to put up her hand to share. This is the first time I have seen her volunteer to read aloud.

- Because we are seeking to highlight our students' strengths, let your observations capture what you see happening rather than what your student is not doing. Collecting what a student can do will prove more instructional when looking at next steps.
- Noticing whether an observation triggers or raises your frustration levels is also worth noting. What does it tell you about your bias or your connection to the stories you have about your students?
- Curriculum guidelines can help frame your observations, but don't be limited by these skills. Take a holistic approach and gather any information that develops a deeper understanding of your students, including body language.

Focus students

Using a focus student approach noted in the first feedback loop systemises your observations and allows you to keep track of all writers in your class. But the question remains: What if your focus students don't volunteer to share their writing that week? Don't stress. This method of record keeping allows you to gather data flexibly across several streams.

While your students are writing, observe your focus students. Look for engagement and note body language. Keep these students in mind as you go about your day and week. Sometimes insights are gained outside of the time set aside for your writing practice. All of this can be valuable. For example, having workshopped a short poem with a Year 6 writer at the start of the day, that same writer found me at the end of the day to tell me about the changes he had made to his poem and why. Understanding and learning doesn't always land on time during your writing practice, so be prepared to gather writing observations during your school day.

Organising your observational records

At first, swapping formal assessment tasks and additional marking for observational records might feel like a weight lifted off your shoulders. But unless you find an effective way to organise and maintain this system, it quickly becomes unmanageable. I find analogue systems work best for observational records. In my experience, the act of handwriting your observations lodges them in your memory. As you file an observation, you reread it, you ponder it.

Apart from being easily accessible, sticky notes allow you to collect brief observational records and store them easily. Start with a stack of sticky notes and one A4 piece of paper per student. You should be able to attach four to six completed notes per page. I find it helps to staple notes to the page to make sure they stay in place and are easy to read. Pop each page into a clear plastic sleeve and place a page divider between each student or group of focus students in a binder.

Another way to collect and organise your observational records is to use sets of coloured index cards. For example, if you have twenty-four students it's possible to create six focus groups of four students each. Each of these focus groups can then be allotted a different colour card, one card for your observations of each student. Index cards can then be filed under student names in a filing box – or simply stacked in alphabetical order and secured with a rubber band.

Of course you can also use digital files to collect your observations, but be mindful of incoming messages, emails and so forth that could distract you from the task at hand.

Feedback loop 3: Self-regulated assessment

Two questions surface time and time again when I work with teachers in their classrooms. How can I help students to generate fresh ideas? And then, once students have something down on the page, how can I motivate (coax, force) them to edit their work? While the first two feedback loops are externally focused, monitoring what is seen and heard in your classroom, the final feedback loop invites your students to analyse and compare pieces of their own writing for evaluation purposes. This allows students to experience their writing as both reader and writer. Reading their own writing, hearing and seeing themselves on the page, offers writers agency and control over the process.

National curriculum guidelines, developmental learning objectives and assessment practices set a clearly defined course through the educational terrain. We pause at regular checkpoints to take stock and mark off skills – then the race is on again. It doesn't take young writers long to absorb the value our culture places on finish lines. Once your writers put down their pens, their energy is spent. Asking our students (or any writer for that matter) to stop, go back and retrace their steps calls for a different mindset and source of motivation altogether.

The collections of writing in your students' notebooks are the most valuable self-evaluation resource you have at your disposal. Because the pieces of writing are naturally short and concise, writers are not forced to confront mountains of text to compare and analyse their work. Self-evaluation skills take time to develop, but cultivating this growth mindset gives your writers an advantage for life and encourages them to take ownership of their writing journey.

Check and reflect

Allowing time for students to revisit and review their pieces of writing is essential for self-evaluation purposes. Reading their own writing helps students see how their ideas and experiences turn up on the page. If you write up to three times a week, students accumulate a range of story seeds that map their progress. Self-evaluation encompasses more than simply editing a piece of writing for grammar, spelling and punctuation. If you want to motivate writers to enjoy reading their work, provide opportunities for them to highlight and acknowledge their creative strengths and abilities as well. Celebrating our progress is a positive, energetic experience that propels us forward.

First, let's get your students reading their own writing. You might choose to set aside one of your writing practice sessions for this or complete your check and reflect at another time. You will develop your own system for encouraging your students to review pieces of writing, but here are four starting points:

- Ask writers to choose one piece of writing and use a highlighter to mark two phrases or sentences that most appeal to them. What did they like about their sentences? What technique or skill have they used that appeals to them?
- Ask writers to check through a series of entries (for example, everything written in the month of March) and mark any pieces of writing they'd like to expand further. This helps writers tune in to the energy behind a piece of writing and learn to generate their own writing topics. One of the lists I suggested including in student notebooks in Chapter 2 was 'Stories I want to write' (page 52). Keeping track of creative ideas and inspirations is an important part of being a writer, and this is the perfect place to capture this information. If your students come across a piece of their writing that inspires them, ask them to create a working title for the idea and add it to their list. Then allow time during your literacy block for students to go back and develop some of these scenes into short stories.
- Ask writers to choose a favourite piece of their writing for the week, month or term, read it to a classmate, then listen carefully while their classmate shares their own favourite

piece of writing. Rather than judge the pieces of writing, ask students to identify the skills and techniques the other used and find evidence of this.

- Ask writers to choose a piece of writing and add one new idea. Could they add a colour detail? Could they add a sentence to help the reader see the setting more clearly? Use a sticky note to add the idea and place it over the top of the story. Alternatively, students might work in pairs to share one piece of writing and ask their partner to offer one additional idea.

Read and edit like a writer

Teaching students to read and edit their own writing is a complex task made much simpler if you're only working with short pieces of writing. Let's explore how discovery writing, workshopping and the skills that surface when responding to a piece of writing naturally link into your student self-evaluation.

In a recent workshop I used a fast piece of instrumental music to inspire students to write an action scene. When we began workshopping, verbs became our focus. One writer had used the word *jog*, but when questioned about how fast his character was moving he agreed that his character wasn't jogging – he was flat out running. *Jog* wasn't a fast enough verb to describe the action. The writer changed the word to *sprint*. Another writer described a scene in which a book fell through a window. I asked her to describe in detail how the book fell through the window. When she described the scene, she automatically swapped in the word *crashed* for *fell*. As soon as she said this, she self-edited her writing. I noted this discussion and during our next check and reflect session the class chose a short scene from their notebooks, isolated the verbs and checked whether their choices carried out the specific action they wanted to convey. Then we shared our upgrades: *cut* became *snip*, *run* became *sprint* and *shake* became *tremble*. Apart from an interesting conversation about the superpowers of the simple verb, this on-the-spot, or 'just-in-time', editing lesson was all recorded in notebooks and became a resource for future learning. We also created a 'Verb upgrade list' for future reference and added a new entry to the list of writing tips they were collecting in their notebooks (see Chapter 2, page 52): 'Match verbs with the action they need to describe. Be specific.'

A writer's level of experience and writing skills directly impacts their ability to edit their work. A writer may sense their story doesn't quite hang together, but they might not know how to fix it. We have already highlighted the fact that, once finished, a writer is often reluctant to make changes. However, the shorter pieces of writing collected during writing practice have instant appeal for editing because they are rough drafts, so writers expect they need a refining and tweaking. More importantly, they are short scenes; it's much easier to dip your toes into one paragraph than to wade through pages and pages of writing.

The skills you model during the workshopping phase of your writing practice become the same skills students use to edit their pieces of writing. In the activity section of this book you will find a range of strategies, positioned as games, that you can use to help students level-up their own writing. In this section you will find activities that help your students engage their senses ('Turn on your senses', page 286), clarify their message ('Dumper', page 278), zoom in on word choice ('Scale up', page 281) and more.

Summary

Flying by the seat of your pants is an aviation idiom that originated in the days before nautical instruments and flight plans, when pilots relied on a combination of instinct, judgement and knowledge to fly from A to B. Their logbooks detailed their flying experience and told the stories of their adventures in the sky. There was no such thing as automatic pilot; flying required a pilot's full attention. Your writing practice draws on this same instinctive and mindful approach to develop writing skills – and your assessment records reflect this philosophy.

Assessment is an essential part of the process, but the data teachers gather helps to build relationships while revealing the opportunities and complexities of the writing process to students and teachers. Nothing is wasted. By using simple tools available to all teachers, it's possible to experience both a sense of control and the thrill of creative freedom and spontaneity. Your end goal is to create independent, engaged writers who love to write. Your assessment processes and systems work to fulfil this fundamental goal. You are not collecting notes to justify your teaching decisions; rather, you will find yourself deeply invested in this process because what you witness will be too instructive to not give it your full attention.

Power points

- Three feedback loops keep your writing practice in balance: program planning and evaluation, teacher–student observational records, and self-regulated assessment.
- Formative assessment tools such as ongoing observational records, class discussion and logbook-style planning allow teachers to collect data that honours each student and measures skill and ability.
- Assessment plays a key role in monitoring progress, guiding teaching practice and developing writing skills.
- This style of assessment is student centred, collaborative and focuses on celebrating strengths as opposed to emphasising deficits.

Pause and reflect

Teachers are so accustomed to multitasking that slowing down and staying fully present can be a challenge. What other obstacles might you personally encounter when it comes to this form of record keeping? How comfortable do you feel 'flying by the seat of your pants' during workshopping and program planning? What steps could you take to ease the transition?

Set a timer for five minutes and write down all the questions that circle in your mind, such as:

- How do I motivate all the writers in my class?
- How do I feel about teaching writing?
- How do I help my students generate ideas?

Answer these questions as best you can now, then return to them as the months progress to see how your writing practice is feeding your teaching practice.

Your action plan

Review your writing practice

A periodic class review keeps your finger on the pulse of your writing practice and gives your writers a platform for sharing their thoughts and ideas. Scheduling your review and briefing your students in advance gives them a chance to incubate ideas.

Start by making sure your writers can see and hear each other clearly. You may like to sit together in a circle. If you would like to give writers a chance to add discussion points, consider tabling an agenda in the days before your meeting. You could also set some of the questions below as homework tasks so writers have a chance to privately think through their responses.

Each class will conduct their review differently, but the following structure, which invites consideration of the good, bad and curious elements of your practice – as put forward by Chris Durham (2003) – is a great springboard for getting the process started. Once you have this structure in place, your class review should not require onerous preparation.

I have included some lead questions in response to each prompt to get you on your way, but don't try to cover them all. Simply start by choosing one for each section and follow the discussion from there.

Good
Start your review by focusing on the positives:

- What aspects of the program are going well for us?
- What part of this process do we like most?
- What creative routines are working for us?
- What positive outcomes are we experiencing as a result of our writing practice?
- How is our code of conduct guiding our behaviour?

Bad
These questions invite students to air any difficulties they have and access their problem-solving skills:

- Where do we encounter roadblocks or obstacles?
- How could we improve our writing practice?
- What could we do to make the session run more smoothly?
- Are there any particular problems we need to air and discuss?
- Do we need to update our code of conduct?

Curious
These questions can be about writing or the structure of the process in your classroom:

- What is creative flow?
- What helps or hinders the creative flow for us?
- What is a mind blank? Why do mind blanks occur?
- How important is it to feel a sense of safety when it comes to creativity?

- What writers do we know that use creative routines to help them access flow?
- What inspires us?
- What other questions come to mind when we think about our writing practice?

Chapter 6
Individualising your writing practice

No doubt there are writers in your class who happily head off into the land of fiction, their pencils moving in time with their imaginations as they race after a story. They'll return soon enough with a tale about a dragon who loved eating golden carrots. Of course, golden carrots were plentiful until a mystery thief appeared. These young writers fish in a lake of vivid images and fresh ideas. You can't help but smile when you read their stories. Then there are the writers at the other end of the continuum; let's call them *cloud writers*. Words and images form like misty clouds before their eyes, but just as they reach out to touch them, they are gone. Instead of returning with a story slung over their shoulder, cloud writers spend their writing time developing an impressive range of avoidance tactics – sharpening pencils, hiding among school bags and searching for missing books and pens.

There are as many different writers as there are students in your classroom, which means teachers are often juggling the needs of twenty or more students, each with their own skill sets, learning styles and natural tendencies. How is it possible to get your class over the line and still be responsive to your students' individual needs?

Your writing practice approaches differentiation from a unique standpoint. There is no hidden agenda for your writers to achieve the same outcomes at the same time. Rather, it acknowledges that students learn in different ways and at different rates. Every component of your practice, from discovery writing and workshopping to gathering observational records, validates the experience of the individual writer. It's designed to support writers in their quest to realise their individual creative potential.

In this chapter I'll guide you through using a three-step framework to dial up the impact of your observations and respond to students' individual needs. This reflective process, together with your observational records and assessment results, paints a detailed picture of the writers in your class, from their mindset and personal associations with writing to their actual writing skills. A narrative arc tracks the journey of a story, it details the many paths that characters take to overcome challenges and achieve their goal. In the same way, the ARC approach I suggest gives teachers a practical tool for understanding, shaping and sustaining their students' individual writing journeys.

A note on labels and classifications

Before we begin, let's return to our golden-carrot and cloud writers. I know you recognise these writers, their labels and their stories. Classifications and labels allow teachers to differentiate learning, but these constructs also have a shadow side; they have the potential to lock teachers and students into limiting stories and paradigms. In truth, most writers experience golden-carrot and cloud days, as well as the myriad positions in between. Inconsistencies flourish and (thankfully) writers rarely stay neatly within the labels they are assigned. A writing practice acknowledges the writer first and foremost. You get to decide whether the stories and beliefs you have about your writers, as accurate as they may be at a certain point in time, become obstacles and roadblocks or starting points and springboards.

Taking a holistic approach

Despite the fact that your students are expected to achieve the same curriculum goals and master the same set of skills by the end of the school year, every writer in your class is a unique puzzle, made up of many interconnecting pieces. Our writers, however, don't come in a neat box, with all the pieces inside and a guiding image on the lid.

Thankfully, teachers are tenacious problem solvers. Data, such as assessment and test results, are corner pieces: they provide a starting point. Handwriting samples add another piece to the puzzle in terms of motor skills. But these elements only give us part of the picture. When it comes to developing a deeper understanding of what makes each writer tick, teachers are often faced with inconsistencies and missing pieces.

Gardner's model

I first discovered Paul Gardner's (2011) model when I was researching methods for supporting reluctant writers in the classroom. His research explores many factors that influence a writer's motivation and love of writing and identifies five broad domains in a causal model for reluctance towards writing (shown in figure 2): pedagogic causes, physical factors, cognitive processes, cultural ecology and, at the heart of these, the affective resistor (Gardner, 2011).

While Gardner's model started its life as a diagnostic tool for reluctant writers, it's applicable to all writers. It helps us become aware of the wide range of factors that impact writing ability and helps teachers individualise their teaching practice. As I began to gather information and observations across the domains in Gardner's model, it became easier to recognise obstacles, connect ideas and notice patterns; the writer came more clearly into focus.

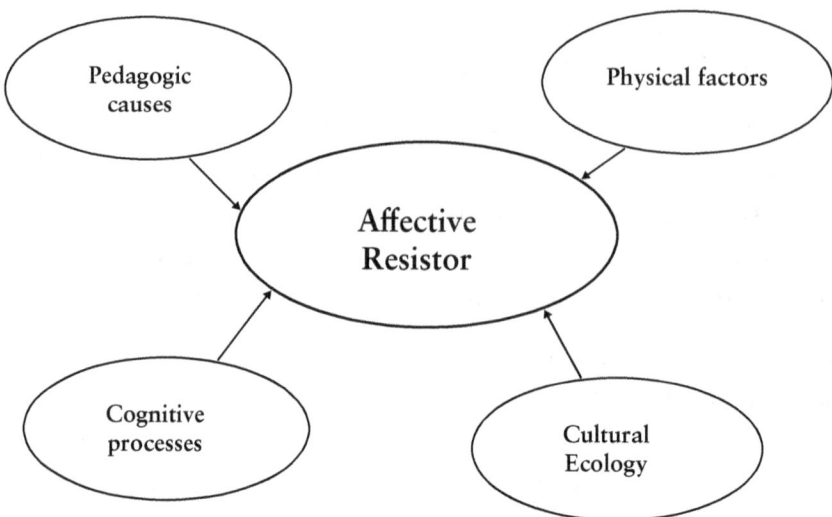

Figure 2: 'The reluctant writer: Towards a causal model'
Source: Gardner, 2011, p. 38

Let's start at the centre with the *affective resistor*, which Gardner (2011) defines as 'the extent to which the writer's emotional and/or psychological state inhibits their motivation to write effectively' (p. 39). That is, the feelings, emotions, attitudes and personal associations the writer holds towards the act of writing directly affects their writing identity. The four remaining domains orbit and contribute to this affective resistor, impacting the affective resistor and ultimately the writer's experience in different ways (Gardner, 2011). *Cognitive processes* includes memory, language processing and literacy skills, as well as creative thinking skills such as visualisation, while *pedagogic causes* refers to both instruction and the wider nuances of teaching practice, such as a teacher's attitudes and deeply held beliefs. *Physical factors* include both fine and gross motor skills, as well physical coordination, and *cultural ecology* captures the many factors outside the classroom that impact a writer. This includes parental expectations, cultural and socio-economic influences such as a writer's range of life experiences and availability of resources outside the classroom. Interestingly, cultural ecology also refers to the learning environment and classroom culture, including cultural norms such as standardised testing.

Inspired by Gardner's (2011) research, I built on his model of causation to help me pose questions and reflect on the factors that influence my students' writing identity and creative potential. Like Gardner, I placed the affective resistor in the centre, but I added another domain: social and emotional capacity. I was interested in how a writer's emotional intelligence played into their writing identity. Self-awareness, motivation and the ability to regulate one's behaviour all impact the quality of a writer's experience. Skills such as social awareness, leadership and empathy inform our sense of belonging and community, which is an integral part of your classroom writing practice. My final adjustment is adding the writer to our version of the model. This illustrates that all of these factors combine to impact the writer and how they experience the writing process.

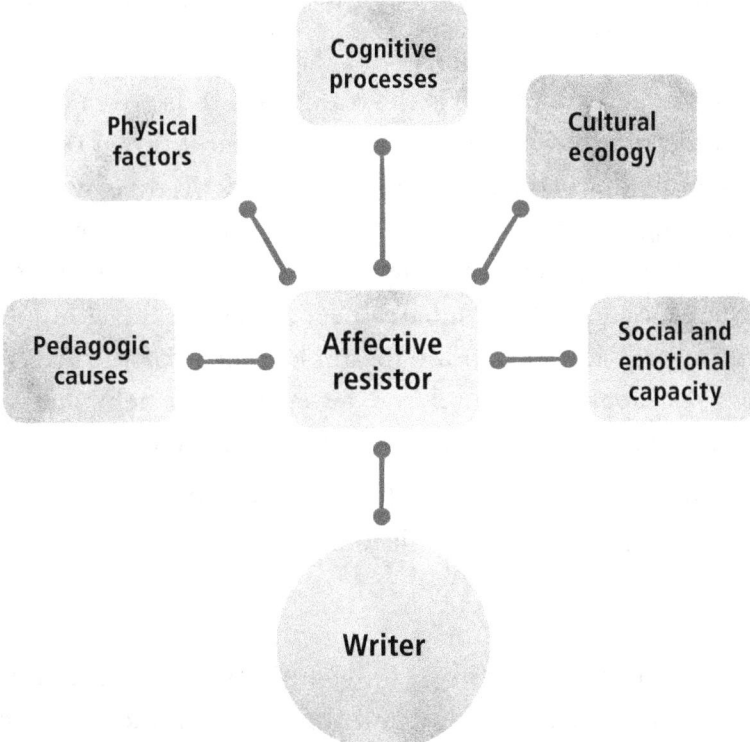

Figure 3: An extended causal model of the affective resistor
Source: Adapted from Gardner, 2011

Working across these six domains allows you to view your students from many angles. Your observational records note body language and conversations, catch the threads of thoughts and ideas, and pinpoint writing strengths, all of which reveal your writers' true natures. When teachers combine these anecdotal records with test results and additional assessment data, they have a powerful tool for understanding the skills, mindset, behaviours and motivations of their writers.

A three-step framework

In any plot or story arc, characters face a series of challenges in order to achieve their goal; your students are no different. To reach their creative potential, they scale a series of obstacles, one after another. Our task, as teachers, is to be aware of the roadblocks and ready to find ways around them.

Ask, respond, create (ARC) is the framework I use to take the thinking and pondering that naturally occurs and get it down on paper so I can clarify individual goals and support writers on their writing quest. The process begins with a question. Start by posing an open question related to one of your writers. Then make a list of possible ways you could best respond to this student's need, keeping the components of your writing practice in mind. The final element of the ARC framework involves creating a simple next-step goal to help the writer in question pivot or course-correct to get back on track.

Let me guide you through the ARC process and share two case studies so you can see how the steps fit together.

Ask

This reflective process begins by asking curious questions that increase your awareness and understanding of the writer in question. This process of questioning is not linear or product-driven and it's not focused on the deficits or shortfalls of the student or the educational system. Rather, this style of questioning is designed to awaken your creativity, intuition and problem-solving skills.

Questions are powerful; they hold space for a wealth of imaginative possibilities. Here are some suggestions of open questions that you might find useful throughout the process:

- What do I need to know about this writer?
- Looking holistically at this writer, which domains from the causal model feed into what I am observing?
- What am I curious to discover?
- What would help this writer feel safe?
- What is one small action that supports this writer to stay connected to self, their writing community, the creative process or the writing process?

Choose one or two questions at a time that relate to your focus student and help make sense of your observations. Be led by your intuition. Take a moment to quickly mind map any ideas that immediately rise to the surface upon asking your questions.

Let this also prompt you to ask the student in question for some feedback. Consider too how a conversation with that student could widen your perspective and provide information about their experience of the writing process. Too often we focus on the deficits of a writer, but posing open questions breathes life into a writer's potential.

Respond

Now it's time to respond to the questions that have surfaced as you focus in on your writer. One of the best approaches is to match possible responses against the four components of your writing practice:

1. Discovery writing – what prompts or activities might enable this student to develop the particular writing or mindset skills that would be most helpful at this time?
2. Workshopping – what focus skills would be useful for this writer?
3. Check and reflect – what self-evaluation strategies would enable this writer to critically analyse or unlock insights about their writing and creative process?

4. Writing practice review – what topics could you add to your class discussions about your writing practice that could support this writer, and what broader topics relating to writing or creativity could be explored?

Remember, you don't need to brainstorm multiple strategies across every stage of your writing practice or create a long list of possible responses. In this stage, you are simply responding to the questions by using your writing practice as a way of mapping options to support your writer.

Create

Because this process starts with open questions and works through the stages of your writing practice, you will end up with more than one possibility for taking action. But rather than focusing on several goals across multiple domains, start with the next small step that could best support this writer.

This process needs to be kept manageable, easy to implement and simple to follow up. Small next-step goals keep goal-setting fluid, open to iterations and, most importantly, centred on the writer. In the race to move our students from A to B, we often jump ahead to the big picture and overlook that change can be achieved with a series of small next-step goals.

The next-step goals that you develop for individual writers will often set the collective direction of your practice because they highlight the natural similarities that exist between writers. Some next-step goals, such as those supporting writing confidence, will be applicable to many writers in your group. Keeping your finger on the pulse of the skills and concepts that support individual writers makes planning your writing practice more streamlined and responsive.

ARC in action

ARC has a wide range of applications within your writing practice and your literacy program as a whole. When I started to use the six domains of my updated causal model in concert with the three-step ARC framework to guide my observations and anecdotal records, I finally felt I had the tools to piece together each writer's unique story – and, best of all, take action.

Teachers can use this process to regularly check in with their writers or more formally as part of students' individual educational goals. It can be used to pinpoint a change in behaviour so you can address any underlying issues before they become major obstacles. It can help map goals for students with special needs as well as help extending talented writers.

I think it would help us to see ARC in action. Let's step through the process of ask, respond, create with two different students, Sarah and Marco.

Sarah's story

Sarah started strong in my after-school writing program. My observational records showed she was an active participant in group discussions and motivated to share her writing, but as the weeks progressed her behaviour slowly changed. She became frustrated and distracted during writing sessions and was disengaged during workshopping. Sometimes she read a book under the table while her classmates shared their writing.

Ask

I was curious. What had triggered this change in Sarah's behaviour? With this question as my starting point, I decided my first step was to check in with Sarah informally and ask her for some feedback about how she was experiencing the writing program. For example, what activities did she like or not like? How was she feeling during class?

Her feedback revealed some interesting contradictions. Sarah thought the prompts we used were boring and too easy, but discovery writing was too hard. She didn't have enough time to finish writing. Often 'It's too hard' or 'It's boring' are blanket phrases that can indicate a range of complex feelings, so my first instinct was to get more clarity.

'What goes through your mind when it's too hard?' I asked.

'Nothing,' she replied. 'I can't think of ideas. My mind just goes blank.'

'When you're in that space, where your mind is blank, how does that feel?'

Her answer was telling.

'Everyone has a good story, except me,' she said. 'My ideas aren't that good.'

Now I could understand Sarah's behaviour more clearly. It's natural to compare our skills against our peers. Workshopping takes the private act of writing and pushes it into the public domain, so naturally our fears and vulnerability can be heightened. And it's definitely harder for some of us to think creatively under pressure. For Sarah, it seemed that discovery writing had gone from feeling expressive and fun to feeling loaded with expectation to compete with her peers. Knowing this, I could see that reading a book under the table might have been a way of managing her anxiety. It also prompted some curiosity in terms of parental expectations. My questions also crossed into Sarah's social and emotional capacity. How self-aware is Sarah? How does she manage negative self-talk? I may not have been able to change these factors immediately, but I knew that equipping Sarah with some strategies would assist her ability to cope.

After my conversation with Sarah I could fine-tune my questions a little further:

- What would make Sarah feel safe?
- What would bolster her confidence?
- What strategies would help Sarah regain confidence in her ability to generate ideas?

Respond

Next let's work through the components of a writing practice to see how I could respond to my curious questions.

Discovery writing

Sarah needs to build her creative confidence and experience some personal success in her writing, so first I'm looking for ways to scaffold her process for generating writing ideas.

'List poetry' (page 159)

Writing list poetry allows writers to play with imagery, repetition and rhythm rather than spinning a story. It still requires visualisation skills, but Sarah has a solid starting point because she is using her own experiences as writing inspiration. In this prompt writers are also drawing on a given poetic structure, which gives Sarah a container for playing with ideas. This may actually alleviate some of the pressure she feels to come up with ideas. It also lightens the decision-making load and helps to scaffold the process of generating ideas. This prompt has a solid start and finish point. Although writers may not complete the exercise in the timed writing frame, Sarah is working within finite boundaries. And because the students' life experiences will share some similarities, writers might even 'borrow' ideas and add to their poems after workshopping. Taking a collaborative approach may break down some of Sarah's comparison-itis.

Various 'Hello writer' (reflective) prompts (from page 229)

Using 'Hello writer' prompts to encourage writers to reflect on their experience of writing may also help normalise Sarah's feelings. Prompts like these could be helpful in this instance:

- What are your top tips for surviving a mind blank?
- When is comparing yourself to other writers useful? When is it harmful?

Workshopping

Sometimes, if an imaginative idea for a story doesn't quickly come to mind, writers can freeze up during discovery writing. I could use the next workshopping and modelled teaching time to remind all the writers in the group, including Sarah, that there are many genres and writing styles available to them when responding to a prompt.

Over the next workshopping sessions, as each writer shares I could note the genre or style the writer has used, such as imaginative, personal reflection, personal narrative, poetry, lists or brainstorming. This works as a reminder of all the options available to writers when responding to a prompt. Generating a story idea is just one option. Writing a series of haiku poetry around the theme of the prompt is also an option. Storyboarding or sketching could be yet another option. Writing about having no ideas is another possibility. Having a list of possible approaches can relieve anxiety and support all writers in your class.

Writing practice review

When we have our next writing practice review, we could explore how writers (even some of our favourite authors) manage their self-talk, otherwise known as the inner critic. Simply opening a discussion about this topic gives language to the shame and frustration some students can feel when ideas are not flowing easily. Is there an author interview on YouTube you could plan to watch together? Could this become a homework activity so parents can watch too?

Check and reflect

In our next check and reflect session, I could ask students to find evidence of skills they have used in their writing. This can be achieved simply and effectively by initiating a skills treasure hunt with questions like these:

- Do you use dialogue to give information about your characters and move your story forward? Underline a piece of dialogue in your writing.

- Have you used an adjective to describe an object or a character? Highlight two adjectives in your writing.

We often ask students to edit and change their writing without giving them ample opportunities to highlight their skills and strengths, but these sorts of activities are a simple remedy.

Once writers have identified some of the skills they are using, these same skills could be transformed into affirmation cards (for example, 'I can use dialogue in my writing' or 'I use adjectives to describe my characters'). Reading through these affirmation cards could become part of your classes' creative ritual, bolstering confidence before discovery writing begins.

Create

My set of responses form an overall plan of action for Sarah and will be a good reference to carry on through our writing journey, but I now need to choose the next small step that will move Sarah through this crisis of confidence (and I say 'this' crisis because developing self-awareness and creative confidence is an ongoing skill).

I decide to target discovery writing and start with the 'List poetry' activity prompt 'Things I have been doing lately' (page 159). I am going to share Hudson's poem (also on page 159) as an example because it highlights the idea that tuning into our physical sensations, our bodies and the thoughts running through our heads can be the inspiration for a piece of writing. I am also going to use workshopping to help us share ideas and invite some collaboration into the writing process.

Will choosing prompts that contain and scaffold the writing experience help Sarah tune in to her creativity? I'm curious to find out.

Marco's story

When I work with teachers, one question that surfaces again and again is 'How can I engage my reluctant writers?' Reluctant writers come in all shapes and sizes from disruptive non-participators to students who quietly fly under the radar. A reluctant writer may have learning difficulties which make writing a challenge or they may present as a highly able student who struggles with perfectionism. Reluctant or resistant writers are formidable challenges for even the most passionate teachers.

Marco was a student in one of the classes I visited. In the workshop I did with Marco's class, I used prompts from all three streams of activities and cycled through the components of our writing practice from discovery writing, workshopping and modelled teaching. Over the course of the workshop, I had a chance to observe his behaviour and his teacher filled in some of the gaps.

During the workshop, Marco sat, pencil in hand, tapping on the table, trying to get the attention of the student sitting next to him. The word *boring* floated to the surface more than once during our five minutes of timed writing. His teacher told me that this behaviour was consistent. Some days Marco engages with writing, especially if it aligns with his specific interests, but today he wasn't keen to participate. He drew patterns around the edges of his page and checked his iPad when he thought no one was watching. He stopped and listened to his peers during workshopping, but when Marco shared his writing his main goal was to make them laugh. At times, Marco's behaviour was disruptive and challenging to manage.

Ask

As a visiting teacher, it's easier for me to stay connected to Marco. I haven't had to deal with this behaviour in an ongoing way. I also know if his teacher can cut through Marco's defensive behaviour (which isn't easy) she is in a better position to offer him some valuable support. The story your students have about their writing abilities is often a greater hurdle than their skills. Marco needs a new story.

After sharing the ARC process with Marco's teacher, she chose to start with a focus on the following questions:

- What are Marco's strengths as a writer?

- What teaching strategies and activities would spark his interest and increase his engagement?

Respond

If his teacher focuses on the skills that Marco lacks, there's a good chance she will split him from the group and unintentionally raise his resistance further. Instead, we brainstormed how their classroom writing practice could build on Marco's interests and strengths as a writer.

Discovery writing

Like Sarah, Marco feels defensive. He does, however, like maths and works well with more structure. In order to create a safe space for him to explore his creativity, we considered prompts that have more structure and ideally less writing to begin with. The goal here is to increase Marco's engagement levels and get him writing alongside his peers.

A variation on 'Playing with poetry' (page 220)

Poetry with a specific structure such as haiku is worth trying. A traditional haiku is a three-line poem that uses a set number of syllables per line – (1) five syllables, (2) seven syllables, (3) five syllables – and can be particularly appealing to writers like Marco.

Students can choose a theme from their interests and then write one or a series of poems about their chosen topic. I have seen writers get so caught up in counting their syllables and working within the structure that they forget they are actually constructing poetry. Imposing boundaries on everyone in the class also evens the playing field a little.

'Shape a story' (page 223)

The second option relates to changing the mode in which a writer responds to a prompt. Instead of writing, 'Shape a story' allows writers to use a range of shapes to create objects that they then connect in some way. This could help unlock Marco's visualisation skills and kickstart his imagination. Marco is a confident artist, so this option allows him to develop storytelling skills and share stories without focusing so much on writing to begin with.

Workshopping

Marco's motivation to make his friends laugh may be driven by his need to belong to the group in some way. For the 'Shape a story' writing activity, it can make sense for writers to share in pairs rather than as a class group because they will also need to talk about their pictures. This could give Marco an opportunity to contribute and share his ideas one on one, which may be less disruptive for him and his peers.

Writing practice review

Ways of refining creative rituals and routines is always open for discussion when reviewing your practice. Without naming or bringing attention to students, could some writers choose to sit alone or wear noise-cancelling headphones? Then Marco could be actively involved in trialling what practices might work best for him.

Check and reflect

I know from Marco's teacher that one of his writing strengths is character development and dialogue. He may not always successfully weave parts of the plot together, but he does capture pieces of dialogue and comedic details that are genuinely funny.

In a check and reflect session, Marco could make a list of the characters he has enjoyed creating. He could keep the list in his notebook, or perhaps writers could each contribute a favourite character and make a class book. It's important to affirm Marco's strengths and building a list enables him to see his body of work and identify as a writer in the group.

Create

Marco's teacher decided that haiku on the writer's topic of choice would be her first course of action. It ticked many of the boxes in terms of structuring and scaffolding the writing experience, while also playing to Marco's strengths. Marco loves cricket and video games which are playful themes for contemporary haiku. Observing how Marco responds to this writing task will give his teacher valuable information about what step to take next. Haiku won't transform Marco's behaviour or writing skills overnight. This isn't a magic fix. It's a small goal that allows Marco and his teacher to engage with the creative process.

Summary

ARC is a reflective goal-setting process that can be used with all students in your class, from talented writers to students for whom English is an additional language or dialect to students with special needs. My hope is that posing open questions ignites your creativity and helps you to explore the authentic craft of writing. It has as much to offer teachers as it does students. There is no right or wrong way to use this process. Teachers can determine how often they want to set individual writing goals for their students.

Your writing practice is not a set-and-forget system; it's a dynamic, organic writing experience that bends and sways to accommodate and affirm your writers. A strange paradox exists at the heart of this reflective process. We might imagine that zooming in and focusing on the unique traits of each writer means teachers are pulled in twenty different directions at once, but in fact the opposite is true. Tuning in to the needs of each writer builds a strong sense of community and makes planning easier, not harder. The key to catering effectively for individual differences lies in the teacher's ability to see each writer as a complex system with many moving parts. If we want our writers to reach their creative potential, we need to recognise that cognitive ability is only one of many factors influencing writing potential.

This approach gives teachers a wide lens for understanding their writers and doesn't shy away from the fact that writers will encounter roadblocks and resistance. Roadblocks are a necessary part of the creative process, so every chance you get to normalise frustrations and model problem-solving strategies gives your students an opportunity to learn skills that will serve them long after leaving your class.

Power points

- Every component of your practice is designed to validate the individual experience of your writers.
- Gardner (2011) offers us a holistic approach to individual differences by identifying five broad factors affecting writing development: affective resistor, pedagogic causes, physical factors, cognitive processes and cultural ecology. I suggest a sixth domain for consideration: social and emotional capacity.
- Ask, respond, create (ARC) is a process of posing questions, igniting your intuition and activating your creative problem-solving skills. This three-step framework helps teachers individualise their writing practice as well as set actionable goals within their classroom practice to support their writers.
- Using the ARC framework, all four writing practice components – discovery writing, workshopping, writing practice reviews, and check and reflect – provide opportunities to respond to the unique needs of your students.
- ARC is inclusive; it can be used to brainstorm next-step goals for gifted students, students with special needs and students for whom English is an additional language or dialect. Apply the broader questions as a way of analysing your observation and then brainstorm possibilities across the stages.
- When you combine ARC with formal assessment results in your literacy program, the result is a powerful tool for understanding the skills, mindset, behaviours and motivations of your writers.

Pause and reflect

- What is your instinctive response to widening the assessment process and taking a more reflective pose?
- How could you see this working for the writers in your class?
- Think of a writer in your class and consider the following questions:
    - What might success look like for this writer?
    - What are this student's creative strengths? What creative thinking processes do they use?
    - What are this student's top five writing strengths?
    - What is the next simple step this writer could take in their writing?
    - What is the next brave step this writer could take in their writing?
    - What dream do I have for this writer? How might they embody their creative potential?

Can you add any other useful curious questions to the list?

Your action plan

Try the ARC process

Let's try working through the simple and practical ARC process for one of your writers.

1. Your first action step is to allocate and set up a notebook (separate to your action research journal, if possible) to collect ARC reflections and next-step goals.
2. Choose one of the writers in your class who you suspect may be having difficulty in some way. This student may have come to mind while reading the chapter.

3. Use Gardner's (2011) model (figure 2, page 112) to brainstorm any domains that are significant for this writer. Would you like to know more about this writer's cultural ecology? What sorts of literacy and writing experiences are part of their life at home?
4. With this in mind, begin the first stage of the ARC framework – ask – by asking curious questions.
5. Read through, add to and then circle one or two questions that allow you to focus on this writer.
6. Respond to these questions by brainstorming strategies across your writing practice that might support this particular writer.
7. Create a next-step goal for this writer based on your brainstorming and add any ideas to your weekly planner.

Chapter 7
A community of writers

When I started writing this chapter, schools in Melbourne, Australia, had recently opened their doors for the first time after one of the longest and most stringent COVID-19 lockdown measures the world had seen. And while there is no doubt that the social and educational impacts of remote learning will reverberate over the coming months (and years), this reality was silenced on that first day back by the simple joy of face-to-face reunions. It was a poignant reminder that when all the dust and debris of teaching and learning is carefully brushed away, we discover, once again, that relationships and a sense of connection are the true backbone of our school communities.

Recent global events see us examining the idea of community more closely and reassessing its true value in our schools and lives. This is the perfect landing point to begin our exploration of the fundamental role that community plays in supporting students on their writing journey. You set out to teach the skills of writing and discover along the way that your writing practice has the power to transform the narratives your students have about themselves as writers. The benefits of writing in community aren't contained within the walls of your classroom, either. Your practice is a powerful platform for engaging parents and inviting the global world of writers and literature into your classroom. This cross-pollination of diverse ideas, understandings and experiences allows your students to see writing as so much more than an in-school activity. Rather, writing becomes a vital form of self-expression, a way of being in the world (Yagelski, 2011).

In this chapter I'll show you how fostering a sense of belonging and community in your writing program can influence your students' immediate and long-term literacy outcomes. I'll also share practical ways to collaborate with your school community and boost the cooperation and support of parents and guardians. It's time to get the whole family on board and involved in your writing adventures. It's also time to anchor your writing practice within the brains trust of the wider literary community. I'll show you how to leverage the working knowledge and vast creativity of writers and literature across the ages to underpin your writing practice.

Community, connection and your writing practice

Let's start by unwrapping the word *community*. A community is a group of people, drawn together by a set of distinct commonalities, from family and locality to shared values, beliefs, shared goals and interests. It's likely that you're an active member of multiple communities, from family, friendship groups, your workplace, clubs, social media platforms and more. Still, despite sharing a common purpose with fellow group members, you know from experience that not all communities engage your attention in the same way. So what factors foster a strong sense of connection and engagement between community members?

Communities that have a distinguishable group identity show higher levels of engagement. Quate and McDermott (2009) suggest that specific routines, rituals and established norms of behaviour that are unique to the group, form a recognisable group culture and move members towards a collective experience. This identification process is even more powerful if community members hear their experiences and emotions mirrored in the stories and faces of those around them. Bickford and Wright (2006) make a similar argument, stating that 'real community ... exists only when its members interact in a meaningful way that deepens their understanding of each other and leads to learning' (p. 4.2). Interaction, authentic communication and vulnerability are powerful human connectors.

Building the writing community in your classroom

Why is a sense of community so important for young writers? Most accept that we learn best in community (explored in detail by Kuh et al., 2005), a position supported by much of learning theory and human psychology bodies of research. As summarised by Bickford and Wright (2006), 'Despite multiple theories about how people learn, they agree on one point: the critical role of interaction' (p. 4.3). And this need for human interaction and connection can be summed up in one evocative word: *belongingness*.

Belongingness theory proposes that 'human beings are fundamentally and pervasively motivated by a need to belong' (Baumeister & Leary, 1995, p. 522). This instinctive human desire to be an accepted member of the group informs our thinking and motivates our behaviour. It shapes our identity and impacts our ability to learn. A sense of belonging is an important learning outcome in and of itself, and for some students it is indicative of educational success and long-term health and wellbeing (Longmuir et al., 2020). The Organisation for Economic Co-operation and Development (OECD) Programme for International Student Assessment 2018 measured the sense of belonging at school in adolescents aged 15–16 across seventy-nine countries and found that Australian students' sense of belonging at school significantly declined between 2003 and 2015, and was in fact lower than many participating OECD countries (De Bortoli, 2018).

In their 2018 article 'Why don't Australian school kids feel a sense of belonging?' Allen et al. report that belonging 'relates to higher levels of student emotional wellbeing and better academic performance and achievement. It also reduces the likelihood of mental health problems' ('Belonging at a vulnerable time' section). The authors point to respectful and valued relationships as being the key factors in helping students feel a greater connection to their school, which they argue lead to far-reaching positive effects. This article highlights the student–teacher relationship as having the greatest influence on a student's sense of belonging at school, followed by positive relationships with parents and peers. A student's sense of self and interpersonal skills, such as optimism and self-efficacy, also contribute to their sense of belonging (Allen et al., 2018).

When we view our writing practice through the lens of belongingness the value of writing in community suddenly comes into sharp focus. Your writing community serves a deeper purpose than you might have imagined. Every step of your writing practice is designed to open the channels of communication and foster positive relationships between students, teachers, peers and the wider community. As well as laying the optimal foundation for teaching writing skills, your writing practice gives students the best possible chance to experience writing as a pathway to belongingness and acceptance. Far from being a by-product of spending six hours a day in a shared space, your classroom community is a living entity, mirroring the personalities of your students as it shapes and transform them in return.

Writing identity

Defining our identity is a concrete way of nailing down where and how we belong in the world. Identity is the interface between our emotions, thoughts and actions. Our writing experiences, especially our early writing experiences, shape how we identify with the writing process and define ourselves as writers.

Seban and Tavşanlı (2015) highlight the many complex factors that impact writing identity in your classroom:

> *Students' literate identity development is a complex social process and influenced by a variety of factors (school practices, home literacy, practices, race, gender, second language learning etc.) however, schools, including the classroom teacher and literacy practices in the classroom, are the most influential factor in students' literacy learning life and identity (Smith, 2008; Martens & Adamson, 2001). (p. 218)*

When it comes to supporting your students' writing identities, there are many variables that teachers can't control or even change, but knowing that the quality of the relationships you develop in your classroom is the most influential factor in literacy learning lands you on solid ground.

Recently I visited a Year 2 class to present a writing workshop. I was introduced to the class as a 'fellow writer' (which I loved) and before I even sat down the students were pointing excitedly in the direction of their class library, where lines of their self-published books were available for reading and borrowing. Writing and authorship held real currency in this classroom. One student had a book in his lap that he had finished the night before, he was waiting patiently for a chance to read his story to the group.

Crossing the threshold from *learning* about writing to *being* a writer is a powerful shift of consciousness. If you identify as a writer, you see yourself as belonging to the wider community of writers. You have a growing investment in improving your skills. You want to talk about your struggles and triumphs with other writers and you look for audiences to share your work, just like that young boy with a homemade book in his lap. We can't erase the experiences our students have had in the past but writing every day in community ensures that students leave your class believing they are writers.

A teacher's writing identity

Teachers also carry a story about themselves as writers. In my professional development workshops, when I ask teachers to define themselves as writers, the room usually goes silent for a moment before animated stories of early writing experiences, formative teachers, shared successes and memorable failings spill out. This provides valuable data, because I know from experience that how a person defines themselves as writer almost always indicates how they approach writing tasks. Those teachers with a natural flair for language and writing are typically eager to get started, while those who view writing as a necessary evil tend to slide down in their seat, resigned to endure the next hour.

A teacher's formative writing experiences, expectations and personality all influence how they define themselves as a writer. Defining our writing identity is often a complex undertaking, it comes loaded with subjective judgements about our creativity and writing skills. Somehow, most of us have it in our minds that to be a writer we must be undeniably creative, talented and published. This belief leaves most of us, even if we enjoy writing, feeling like outsiders, looking in. Whether you identify as a writer or not, it's worth remembering that your relationship with writing filters through to your teaching practice.

You would be right in assuming that the teacher of the Year 2 class I described earlier in this chapter loved reading and writing, but do you have to feel that way about writing to get the same results in your classroom? And more importantly, what can you do to shore up your writing identity so it's fit for the task of developing and supporting young writers?

Let's address how you feel about writing first. The success of your writing practice does not hinge on your creative potential or your natural writing talent. However, as we discovered in Chapter 1, students will model themselves on their teacher's approach (Jeffrey & Craft, 2004). If you approach your writing practice with curiosity and a growth mindset, you inspire your students to do the same. If you offer a range of process-driven activities with opportunities to discuss, debate and reflect on the writing and the creative process, you invite your students to connect with and support each other. If you share your writing practice with your students' families, you bridge the gap between home and school and allow writing to flow into all areas of their lives. If you open your doors to the wider literary community, you summon the wisdom and guidance of working writers into your classroom and connect your students to this invaluable resource. These actions are governed by the decisions you make and the way you plan your program – and this need not be limited by your current writing identity.

Writing identity and teaching practice

Now to the question of how to get your writing identity match ready for the task of teaching writing. Regardless of your past and current writing experiences and associations, your writing identity is malleable and transitory. Every writing experience – even lists, reports and emails – has the potential to deepen your self-awareness and understanding of the writing process, but one of the best ways to strengthen your writing identity is to start writing regularly.

Knowing writing from the inside helps students trust you're on their side. In her Donald Graves Address at the 2012 Australian Literacy Educators' Association (ALEA) conference, well-known Australian author Mem Fox (2013) outlined Graves's pedagogy for writing:

> *His first point about the pedagogy of writing – and this was the truth that threatened us most – was that only writers should be allowed to teach writing because writers alone understand the circumstances of creation. They know first-hand how writing happens and why.*
> ('Only writers should teach writing' section)

Though he was an acclaimed literacy education specialist, Graves was a teacher at heart. I don't believe he was suggesting that only professional writers are qualified to teach writing. Rather, he was making the point that students benefit most when teachers stop giving instructions from the sidelines and get some skin in the game.

Fox (2013), a former teacher, went on to describe the impact this comment had on her and her colleagues at the time:

> *Becoming writers ourselves was the best in-service ever. It changed our lives; it changed our teaching; and it radically changed the outcomes of the students in our classes.* ('What did we do as a result?' section)

Graves was encouraging teachers to get to know writing from the inside out, to be active participants in the creation of their writing identity.

Nurturing your writing identity

So, what are some of the ways you can build writing into your day and nurture your writing identity?

Rather than add to your load of meetings, try incorporating a short writing time into your weekly staff or team meeting. One short prompt and time to share, either as a whole group or in teams, sparks your imagination and strengthens your writing muscle. If that feels like too much of a stretch to begin with, try scheduling in some time to write alongside your students during discovery writing. In my experience, this does more to encourage students to write and share than anything else I have tried. Your students come to see you as a fellow writer and trust that you are prepared to take risks and be vulnerable with them.

Where possible, try to find even a short period of time to bring writing into your life. In *The Artist's Way*, Julia Cameron (1992) introduces a style of journalling called 'morning pages'. This practice, which involves producing three pages of free writing first thing in the morning, might be your starting point. Free writing untangles thoughts and ideas and allows you to let go and experience the release that writing can bring. One of my friends who has particularly limited time has ditched the idea of three pages of free writing and instead writes a daily haiku as her morning pages. This short, regular practice has allowed her to rekindle her love of words. Find what works for you.

Finally, teach yourself to read like a writer. Pay attention to the way words work and the writing techniques you encounter in books and other reading materials. Take notes. Highlight quotes. Share them with colleagues and students and use them to start a collection of mentor texts (more about that soon). You might also make a commitment to read more about the writing process. Many writers write about their process in ways that can be both inspiring and instructive. I use this genre of writing to inform and nurture my teaching practice.

Whether you decide to join in with your students, write with colleagues or take on a reading project, decide today to understand more about your writing identity and its influences. Writing yourself undoubtedly gives you a wealth of firsthand information to share with your students. Challenge your old stories and be prepared to offer yourself the same gentle support you extend to your students.

Sharing the journey with the school community

Welcoming parents and guardians into the classroom has widely accepted benefits, and when it comes to your writing practice, family involvement can significantly improve writing outcomes for your students.

Gardner's (2011) model, see page 111, acknowledges that a young writer's cultural ecology – that is, their life outside the classroom – affects their motivation and engagement in writing. Parental beliefs and expectations, cultural and socio-economic influences, life experiences, and the availability of books and reading material at home all play a crucial role in the relationship your writers have with writing. Your writing practice is one of the best resources you have at your disposal to share the many practical ways parents can influence and support young writers. Parents are working with a range of challenges too – from time constraints to language barriers – so you may need to experiment to find what bridges the gap but, as we know, influencing a student's cultural ecology will also impact their writing identity. The interactive writing activities that follow work to gradually level-up parent participation and collaboration, starting with simple ways to get your student writing for fun at home.

Home writing tasks

Students often complete writing activities as part of their regular homework tasks, but encouraging your students to write for fun at home sometimes calls for a fresh approach.

Celebrations and events provide the perfect opportunity to add a touch of novelty to the activities and resources you send home with your writers. For example, if students celebrate Easter, teachers often send home a small bag with one or two small chocolate eggs. Why not include a set of a random words to inspire writing (page 202)? This idea can be adapted to any celebration you share with your students. I know one family who took the set of random words on their annual camping trip and it's now a family tradition to write around the campfire. Seasonal opportunities such as the first day of winter can also be springboards for home writing activities. I once sent home a sachet of hot chocolate mix in a coloured envelope with a set of journalling cards and a personal note to motivate writers to curl up somewhere warm and take some time to journal. Perhaps students could take a photo of themselves with their hot chocolate and writing so you can create a class slideshow or poster. Consider popping in a note to parents to share your expectations and methodology, but keep it fun. The aim is to create an easy flow between your writing at school and home.

A home writing project: Creating a writing space

Many of the activities in the activity section of this book make great home writing tasks and projects. 'Writing spaces' (page 244) is one such example. Our writing space impacts our productivity and focus, so asking students to explore their personal preferences is a valuable home writing task. Because your students are exploring their writing routines and habits at school, it makes sense to trial whether these same habits work for them at home. This home writing project requires some prior planning at school before students start.

Begin first by introducing the idea of creating personal writing spaces by selecting discovery writing prompts to use in your daily practice at school. This not only gets students reflecting and writing on the topic of writing spaces, but they can discuss and share ideas with their peers.

At school, choose discovery prompts such as:

- Does where you write influence your concentration or focus? How?
- Do you work best in a consistent writing space, or can you move from space to space?
- If you could write anywhere in the world, where would you choose? Describe your exact location. Why are you writing there? Why is this place so perfect – or not perfect – for writing?
- Describe a place that wouldn't work for you at all and tell us why.
- Describe the best place you've ever opened your notebook to write.

An extended list of suggested prompts can be found in the 'Writing spaces' activity (page 244).

After your writers have considered writing spaces, it's time to get started with your home writing project. Ask them to nominate three different writing spaces at home. They can choose any space from a desk in their room to a tent out under the stars in the backyard. Over the course of the next week, students should write for five minutes in each of their nominated places. Then they can compare which places worked best for them. Start by asking writers to compare factors such as temperature, light, noise and clutter. They can add other variables to the list as they discuss their writing spaces. Your students will end up with a list of conditions that work best for them.

I once did this activity with a group of my students aged 8–12. We had a visiting teacher present when the students shared their findings and he was blown away by how this group analysed their results, distilled their findings and articulated their personal preferences. Printed-off information about your writing program often gets discarded, left in bags or never makes it home, but this sort of hands-on activity is more likely to arouse the interest of parents and guardians, and to spark the conversations we want to have about creativity and the craft of writing.

Holding a reading

Another point that Mem Fox (2013) highlighted in her address to the ALEA was the fact that writers don't write well or willingly without an interested and inquisitive audience. Without the opportunity to workshop writing with various audiences, many young writers find their work is only ever read by an audience of one: their teacher. Reading aloud to an audience brings voice and life into a piece of writing. Readings also allow teachers to publicly acknowledge their students' creative efforts and demonstrate the very real learning that is taking place. Scheduling in time for questions can also give writers a chance to talk about their experience of writing.

If you decide you would like to invite parents to a reading, get the ball rolling by providing your students with an authentic literary context for doing this. Your students may have heard visiting writers and authors read a favourite piece of work aloud, but you can also make use of online interviews and footage of writers' festival panels as well as video and audio of authors giving readings. Ask your students questions about what they notice about the readings and what they found interesting. Providing a context for reading aloud to an audience and talking about writing makes this activity feel like a natural extension of your practice rather than a stage performance.

Once your writers are on board – and I wouldn't attempt a reading unless your writers are enthusiastic – it's time to send out an invitation to parents. I always make it clear in the invitation that reading aloud is voluntary and this decision is made by each writer.

In the days before the reading, ask writers to choose two to three short paragraphs or a short piece of writing to share. Encourage your writers to give the piece of writing a title if it doesn't already have one and jot down one or two ideas about the initial inspiration for the piece. Sharing your writing can feel daunting, but starting with these small details helps writers find their feet and gain confidence. Once they have chosen their writing, give your writers time over the next few days to read aloud to themselves and peers to build their confidence.

Here are my tips for organising the physical space so your reading runs smoothly:

- Hold the reading in a space that allows the audience to be close to the group of writers so you can keep it simple.
- Set writers up in a semicircle in front of the audience. I find it works best to keep writers together. There's a collective energy in the group that supports the process.
- Think about how you can organise the reading to showcase a maximum of 12–15 writers and allow time for discussion afterwards.
- I suggest writers leave their notebook or papers on the floor until it's their turn to read. This avoids rustling-paper syndrome.
- I ask writers to let me know beforehand if they do not want to read, but I encourage them to sit with the group so they identify as one of the writers. They may decide not to read but can be included in answering questions from the audience.

Let's see this in action by walking through a reading I held with my students recently:

> *Traditionally we throw open the doors in the last session of the term and invite parents and guardians to come and hear writers read a part of their story.*

Soon parents and family members arrive. One writer volunteers to start us off; he reads with conviction. He knows exactly how his character would say the words. Suddenly all those weeks of chasing ideas, developing characters and writing intersect. And then the next writer shares, and then the next.

After the readings, writers answer questions and discuss their writing processes. They talk about the aspects they find most challenging, as well as the moments when ideas come together effortlessly and the words do what they want them to do. In an impermanent world where ideas come and go, this group of writers have followed their imagination and, against all odds, created something from nothing. I love watching the interaction between audience members and writers. During every reading I've hosted, there is a notable shift of energy in the room. This reading is no different: the children move from being students of writing to being writers. They own the room.

Afterwards, I watch parents and guardians congratulate their young writers. I was in earshot of a parent seeking out another writer to say how taken she was with this girl's prose and her use of imagery. The parent even repeated back the phrases she loved most. The writer blushed and beamed. I know from experience that feedback like this keeps a writer motivated and engaged long after the conversation ends. Another parent recounted to me afterwards how she had watched her son's original idea change and develop into a story. 'Writers,' she said, 'need to be flexible and adaptable thinkers. You can't have rock brain.'

(adapted from Cregan, 2020)

Family writing nights

Family writing nights take participation one step further by encouraging parents and guardians to experience writing alongside their children. The key objectives are to spark conversation about the craft of writing, share understandings and strengthen relationships between home and school, but for busy parents this can also be a chance to reconnect with their creativity and writing identity.

The stories we have about ourselves as writers run deep, so be prepared for some of the adults in the room to feel vulnerable and exposed at first. I'll share some tips to help you put them at ease shortly. It's also an opportunity for roles to shift and change as students become teachers and facilitators, introducing writing activities and taking responsibility and ownership for their writing practice. Your students can introduce prompts, lead workshopping sessions and share their class routines with their families. This is such a valuable way to consolidate learning. It's a good idea to create a script for your family writing night to bolster confidence and allow the evening to flow from one activity to the next.

Think back to the tortoise enclosure we discussed in Chapter 3 and the importance of creating a sense of safety. Your first writing prompt needs to mark the boundaries and encourage creativity to come out to play. I find one of the best ways to do this is to start by using an icebreaker prompt that gets parents drawing on their personal experience by asking them to write about their name. Every name has some sort of story and these pieces of writing are usually alive with voice, emotion and details. You can find this activity, 'The story of my name', on page 176.

I've found that family writing nights work best if you have a range of activities for parents and children to work on both independently and collaboratively. Shared writing activities that make fun and creative collaborations include developing characters together or planning quick story outlines (consider 'Object writing', page 209, and 'Shape a story', page 223).

Family writing nights also give parents the opportunity to reflect on their beliefs about writing and creativity. Once the group has warmed up, add in a prompt or two that invite parents and guardians to reflect on their early experiences with writing and how they use writing today in their everyday life. Lead with prompts such as:

- Can you remember any stories you wrote at school?
- Has writing together with your child brought back any memories and feelings about your writing experiences at school?

At the end of the family writing night, finish by asking to take a minute to acknowledge each other's participation. If time allows, you might even open discussion about the experience, led by questions such as:

- What did you like most about writing together?
- What did you find challenging?
- What might you take away from this experience?

A variation: Remote writing nights

During numerous lockdowns, remote learning bought the life of the classroom directly into family homes. Parents and guardians suddenly had full access to the activities and interactions that take place in a regular school day. While holding family writing nights at school is ideal, it's also possible to record or livestream these sorts of events to reach those who for any number of reasons – maybe they live too far away or simply feel more comfortable writing with their family group in their own home – are unable to attend in person. Whether you choose to hold your writing night remotely or face to face, asking students to lead activities, introduce prompts and share their writing reflections is invaluable.

Connecting with the wider writing community

Author visits, special events and writing workshops have long been part of school literacy programs. These events give your students a rare glimpse into an author's life and all those decisions and influences that run alongside the stories we read and love. However, too often these are isolated events. Students leave the room buzzing, but soon the creative energy subsides and the learnings fade. But there is a way to link your students with this valuable resource in an ongoing way.

The literary community needs to be an active ongoing component of your writing practice. Because books and storytelling are magical out-of-this-world experiences, we sometimes forget that the business of writing books is, in fact, very real – as are the authors who have devoted time and energy to developing their craft. This wealth of inspiration, creativity, hard-won lessons and hands-on experience is one of the best resources fellow writers have at their disposal. We underestimate what the wider literary community has to offer our students but, thanks to the internet, it's never been easier to connect with writers from around the globe.

As well as face-to-face author visits, there are videos, memoirs, books, articles, podcast interviews, virtual meetings and more – all at our fingertips. The wider literary community also includes local authors and writers who work in related fields or use writing as a way of expression to come to speak about their experiences. This is one of the best ways to expose children to a range of literary voices, purposes, audiences, writing styles and genres, enabling them to add new skills and techniques to their writing repertoire.

There are many compelling and immediate reasons to connect with the wider literary community. Creative inspiration is fuel for writers, but opening your classroom to such influences has lasting benefits for your students in terms of strengthening their writing identity.

The literary community and writing identity

For teachers buckling under the weight of constant daily pressures, setting our sights on the seemingly lofty goal of developing a student's writing identity feels out of our reach. But anchoring this faraway vision in the present moment makes everything we do purposeful and worthwhile – even the assessments. Grounding our writing practice within the wider literary community fosters a sense of belonging to the craft of writing and solidarity with fellow writers who share our struggles and successes. These interactions, in whatever form they take, spark curiosity and encourage us to try new things and refine our processes. Simply knowing that we are not alone bolsters our creative spirit and gives us the inspiration and motivation to keep writing.

Find a writing mentor

A writing mentor is someone we trust and admire, someone who has travelled the path before us and whose wisdom lights our way and guides our creative journey.

The process of researching and narrowing down a list of writers and authors (past and present) to support my journey was a defining experience for me. It helped clarify my values and beliefs about writing. It shone a light on what I love about a piece of writing, the voice and characters, the use of language. As a result, I now have a small band of writers that I refer to as my brains trust. I keep their quotes and thoughts about writing in a digital file and refer to them often, especially when I'm stuck or blocked. Rereading their words of wisdom is often enough to shift my perspective. I also keep a list of articles, podcasts, interviews, videos and other resources that connect me with their experience of writing.

Encouraging your students to go through this same process and choose a writing mentor brings the literary community into your classroom in a very real and personal way. I include a range of writing and thinking prompts to get your students started on this journey in 'Choosing a writing mentor' (page 253).

Read like a writer

Literature and mentor texts bring writing skills to life by giving teachers and students easy access to a wide range of voices, styles, genres and writing techniques. In his article 'Mentors and mentor texts' Lester Laminack (2017) describes his belief that mentor texts only become useful when readers know and understand the piece of writing well. Sharing one-off literary examples doesn't capitalise on the power of mentor texts to teach and support our students. Laminack advises teachers to introduce fewer mentor texts but provide many opportunities for students to develop a relationship with these pieces of writing, even to commit them to memory. His description of this process is poetic:

> *Over time, you will notice small details and how powerful they are in the arc of the story or how they are crucial to the argument being presented. You will notice the power of a single word. You'll see the impact of rhythm and pacing in the language. You'll begin to recognise how the writer assembled the text and employed various text structures with purpose. You will see how and come to understand why.*
> *(Laminack, 2017, p. 754)*

The practice of working with mentor texts takes time. Students need opportunities to pull apart, analyse and play with mentor texts, to try them on for size. Mentor texts can be used to teach writing skills but the process itself also develops critical thinking skills that benefit learning across all areas of the curriculum.

To use mentor texts effectively, you'll need to create a collection of significant samples of writing, but this doesn't have to be an arduous task. The trick is to read with a question in mind. For example, if your class become interested in how to develop rising tension, start to pinpoint the questions you might have about this, such as 'How does punctuation play into developing rising tension?' You might even send your students out to collect samples of rising tension in the books and materials they are reading.

Mentor texts come in many shapes and sizes. Collecting quotes about writing, lines of poems, samples of dialogue from graphic novels and paragraphs from journalistic articles all make effective teaching tools. Finding a piece of writing that speaks to our heart has the power to not only show us writing in action but it can help us feel brave and less alone in the world.

Summary

The true strength of your writing practice is best witnessed through the quality of the relationships your students develop with teachers, peers, the literary community and the craft of writing itself. When we place connection and a sense of belonging at the heart of our writing program, we honour the vital role that community plays in developing writing skills and identity. If you ever wondered how to justify taking regular time to write and workshop, I hope this gives you the courage to stake your claim. The systems you put in place and the foundations you set for learning are the connective tissue that holds your writing community together.

In our current system, teachers are often forced to sacrifice long-term writing goals for immediate results, but it pays to remember that the writing experiences we choose today and the values and beliefs we model leave a lasting imprint on our students' writing identities.

Power points

- Your classroom community is a living entity that mirrors the personalities of your students as it shapes and transforms their writing identities.
- The benefits of writing in community are supported by two powerful bodies of research: learning theory and human psychology. Both agree that interaction is an essential learning tool.
- The relationships your students have with teachers, peers and parents influence their writing identity.
- Your classroom community is a vital, proactive force that develops relationships and connects writers to wider networks to support the development of their skills.
- Writing in community enhances both short- and long-term goals that parents and teachers hold for young writers.
- Writing in community starts at a grassroots level in your classroom and branches out into the school and wider literary communities.

Pause and reflect

- How could you learn more about the cultural expectations of writing practice with your parent community?
- What activities and systems could you put in place to strengthen the bonds between home and school?
- How could you join forces with your colleagues to support each other in your writing and teaching practice?
- Do you have a favourite writer – perhaps someone whose words resonate with your experience of writing? Why?

- How do you define yourself as a writer? What are some of the important factors that have influenced the way you feel about writing?

Your action plan
Create a code of conduct for your writing community

If the quality of your relationships determines the strength and impact of your writing community, your code of conduct needs to protect these relationships at all costs. While it is possible to use phrases or ideas from similar codes of conduct, this is something that is best developed with your class. The choices you make together set out the norms of behaviour which assist behaviour management and strengthen your community identity.

A code of conduct is a work in progress that develops alongside your writing community. Although it shapes and guides behaviour, your code of conduct is more than a set of rules; it is a statement of your shared beliefs and expectations about writing and writers. Refer to it often.

1. Walk through your writing practice as a class and see what behaviours and values are important, noting them down as you go. Here are some ideas to start with:

    - We limit distractions by staying in our seats during discovery writing.
    - We are patient and kind to ourselves if our ideas don't flow easily.
    - We treat each other with respect.

2. Pull apart concepts and define what they mean for your class. For example, 'We treat each other with respect' is an undeniably important principle, but what does respect mean in your class and in your writing practice? What behaviours

demonstrate this respect? Discuss this as a class to make sure every writer understands what is expected of them.

3. Rather than include a long list of items on your code, select the items that matter most to your students. Try to limit your code to no more than ten points. Now is also an opportune time to discuss the options for class members who choose not to follow the code.

4. Finally, print out your classroom code of conduct and make sure it is visible – be that in notebooks or on classroom walls. Your classroom code is an agreed set of behavioural guidelines and a handy reference point as you navigate the creative journey ahead.

Tips

- I've used the plural pronoun *we* in my examples, but you are free to choose how you frame the statements in your code of conduct.
- You might choose to start with an overarching statement and add statements to this. An overarching statement could be something like 'Our classroom is a safe space to write and explore creativity because …'
- Wherever possible, use positive statements to establish norms of behaviour. For example, 'We listen carefully and quietly to other writers when they share their work and offer respectful feedback when called upon' should be chosen over statements like 'We don't interrupt other writers or call out mean comments when they share their work'.
- Classroom dynamics naturally change and develop, so remember to revisit your code of conduct at regular intervals to check whether it needs updating or revising.
- Teachers have shared with me that some writers in their classrooms use their classmates' names in stories, which can be unsettling for some students. Use your code of conduct to establish positive and inclusive behaviour if issues like this arise.

Classroom activities

The writing prompts provided in this section are divided into three categories: personal writing, imaginative writing and reflective writing. Each writing prompt is then broken down into four parts:

1. Introduction – highlights the importance of the prompt and the benefit of sharing it with your students.
2. How to use the prompt – includes any sequential steps and instructions.
3. Tips for working with the prompt – includes any notes about preparation, materials and ways to extend the prompt with your students.
4. Teaching focus – articulates the broad writing skills targeted by the prompt.

An open invitation to write

This collection of writing prompts, extension activities and editing games is an open invitation to explore the craft of writing with your students. I've included some of my favourite tried-and-true activities to guide you through the process of developing a daily writing practice in your classroom. These activities weave together many years of teaching experience with a sense of playfulness and my passionate belief that writing makes life better.

I use these same prompts successfully with writers of all ages and stages from Year 3 and beyond. There are no hard or fast rules. Trust your intuition and modify them as required to support your students.

It can be reassuring to repeat exercises you have done before, especially after a holiday break. Revisiting prompts also invites students to branch out and explore new ways of thinking about their writing.

I know teachers are time-poor, so my overarching goal for this section is to ensure you have enough prompts ready to go. You will soon discover that these prompts are not single-use writing exercises. Many exercises include multiple prompts and several layers of extension possibilities and activities related to the same topic. For example, in 'Journal writing' (page 179) you'll find thirteen different prompts to work with. You'll also find many ways to explore the concept of creative flow in these activities. Making use of multiple prompts allows you to revisit concepts, extend ideas and foster continuity of thought.

The open-ended nature of these exercises means your class can add their unique spin to many of the writing prompts. Ask your students to contribute random words to build your list or create journalling prompts or titles for list poetry. Inviting students to contribute to your bank of writing prompts encourages them to accept some responsibility for generating ideas for discovery writing. Your aim is to develop independent, lifelong writers.

Writing fluency

The main aim of your timed discovery writing is to generate ideas and capture these on the page (or on screen depending on your students' needs). Grammar, spelling, word choice can all be edited, but accessing that sense of fluency and flow – as is our aim here – is exhilarating. It's the very thing that keeps writers writing.

Adrienne Gear (2016) shares a simple acronym to help writers access creative flow and fluency: *GUM*. G stands for 'give it a try' or 'get it down'; *U* is a reminder to underline the word if you aren't sure of the spelling; and *M* is for 'move on'. I love this simple, supportive strategy – and so do my students.

If a writing prompt doesn't inspire an initial idea, encourage writers to sink directly into the present moment and describe how it feels to not have a starting point, that initial spark of an idea. It can be especially daunting to not have a starting point when everyone around you is furiously writing, so encourage students to write directly from this space using the first person or create a character who is feeling all the same emotions.

Suggest students first lean in and describe how their body feels, capturing the physical sensations and sensory details. Try pinning down the anxiety or fear or apathy. How does it look and feel? Then zoom out and describe the room (the setting) in detail.

It may seem counterintuitive but giving students permission to write about not having an idea or how it feels to experience a mind blank means they will always have an available option to get started. This immediately reduces the anxiety around this happening. I've found this strategy not only helps students come into the present moment but results in some hilarious and evocative pieces of writing.

Home writing

Wherever possible, find ways for your writing practice to flourish outside the boundaries of your classroom, until writing becomes a natural extension of your students' lives. See Chapter 7 for a range of possibilities for home writing.

Make your mark

And finally, I want to reassure you that there is no right or wrong way to work with these prompts. Put your stamp on the exercises and your classroom writing practice. I've been lucky enough to be a teacher and a student of the writing process over the last thirty years and I'm excited about having the opportunity to pass the baton on to you. Run with it. Let creativity lead the way.

Personal writing

Mine your life for writing inspiration

Stories generally come from two places: our personal experiences ('I know') and our imagination ('I imagine'). Our personal experiences serve as useful springboards for developing pieces of writing, but in order to make use of our lived experience we need to be skilled observers of our lives.

Young writers do not always understand the power of personal storytelling. If you could choose to write about a zombie controlling a new planet in the solar system, the story of what you ate for dinner last night seems to pale in significance. But our personal stories are the backbone of any piece of writing so this is the perfect place to start. Zooming in on small details gives writing depth and authenticity. Sensory details, in particular, not only engage your readers' imagination but can elicit involuntary physical responses, such as hunger or fear.

Recently in an online writing class, each student developed a character and then created a fictional diary. We had diaries written from the perspective of a bee, a pigeon, a dragon, a balloon, a puppy, an aeroplane and even Sunday, a day of the week. As a final writing reflection, each of us traced the origins of some of our diary entries to see how our interests, daily lives and past experiences intersected in this piece of fictional writing. It was an interesting mapping exercise and highlighted the importance of paying attention to the details of our everyday life.

This section contains ten different personal writing prompts:

1. List poetry
2. I remember
3. Wonderings
4. Mind maps
5. What do I need to know about you?
6. The story of my name
7. Journal writing
8. What if?
9. True, true, false
10. Make up your mind

1. List poetry

List poetry uses a simple repetitive structure to inspire students to catch small details, play with imagery, and express their feelings and experiences in prose. Innovating on a given structure scaffolds learning which is especially helpful for reluctant writers. It also reduces the cognitive and creative load, which frees up writers to work with humour and voice. This writing prompt can be easily modified to suit any topic, theme or age. It's the sort of poetry that really gets your class buzzing, so it works well as an icebreaker activity.

Things I have been doing lately – inspired by Allan Ahlberg's (1991) 'Things I have been doing lately'

Hudson (11 years old)

Writing this poem.
Picking up my pen.
Opening my pen lid.
Picking up my pen lid again.
Moving my arm.
Raising my eyebrow.
Swinging on my chair.
Back and forth.
Side to side.
Looking at the time.
Daydreaming.
Spinning my pen.
Thinking about what I had to eat last night.
Tapping my notepad.
Flicking the pages.
Don't look now.
I've written a poem.

How to use this prompt

Often students write ordinary recounts of their weekends, but using a list poem like 'Things I have been doing lately' from Allan Ahlberg's (1991) *Heard It in the Playground* as inspiration (many others can be found online) can be a much more engaging alternative.

1. Introduce your students to the list poem structure before you use this discovery writing prompt (see the notes in 'Tips for using this prompt' for how to analyse structure).
2. Read through the list poem together and highlight the structure used by the writer.
3. Ask students to think about the activities that featured in their weekends and write a list of ten verbs with an 'ing' ending.
4. Set your timer for five minutes and invite your writers to start turning their list of 'ing' verbs into a poem modelled on the structure of the original poem.

5. Remind students to add a title and a final line to bring their poem together.
6. Workshop responses.

Tips for working with this prompt

Preparation: Introducing a list poem

To introduce list poetry, first try innovating on an established list poem like 'Things I have been doing lately'. This introduction could take up to fifteen or even thirty minutes and sets the stage for following up this activity during your writing practice.

1. Provide a copy of the poem you've chosen, either in hard copy or on screen.

2. A list poem focuses on a single topic or idea so, after reading the poem, ask students questions like these:
    - What is the poem is about?
    - What's the main topic or theme? (This is usually explicit in the title of the poem.)

3. Next mark the repetitive elements that create the backbone or structure of the poem. I find it effective to use some form of highlighting to visually mark these elements either on screen or paper. For example, you might mark all lines starting with the 'ing' form of a verb, as I've demonstrated in figure 4 using Hudson's poem. This repetition gives the poem its structure and rhythm.

4. Allow time to discuss the poem and share some personal responses.

5. You may like to follow up by sharing a sample of student writing. As you can see from Hudson's poem, it's possible to play with the edges of any structure and still keep the poem true to form. For example, most of Hudson's sentences start with the 'ing' form of the verb. The lines 'Back and forth / Side to side' provide a clever break in the regular structure, but the poem quickly returns

Personal writing

to form. There's another variation in structure with the line 'Daydreaming'. This works because the 'ing' form of the verb is still there, just in a slightly different form and place.

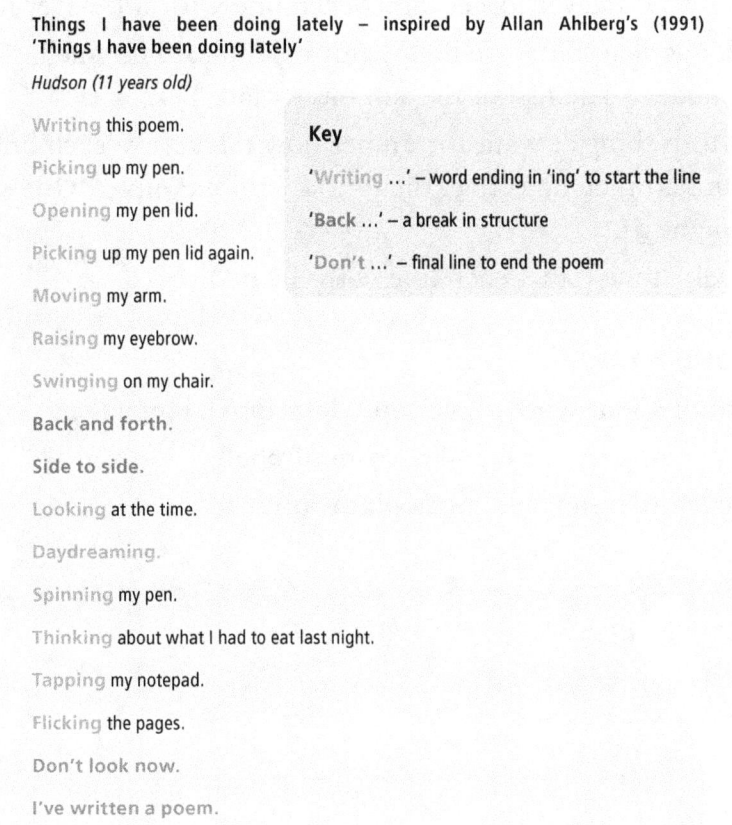

Figure 4: Sample poem with highlighted structural elements

Original list poetry

Once your students have worked with a list poem, they will be ready to create their own using their own topics and repetitive structures.

A list of possible poetry titles that students can use as prompts is handy to add to your class resources. Examples of prompts I have used with young writers follow:

- How to delay your bedtime (Start each line with an action verb – *shout, run, wash, drink* and so on.)

Time to Write

- Things you should know about me (Start each line with the pronoun I.)
- Memories (Start each line with 'I remember'.)
- Things I'll never forget (Start each line with 'I'll never forget'.)
- Things that make me happy (for example, 'The smell of lavender / The feel of the sun on my face')
- Fifteen things I want for dinner now (Structure each line number, then adjective, then food – for example, 'One sloppy lasagne'.)
- Look at me (Start each line with 'I can'.).

Teaching focus

- Think about word choice and descriptive language.
- Play with structure and rhythm of poetry.
- Generate ideas on a particular topic.

2. I remember

When students write about events, their writing often focuses on a string of actions, one after another: 'I went here. I did this.' This writing prompt, centred on the words *I remember*, encourages writers to focus on sensory details and emotions that hide under the events themselves.

Young writers don't always plumb the depths of their own experience for writing material. They need to be reminded their personal stories are important and deeply engaging. If you lived it, you have a better chance of bringing the story to life.

This prompt is inspired by an exercise in Natalie Goldberg's (1990) *Wild Mind: Living the Writer's Life*, in which she encourages writers to use two simple words – *I remember* – to open up the tight spaces in our minds, awaken memories and stir emotions.

> **I remember – first day of school**
>
> I remember the Kraft cheese sandwich my mum wrapped in rainbow-coloured greaseproof paper.
>
> I remember my dad's huge hand wrapped around mine and his gentle push forward, when they called out my name.
>
> I remember the hot, scratchy feel of my school jumper.
>
> I remember my teacher, Mrs D'Cruze, and the way she swept her dark hair into the same perfect bun every day.
>
> I remember her smell.
>
> I remember the sandbox that stood in the corner of our classroom.
>
> I remember that shallow rectangular metal crate, full of fine white sand and interesting little stones, animals and seed pods.
>
> I remember how (on hot days) we were allowed to add water from a thick, blue, plastic jug.
>
> I remember how I loved the easy feel of sand running through my fingers.
>
> I remember how I made tunnels and rivers in the sand tray.
>
> ...
>
> I don't remember any single lessons Mrs D'Cruze taught that year.
>
> I don't remember the names of most of the children in that class.
>
> I don't remember how I got to school in the mornings. Did I walk with my sisters or my mum?

It doesn't matter whether I'm writing myself or working with teachers or students, this prompt is incredibly versatile and goes to work quickly.

How to use this prompt

1. Choose a topic with a common theme that resonates with all students. If you are using this prompt for the first time with young writers, focus on a topic that is not too distant

in memory (such as a shared experience at school or a family event).

2. Set your timer for five minutes and invite writers to wander through their memories and write down any that catch their eye, making sure to start each sentence with the words *I remember*.

3. Encourage your writers to keep coming back to the small sensory details which are the foundation of writing. Explore the colours, details, tastes, smells, textures and feelings locked within the experience.

4. Allow time to workshop responses and highlight any sensory details. Consider collecting a list of vivid sensory details on a class list for future reference.

5. After students have finished writing about what they remember, try repeating this exercise using the words *I don't remember* at the start of each sentence. This suggestion from Goldberg (1990) helps writers turn the memory over and peer at its underbelly.

Tips for working with this prompt

- 'I don't remember' asks writers to make connections that are just under conscious thought. It's interesting how the details of what we don't remember tug at our sleeve to get our attention. You can progress directly to Step 5 with 'I don't remember', or you might return to this second part of the prompt over the next day or so.
- It's possible to leave the prompt open or use it to deep dive into a specific memory or experience as I did in my sample poem about starting school (page 163).
- 'I remember' is a good starting point for a range of writing endeavours, including as a prewriting exercise to gather ideas for an extended piece of writing such as a personal narrative. Creating mind maps (see page 170) of topics and inspiration

that your students can build on can be useful when working with this prompt. For example, if students are exploring memories about their first year at school, they could create a mind map in their notebook with ideas related to fields including the following:
- accidents
- proud moments
- embarrassing moments
- favourite teachers
- school lunches
- special events
- friends
- daily activities and routines.

- The repetitive phrasing of this prompt means this piece of discovery writing can be refined and transformed into a list poem (see page 159).
- If you notice the use of general, sweeping adjectives such as *cool* or *uncomfortable*, ask the writer to get specific: 'How was the jumper uncomfortable?' Encourage writers to keep probing to uncover words like *scratchy* and *itchy*.
- Allow plenty of time for sharing, because from my experience this prompt inspires conversation and uncovers finer details and emotions.

Teaching focus
- Explore the importance of engaging your reader through sensory details such textures, sounds, smells, tastes and visual details (like specific colours) that come to mind.
- Emphasise word choice, in particular zooming in on specific descriptive words like *scratchy* or *itchy* rather than using general descriptions like *uncomfortable*.

3. Wonderings

Teaching philosophy to primary-aged students showed me the value of using questions for inquiry and conversation, but it was Ralph Fletcher's (2003) *A Writer's Notebook* that inspired me to see the potential of collecting questions to generate ideas for writing across a variety of genres.

Keeping a list of questions means your students always have a source of writing material at their disposal. Paying attention to your questions is like shining a torch into the far corners of your mind.

> **Wonderings**
>
> What do you wonder about just before you fall off to sleep?
>
> Some people say space goes on forever but it can't.
>
> Can it?
>
> Do jellyfish have feelings?
>
> Can dogs really smell fear?
>
> Do you ever wonder what you are doing here?
>
> On earth?
>
> All these questions swim inside my head
>
> coming up for air
>
> every now and then.
>
> What do you wonder about just before you fall off to sleep?
>
> A free reproducible version of this sample is available

How to use this prompt

Part 1: Start wondering

1. Share my sample poem, 'Wonderings', first to get your class thinking and talking about the questions that circle inside their minds. (Downloadable copy of 'Wonderings' available.)

2. Invite your students to begin creating a list of any questions that puzzle, intrigue, unsettle or scare them. All questions, big and small, can be added to their list.

3. Set your timer for five minutes and ask your students compose their own list of wonderings. You may wish to play some quiet music as they work.

4. After writing, allow time for workshopping. Students share some of their wonderings with the group, keeping in mind that some questions are private and that sharing is voluntary.

5. As students share, encourage the group to cross-pollinate their

lists. Sometimes it's not until we hear someone else ask a question aloud that we recognise the same thought lives within us too.

6. If time permits after sharing, give students another short block of time to continue writing their lists. They will have warmed up a little by this point and be ready to keep going.

Creating a list of questions and opening this topic up for discussion are the first steps in using this prompt to generate ideas for writing. This is important work. I have seen students come back and add questions to their list after this introduction, so allow time for this process to settle before proceeding with Part 2.

Part 2: From wondering to writing

Now your writers are ready to start developing their questions into writing prompts. This is not a one-off writing activity – I suggest you circle back to this activity regularly as part of your writing practice. Some questions will find answers. Some will simply live on the page, while others will inspire stories, poems and inventions. Some questions give your writers plenty to think and write about in their writer's notebook.

1. Introduce the following code to your students as a starting point for working with their questions:

    - F – fiction
    - RP – research project
    - NF – non-fiction or persuasive writing
    - R – reflective writing
    - D – draw a diagram to clarify the idea
    - M – create a mind map.

    More categories can be added by students as they go but this is a good place to start.

2. Next provide examples of how questions raised in using the

'Wonderings' prompt can lead to more writing. Here are two examples I share to show how wonderings can lead to fiction writing:

- Bluetooth was a relatively new concept when I purchased my speaker. I wrote in my notebook 'How does Bluetooth actually work?' I fully intended to research this question, but instead a character knocked on the door of my imagination. This character had super slick, black hair and, you guessed it, one long, sharp, blue tooth. Instead of researching how Bluetooth worked, I spent some time that morning mapping out possible plots for this character.

- In one of my workshops, a young writer posed some questions about hair colour: 'Why were there so many colours in the world, but only blond, brown, red and black hair? Why couldn't we be born with rainbow-coloured hair?' It was a great question that then inspired a story about a character born with pink hair.

3. After sharing these examples, ask students to apply any of the codes to their questions. Would they like to research a question or create a mind map or use it to inspire an interesting character?

4. Set your timer for five minutes and invite students to choose a question to explore further. If you played music when students were working through the first part of this prompt, play the same music again this time.

5. Workshop students' responses.

Tips for working with this prompt

- On a new page at the start of their notebooks, ask students to add the heading 'Curiosity challenge' and number each line down the left side of their page from one to fifty. This will likely take up two or more pages. The challenge is to note down fifty questions – one on each line – sparked by their own curiosity as time goes on. This central place to store what they wonder about allows students to return to and write on their curiosity regularly.
- Alternatively, you might like to give students a pocket-sized spiral notebook titled 'A book of wonderings' in which to collect questions as they arise. This will teach them to pay attention to their thoughts and writing inspiration.
- I often use this activity when working with adults in my professional development workshops. Paying attention to your questions frees up space for creativity and means teachers have experience using this same practice in their own lives.

Teaching focus

- Give students full ownership and control by helping them to generate their own writing topics.
- Use writing for different purposes across a range of genres, from critical and reflective thinking to works of fiction.
- Build general knowledge.
- Spark students' curiosity, creativity and imagination.

Resources

'Wonderings' sample poem

A downloadable copy of my sample poem, 'Wonderings' is available. You can use 'Wonderings' to introduce the prompt and to get students thinking and talking about the questions that circle inside their minds.

4. Mind maps

Mind-mapping, a thinking tool made famous by Tony Buzan (2002) in *How to Mind Map*, engages both the creative and the logical parts of the brain to gather and classify a wide range of information about any topic. Writers use symbols, pictures and words to deep-dive and download thoughts and ideas on a given topic.

This prompt encourages writers to make decisions and trust their intuition. Mind maps are also an effective prewriting and planning tool, and in this activity we use mind maps in a structured way to capture the source of writing inspiration.

How to use this prompt

1. Ask students to orientate their notebooks in landscape to give themselves more space to work.
2. Draw a circle in the middle of the page and add a title. Students can come up with their own titles, but some examples follow:
    - 'Writing inspiration'
    - 'What inspires me'
    - 'Digging for ideas'
    - 'Real-life inspiration'.
3. Ask students to think back on their writing and name some possible sources of inspiration. You can support their thinking by asking them what they like to write about and why. You might also ask students to think about a time when they thought, 'This would make a good story.' Where were they? What were they doing?

Personal writing

4. Once students have had a chance to think about what inspires their writing, as a class, create a quick list of the categories you've discussed, such as places, experiences, activities, holidays, people, objects and so on.

5. Ask students to choose two to four categories from the list to focus on and add these to their pages. Draw circles around these categories and connect each to the title in the centre of the page as in figure 5.

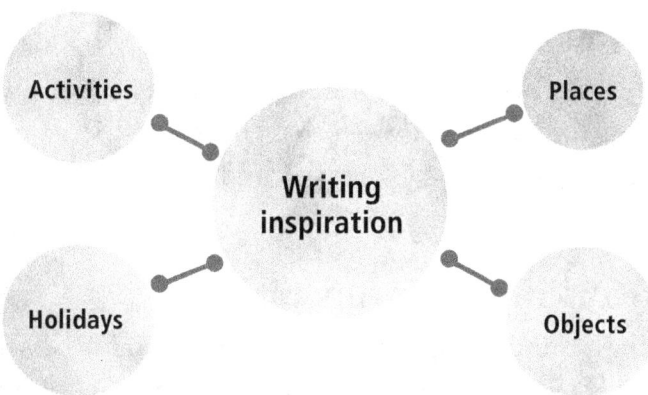

Figure 5: Partially scaffolded mind map

6. Ask writers to work on capturing four specific ideas within each category they have chosen to add to their mind map – that is, four ideas that branch out from each circle. For example, as illustrated in figure 6, the category of *activity* might result in ideas like *playing soccer*, *going to the shops*, *getting lost* and *packing my school bag*. As this activity invites associative thinking, students are free to use images and symbols along with words to represent their ideas and complete their mind maps in colour.

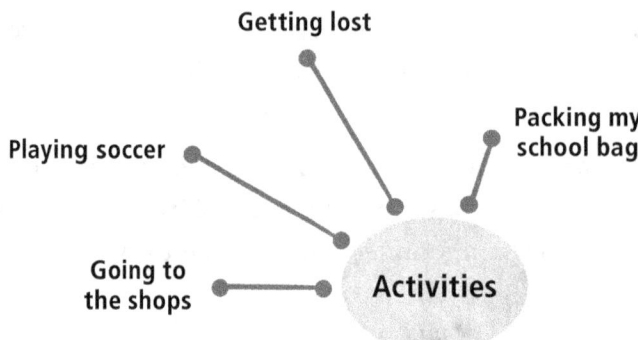

Figure 6: Connecting ideas to a category in a mind map

7. Set the timer for five minutes and let writers get to work making connection between their lives and their writing inspiration, add more categories and subcategories as time permits.

Tips for working with this prompt

- Although mind-mapping is a slight variation on discovery writing, the same guidelines apply: get specific, write from your heart and don't edit or self-censor.
- Using a mind map, writers can collect a vast number of ideas in a relatively short space of time. Visualising and bringing ideas to life in their imagination gives writers a solid base for writing. The fact that the outcome is not predetermined often frees up writers to explore a wide range of ideas without the pressure of immediately finding a narrative.
- Consider collecting mind maps like these in writers' notebooks. Having a map of possible writing ideas ready to go means writers have a range of possible story ideas to choose from at any time. This is an effective way to support reluctant writers, as it starves off that 'I don't have any ideas' feeling.
- Mind-mapping can be used across all three categories of prompts presented in this book. I've outlined how to use mind-

mapping to gather writing inspiration from students' own lives, but it can be used equally to develop characters and ideas for persuasive writing.

Teaching focus

- Generate and classify a wide range of writing ideas on a given topic, from fiction to non-fiction.
- Practise whole-brain thinking by igniting both creative and logical parts of the brain to complete a task.
- Be independent and responsible for generating their own writing topics.

5. What do I need to know about you?

When I went in search of icebreaker activities to kick off the new year at The Writer's Club, I discovered a list: '30 questions every student should be able to answer' (Heick, n.d.). Many of the questions on this list make excellent, thought-provoking writing prompts, but 'What is something everyone should know about you?' cut right to the chase.

What you need to know about me

One thing you need to know about me is that I'm not all that comfortable with getting things wrong. I never have been.

Sometimes if I don't think I can do something well enough, I sidestep it. Perfectionism is especially hard if you love to write because writing is rarely perfect on the first try.

I keep reminding myself, even at my age, to go with the flow and get my ideas down on paper first. Even the phrase *go with the flow* makes me feel excited and a little nervous.

So be prepared for the fact that, during this year, when I share my writing, it's going to be unedited and a bit clunky, but I will share it anyway. It's my way of saying I will not let perfectionism and fear get in the way of me enjoying the writing process.

I use a slight variation – 'What do I need to know about you?' – to invite writers to focus on personal insights that are not immediately obvious to others. The main aim of this prompt is to evoke personal insights and allow writers to reflect on their experiences and natural tendencies. This prompt invites reflection, self-awareness, honesty, and vulnerability: the very qualities that build community and connection.

How to use this prompt

1. Ask your students the question at the centre of this exercise: 'What do I need to know about you?'

2. Set your timer for five minutes and invite your students to respond to the prompt in any way they like, reminding them to write from the heart. There are no right or wrong answers. There's no need to censor or edit.

3. Sharing is optional, but do allow workshopping time for any students who wish to speak.

Tips for working with this prompt

- When I choose this prompt I always sit down and write with the group. I recommend teachers taking time to write alongside their class for this activity. Sharing your response first builds trust and models risk-taking and vulnerability.
- Consider selecting and working with other questions from the full list that this prompt is inspired from, available at www.teachthought.com/critical-thinking/student-should-be-able-to/.
- This is a good prompt for early in the year, but be prepared to come back to it again at intervals as your class's needs and wants change.
- Personal insights or thoughts can be transformed into individual writing goals. For example, in my sample, I refer to my perfectionism, I could challenge this tendency by aiming to share my writing at least once a week.

Teaching focus

- Clarify thoughts and ideas.
- Develop self-awareness and self-identity.
- Reflect and express wants and needs in writing.
- Develop empathy and compassion.

6. The story of my name

I first read about the idea of asking students to write about their names in Aimee Buckner's (2005) *Notebook Know-How: Strategies for the Writer's Notebook*. Over the years I've put my own spin on this prompt, which I use with adults and students alike. It's always a great icebreaker and gets a group talking.

Our names are such a strong part of our personal identity. If a child has never been curious about the origin of their name, this prompt will send them home with lots of questions. Once writers see the time and effort behind choosing names, they may feel inspired to offer their literary characters the same consideration.

> **The story of my name**
>
> My mother was from a Catholic family. Her name was Mary. My father wanted to continue this tradition in our family and name one of his daughter's Mary, but my mum wasn't so keen.
>
> She didn't like the idea of a young Mary and an old Mary, or a big Mary and a small Mary. I think she wanted to be the only Mary, and fair enough! (In the sixties and seventies children were often given the same name as their parents. My little brother and my father are both named Thomas.)
>
> My mother obviously felt some pressure to name her daughter Mary, but her heart wasn't in it. Instead, she found a way to fly under the radar. The name on my birth certificate reads Mary Elizabeth Cregan, but as soon as I came home I became known as Beth, which was a name she loved
>
> Occasionally, if I was being especially naughty, she would raise her voice and start the sentence with 'Mary Elizabeth!' At home, there was no confusion, but I dreaded substitute teachers. If they didn't know me, they would read down the roll, and the class would roar with laughter. I'd turn a shade of red. I was mortified.
>
> In doctors' surgeries and at airports, I'm always called Mary, but it doesn't embarrass me at all. Now when someone calls me Mary Cregan, it reminds me that my mum is never far away.
>
> I love that connection between us and the fact that we share the same name.

How to use this prompt

1. Share an example like the one I've given here to get your students thinking about the origins and backstories of names.
2. Ask some students to share their name story with the class.
3. As students share what they know about their names, write any broad headings or ideas that surface on a large piece of paper or blank whiteboard. Here are some fields that may end up on your list:
    - family history
    - cultural and religious traditions

- famous people
- characters from books or movies
- symbols and meanings behind names
- names that have significance for parents
- shadow names (other names that were on the list of options)
- gender-neutral names.

4. Now build on that list as a class to include what else they know about the various inspirations for names. For example, names can be inspired by:
   - places, such as Paris
   - colours, such as Scarlet
   - precious stones, such as Ruby and Crystal
   - nature, such as Summer and Reid
   - values and emotions, such as Joy and Hope
   - flowers, such as Lily and Violet.

5. Set the timer and invite students to write about their names. Some may not know the story behind their name, in which case they can write about what they like or don't like about their name. They can also write about their favourite names, their nicknames or use names as an open prompt.

6. Allow time to workshop responses and continue adding any categories to the list you started earlier.

Tips for working with this prompt

- This is a great prompt to help your class get to know each other. I encourage teachers to join in with this prompt and share their own response to build relationships and help establish their writing community.

- These short pieces of writing can be extended and edited to create personal narratives, which can then be published in a class book with illustrations and photos.
- Keep the list of what your class knows about the origins of names visible in your room. We will refer to this list when we are developing characters and plots in the next section.

Teaching focus
- Reflect on personal and family history.
- Practise a range of storytelling skills.
- Develop an awareness of personal identity.
- Develop voice and style.

7. Journal writing

Journal writing is a portal into the world of our innermost thoughts and dreams. There are no rules, no right or wrong. The blank page becomes a space where we're free to express ourselves.

We underestimate the importance of writing as a personal thinking tool, but once an idea is down on paper it becomes part of our consciousness. This style of writing plays a critical role in the development of a writer's self-awareness and emotional intelligence. In my own journalling practice, I'm often surprised by the thoughts that tumble out onto my page. I use journalling for many purposes, from problem-solving to imagining and dreaming about the future.

How to use this prompt

1. Select a journalling prompt from the list starting on page 180 and share it with your students. Write it on the whiteboard.
2. Remind students that the prompt is only there to get them started and they are free to head off in any direction they choose.
3. Set your timer for five minutes and invite students to respond to the chosen prompt.
4. Allow time for workshopping afterwards.

Tips for working with this prompt

- Journal writing teaches us to let go and experience the release writing can bring. To experience this sense of freedom, encourage your students not to continually read back over their writing and edit as they go. They can read back over their writing once they have finished.
- It's easy and fun to make what I call a 'journal in a jar'. Print the list of journal prompts provided and cut into single prompts. Fold and add each prompt to your jar, then select a

prompt any time you need one. This simple resource means you always have a writing activity ready to go.

- Ask your students to contribute journalling prompts to your class collection so they carry some ownership and responsibility for generating ideas for writing.
- In Chapter 1 we talked about the role of decision-making within the creative process (page 32). *Would You Rather?*, a popular picture book by John Burningham (1994), provides a range of fun writing prompts that encourage your students to access the options and make decisions – for example: 'Would you rather be covered in jam, soaked in water, or pulled through the mud by a dog?' (pp. 6–7). Journalling about these sorts of questions can be a fun way to practise decision-making skills.
- Use journal prompts to inspire thinking and writing on a range of topics or themes you are exploring across the curriculum areas.

Teaching focus

- Use writing as a tool for personal reflection and self-expression.
- Develop self-awareness and personal identity.
- Recognise the value of writing as a tool for clarifying ideas and solving problems.

Resources

Journalling prompts

Here's a list of some of the journalling prompts I've used over the year with a range of writers:

- What's the most creative thing you've ever done?
- What's your proudest moment?
- What is your personal philosophy or motto?

- What's most important to you?
- Who are your heroes or role models in real life?
- What are your hidden talents?
- What is your favourite season of the year and why?
- Take us through your favourite meal of all time from beginning to end.
- If you could meet any person, alive or dead, who would you choose?
- If you could spend the day with one of your favourite fictional characters, who would you choose and where would you go?
- What scares you the most?
- Describe one of your most treasured items.
- If the choice was yours, what pet would you choose and why?

Download a reproducible version of this list.

8. What if?

Our personal experiences are a springboard for developing writing across all genres, but when you mix real life with a touch of imagination, wonderful things can happen!

'Write what you know' is a common piece of advice given to writers, but so often, writers can't see how they can turn ordinary events into storytelling magic. It's much easier for your students to visualise a story if they can draw on lived experiences.

Once I was dropping my daughter Molly at school, and as we rounded the corner, her sister Neve, who was three years old at the time, started to cry.

'It's not what I wanted,' she sobbed.

'What do you mean, not what you wanted?' I asked.

'I wished that when we turned the corner the school would be all gone, and Molly would come home and play with me. I hate school!' she snarled.

Molly and I laughed, but I went straight home and wrote that conversation into my notebook. Could something as ordinary as school drop-off trigger an extraordinary story? What if we turned the corner that day, and found the school was gone? Where might it have gone? Who made it disappear and why? What if we were running late, and now Molly was the only student who could solve the mystery and bring back her school?

Simply applying the question 'What if?' blurs the edges of this everyday task and invites in a little magic. In this prompt I'll show you some ways to anchor flights of fancy in the real world.

How to use this prompt

1. Start by setting your timer for three minutes and ask writers to make a quick list of ten or more ordinary actions they did that morning or the night before. As an example, here is the start of my list:
   - went to supermarket to buy milk
   - listened to an audiobook
   - went for a walk
   - cooked dinner
   - had a bath ...

2. Next, choose one action on your list and circle it. For example, I might choose 'went to supermarket to buy milk' from my list.

3. Ask writers to close their eyes and visualise themselves in the space where this action occurred, paying attention to the sounds, colours and other sensory details around them.

4. Now ask writers to visualise the scene in slow motion, breaking it down to a series of actions.

5. Here's where it starts to get interesting. Ask your writers to create a series of 'What if?' questions related to their scene and recreate the action in a whole new way. For example:
   - What if, when the doors of the supermarket opened, a strange-looking gnome-like character, dressed in green, was standing right next to the trays of mangoes, giving out samples of lollies as shoppers walked in?
   - What if he gave me a sample of the bright-pink lollies in a small clear plastic cup, which I drained into my mouth?
   - What if, as soon as the pink lollies hit my tongue, there was an explosion in my mouth, a sensation took over and a trapdoor appeared in front of me.

- What if, when I turned around, the gnome-like character was gone?
- What if I asked the man getting a trolley whether he had seen the gnome leave?
- What if the man said he hadn't seen anyone, especially not someone dressed in green with a big, red, pointy hat?
- What if I reached down and creaked open the wooden trapdoor?

6. Set the timer for five minutes and watch reluctant writers jump into this activity. Without realising it, this series of questions will actually become a plan for their stories.

Tips for working with this prompt

Media madness

This spin on 'What if?' blends fact and fiction with the support of media relating to real-life events.

1. Collect a series of pictures from newspapers, magazines or online. Choose pictures that relate to real-life events.
2. Make a class set by printing and laminating your images.
3. Organise your students into groups of three or four.
4. Ask writers to each select an image. Students will start and end with their own image, but will share images around the group.
5. Explain to students that that their goal is to pose an interesting question related to their image. You might support creative thinking by suggesting they start each entry with words like *perhaps*, *maybe* and *what if*.
6. Set the timer for a minute or two and ask students to write their question on a sticky note.

7. When the timer rings, instruct students to affix the sticky note to the back of their image and then pass the image along to the student next to them.

8. Repeat Steps 6 and 7 until each student has posed a question related to all the images in circulation in their group and their original images have been returned to them. At this point, students will have an additional two or three questions to consider.

9. Allow a short amount of time to share images and resulting questions within the small groups.

10. Ask students to select a question to use as a prompt for writing, then set the timer for five minutes.

11. Allow time to workshop responses.

Teaching focus

- Pay attention to the storytelling potential lurking behind ordinary, everyday events.
- Draw on personal lives and experiences to generate ideas for writing.
- Learn prewriting techniques to scaffold storytelling.
- Generate a series of sequential ideas to create a basic story plan.

9. True, true, false

This activity has been a popular icebreaker on many school camps and here it becomes a multifaceted writing prompt. The aim of this prompt is to write three statements about yourself to share with the group. Two of these statements will be true and one will be false. The trick is to try to make all three statements sound equally believable.

The first part of this writing activity is fast-paced and fun making it an effective icebreaker. It's the perfect way to get a group of writers talking and laughing. Then, in the second part of this activity, writers have the chance to use their three statements to inspire a piece of writing. You will need more than one session of discovery writing to work with this prompt.

How to use this prompt

Get started

1. Model the game first by sharing three statements about yourself – two true and one false – and allowing the class to guess which one is false.
2. Ask students to write two facts and one falsehood about themselves – so three sentences in all.
3. Set a timer for two to three minutes. Keep the time frame short to encourage writers to think fast and make decisions. It's possible to add more time if required, but the timer provides an initial deadline and helps eliminate the inevitable 'I don't know what to write.'
4. Facilitate writers taking turns in sharing their three statements and having their audience try to identify which detail is false. Depending on your group numbers, you can share as a whole class or work in pairs or smaller groups.

Get writing

In the second part of this prompt, writers work with their true and false statements to generate writing ideas.

1. Ask writers to expand on their false statement first. For example, one untruth I often use is that I have flown over the Yarra Valley in a hot air balloon. I'd love to do this, but the truth is I'm just plain scared! However, if I were to write about it, I'd have the chance to imagine myself in a hot air balloon. I'd describe the lift-off, the view, my feelings, my fear of heights.

2. Use one of the truths (for example, I love chocolate gelato) to inspire a personal narrative. Tell the story in as much detail as possible.

Tips for working with this prompt

- Allow time between planning and playing with ideas and coming back to do some writing. This gives writers a chance to incubate ideas.

- Building on your writers' previous experience, it's possible to blur the lines between fact and fiction by asking 'What if?' (page 182). For example, one of my truths is that I can ride a unicycle. That fact could trigger the question 'What if I'm a unicycle-riding clown at the circus?' Just like that, I've used my fact to inspire a fictional character and a setting. What could happen to a clown at the circus? Brainstorm possibilities and I have a possible scene and a story.

- Having a series of skeleton sketches (like the ones generated in this prompt) in your students' notebooks means they always have a possible story ready to take flight. This is especially important for reluctant writers.

Teaching focus
- Use writing to record and share facts and ideas.
- Find ways to use their own feelings, actions and more to inspire writing.
- Practise active and sustained listening.
- Practise writer's voice and style.

10. Make up your mind

I like giving students as many chances as possible to practise critical and analytical thinking on paper. It's important for young writers to mull over ideas and form opinions without the pressure of having to complete a piece of persuasive writing.

Low-stakes writing opportunities such as these persuasive prompts encourage your students to play with topics, chase ideas, make decisions and develop opinions. Having the time and space to make up your mind and share and discuss topics with peers is a crucial part of developing critical thinking skills. Sharing responses and workshopping these prompts also gives students an opportunity to hear a range of ideas from their peers which sparks curiosity and builds general knowledge.

How to use this prompt

1. Select and share a persuasive writing prompt from the list on page 192 with your students. Sometimes it helps to have a printed copy of the prompt for students, but I will often write it on the whiteboard.
2. Ask students to consider the prompt and express any ideas that come to mind. They may find they have a strong opinion, or they may simply choose to write through their thoughts. As this is an unstructured activity, your writers do not necessarily have to work with any formula or set response. They are free to express their ideas in any way they like.
3. Set your timer for five minutes of discovery writing.
4. Allow time for workshopping so that writers can hear their peers' ideas and opinions.

Tips for working with this prompt

Double-time debates
To extend this activity, try this debate-centred variation.

1. Organise your students into pairs.
2. Choose a prompt from the list, such as 'All children should play sport'.
3. Ask one student to write from the affirmative position and the other in opposition to the statement, then set the timer for five minutes.
4. Instead of workshopping as a group, allow partners to share with each other. This is a great way to give students an opportunity to share and compare their thinking and writing in a less formal way.

Binary opposites
Take another variation by focusing on binary opposites.

1. List sets of binary opposites, such as:
   - cats / dogs
   - city / country
   - winter / summer.
2. Select a set from the list.
3. Ask students make an instinctive choice between the two options and write to persuade their audience to agree with their choice. Once again, it's not always necessary to work with sequential ideas or use set structures. Discovery writing gives students a chance to try on opinions and ideas in a low-risk atmosphere.

Who am I?

This variation gives a fun twist to persuasive writing while developing the skills of using character voice.

1. Choose a prompt from the list, such as 'Recess should be longer.'
2. Create a quick list of possible stakeholders. For example, the people with an interest in the argument about the length of recess would include:
   - teachers
   - students
   - parents
   - canteen managers.
3. Ask students to choose one of these stakeholders and to write persuasively about the prompt from that stakeholder's perspective. This gives students the experience of writing for a particular audience or point of view.
4. Allow time to workshop responses, ideally selecting students who have chosen to write from different stakeholder perspectives. I find writers often shape their writing to match the language the character might use and will often share their writing using their character's voice.

Teaching focus

- Collaborate to develop general knowledge and understanding of persuasive writing skills.
- Develop critical thinking skills.
- Practise using writer and character voice to present thoughts and opinions.
- Reflect on issues and develop opinions.
- Communicate opinions clearly and effectively.

Time to Write

Resources

'Make up your mind' prompts

Here are some prompt suggestions to get students thinking:

- All children should play sport.
- Cats make better pets than dogs.
- Public transport is the way to go.
- Junk food should be banned at school canteens.
- Computer games are a waste of time.
- Family is more important than friends.
- Animals should not be kept in zoos.
- School uniforms should be compulsory.
- Parents should have access to their children's passwords.
- Australia should accept more refugees.
- Homework should be banned.
- All plastic bags should be banned.
- Recess should be longer.
- The school day should be shorter.
- Recycling should be mandatory.
- Downloading music and movies should carry a fine.
- Smoking should be illegal.

Download a reproducible list.

Imaginative writing
Just imagine

When I first began teaching in the eighties, stoking the fire of our students' imaginations was an important part of our writing programs. Telling and listening to stories, poetry and songs kept imagery and metaphor alive in our minds and our classrooms. Time constraints mean that classroom activities such as oral storytelling are on the decline, but our students suffer no shortage of stimulation. On the contrary, they consume imagery all day and night across numerous devices. Our task now is to teach our students the visualisation skills they need to create their own imagery.

It's not just our bodies that need exercise – our minds and imaginations do too. Writers of all ages need time and space to practise generating ideas and imagery. They need tools and strategies that develop a sense of trust in their ability to come up with ideas, especially under pressure. There are many parts of our writing programs that we can't change, but your classroom writing practice ensures the building blocks of imagination and visualisation – the prerequisites of writing – are firmly in place.

If you're writing from personal experience, you can rely a little on memory to furnish your writing with description and details. But works of fiction require writers to generate ideas and create scenes, develop characters, settings, details and dialogue that flow along the length of a narrative arc. As complex as this sounds, our brains are geared for this type of activity, but we need to activate both sides of our brain to make it happen. Wherever possible, encourage writers to activate both the logical and creative sides of the brain by including opportunities to sketch, create storyboards, and use colour and pictures to support the visualisation process. This is important for all writers, but I've found it especially supports reluctant writers.

Activities in this section focus on concepts aligned with narratives, such as setting, plot, character, mood, idea generation and descriptive imagery. The first five activities are unstructured, while the five that follow present your students with a writing challenge. All prompts are open-ended.

This section contains ten different imaginative writing prompts:

1. Ink-blot writing
2. Musical moods
3. Random words
4. It's all in the name
5. Object writing
6. Flip the switch
7. Show, don't tell
8. Playing with poetry
9. Shape a story
10. What a place!

1. Ink-blot writing

We often use images to inspire ideas for writing, but ink blots take this concept in a slightly different direction. Picture prompts tend to include possibilities for characters, settings, objects, themes and moods. Ink blots on the other hand are subjective and open to personal interpretation.

Writers can hold the image in their hands and twist it around to see the shape from different perspectives. I've seen the same ink blot inspire rhyming poetry, free verse and a story about a menacing ink-blot character. Another student wrote such a clear description of the ink blot that we could almost see it in our mind's eye. I've never focused on the psychological interpretations of these images; instead we focus on shape, colour, patterns and personal associations. There are no set outcomes, so writers are free to respond in any way they wish.

How to use this prompt

1. Share a printed image of an ink blot with each student. A quick Google search will uncover hundreds of images that can be used for this activity. You can provide students with the same ink blot or print a class set of different images and have students select their own.

2. Once students have their ink blot, give them a few minutes to explore it carefully from different angles.

3. Ask questions that activate your writers' senses, memory and imagination. For example:
    - What shapes or patterns can you see within the image?
    - Does it remind you of anything?
    - What do you immediately think of when you look at this picture?
    - Does the image inspire a mood or a feeling?

- What questions would you ask the ink blot?
- What would you like to know about this image?

4. Remind students of the many genres and structures they have at their disposal when responding to this image. Possibilities include:
   - personal narrative
   - non-fiction description of the image in bullet form or prose
   - fictional narrative
   - poetry of any form, from free verse to haiku
   - personal reflection.
5. Set your timer for up to five minutes for discovery writing.
6. When you begin workshopping pieces of writing, record the genres and styles your writers use to respond to the prompt. This list reminds writers of the many possible options for discovery writing and that they do not have to rely on fiction.

Tips for working with this prompt

- To expand your students' writing repertoire, ask them to take the same ink blot they used to inspire their first piece of writing and try again using a different style of writing. For example, if a writer used their ink blot to inspire a story, they might try a poem or a detailed description. This approach develops flexible thinking skills.
- Consider laminating your class set of ink blots. I can guarantee they'll be put to good use.
- I've also encouraged students to use ink-blowing to create original ink-blot imagery.
- Instead of ink blots, try varying the imagery you use. I collect all sorts of postcards, especially those found in art galleries that feature abstract works of art. Abstract images give young writers a wide scope for imaginative interpretations.

Teaching focus
- Create original ideas for writing across multiple genres.
- Practise visualisation and creative thinking skills.
- Make interesting associations between shapes and ideas.

2. Musical moods

The atmosphere of a story is often connected to its setting, while mood taps into feelings and emotions. These two elements are crucial storytelling devices for both fiction and non-fiction writing. Many young writers rely on strings of adjectives (*scary*, *cold*, *dark*) to build mood and atmosphere, the 'tell rather than show' approach, so I'm always on the lookout for ways to help writers recognise, define and practise using the subtle elements of mood and atmosphere in their writing.

> **Musings on Schubert's 'Piano sonata no. 8 in F-sharp minor'**
>
> *Tate (7 years old)*
>
> Thinking of a butterfly flying peacefully through a light wind.
>
> Some bees, buzzing through a paddock searching for flowers.
>
> A sad miserable person, walking home through the rain.
>
> A happy polar bear coming out of hibernation.
>
> A lost man dying of thirst.
>
> The people in the village coming back home after a terrible storm.
>
> A badly wounded person being healed as if by magic.
>
> The *Titanic* sinking.
>
> The end of the dinosaurs.

When one of my students, Tate, brought in this piece of writing inspired by Schubert's sonata in F-sharp minor, I saw how music could help writers explore these elements. Tate had a musician, Jovanni, visiting his home. While he played, Tate captured the images this music stirred in his imagination and emotions. His evocative prose beautifully captured the mood and personality of this piece of music, without the pressure of fleshing out a complete story. Tate's response inspired my use of musical prompts to stimulate writing.

How to use this prompt

1. Select a piece of music to play as a musical prompt (see the list starting on page 200 for inspiration). I use short pieces because I find this allows students to hear the music more than once during discovery writing. One of my most successful pieces of music is just twenty seconds long.

2. The first time students listen to the musical prompt, I ask them to close their eyes or rest their head on their tables.

3. After the students have experienced the music, choose one of the questions below to stimulate discussion:
    - What is the mood of the piece of music? Does the mood change during the piece of music?
    - How did the piece of music make you feel?
    - What did it make you think about? Memories or past experiences?
    - If this piece of music had a voice, what would it say to you?
    - What pictures did you visualise in your mind while the music was playing?

4. Play the piece of music again and set the timer for five minutes.

5. Ask students to use writing to capture what they see, feel and hear in this piece of music. The prompt is open-ended so students are free to choose how they respond. They can experiment with prose, narrative or poetry.

6. Workshop students' responses.

Tips for working with this prompt

Matching moods

This is another way to use musical prompts to explore mood and atmosphere.

1. Follow the initial instructions for this prompt up to and including Step 4.

2. After playing the music a second time, ask students to write down three words that capture the mood of the music. Depending on the piece of music, responses could include words such as *scary, uplifting, foreboding* and *menacing*.

3. Set the timer for five minutes and challenge your students to use these mood words to inspire a fictional scene.
4. Workshop the responses.

Playing with action scenes

Soundtracks accompanying action scenes in movies provide the perfect vehicle for developing mood and atmosphere in writing. I save similar pieces of music on a playlist so they are easily accessible for discovery writing prompts.

Remember: if you are using a movie soundtrack, don't introduce the name of the movie or the title of the music before writing as this tends to colour students' responses.

> A response to 'Mutiny', Hans Zimmer, from *Pirates of the Caribbean: On Stranger Tides* (00.00–00.20)
>
> *Kara (12 years old)*
>
> My heart beats.
>
> Where is he?
>
> He was just behind me.
>
> I've no idea.
>
> Do I jump left or right?
>
> I sprint left.
>
> I stumble. Then fall.
>
> I feel his cold, clammy hand on my shoulder.
>
> You're it!

Teaching focus

- Play with narrative elements such as mood and atmosphere.
- Develop technical writing skills such as pacing, building suspense and drama.
- Engage sensory perception and experience writing prompts across different learning channels.
- Develop visualisation skills and mental imagery to inspire storytelling.

Resources

'Musical moods' suggestions

Here are some suggested pieces for you to get started with:

- 'PM's love theme', Chris Armstrong
- 'Motorcycle chase', David Buckley and John Powell

- 'Woven song – Pukumani', Deborah Cheetam
- 'Glocken blocken', Amanda Cole
- 'Extremely loud and incredibly close', Alexandre Desplat and Jean-Yves Thibaudet
- 'Nuvole bianche', Ludovico Einaudi
- 'Butterflying', Elena Kats-Chernin
- 'Guru bandana (Prayer)', Ali Akbar Khan
- 'First steps', Lena Raine
- 'Earth's angels', Robbins Island Music Group
- 'Forrest Gump theme', Alan Silvestri
- 'The southern sea', Garth Stevenson
- 'The quickening', Katia Tiutiunnik
- 'My sanctuary', Amelia Warner
- 'Kiss the rain', Yiruma
- 'Wait there', Yiruma (look for the arrangement for flute and piano, performed by Jasmine Choi and Hugh Sung)
- 'Maestro', Hans Zimmer
- 'Mutiny', Hans Zimmer.

3. Random words

Having the ability to make random connections between ideas is a marker of creative thinkers and innovators. I'm not sure exactly where I first came upon the idea of using random words to inspire writing, but I have been using it now for many years with great success.

It's easy to cater for a range of ages, stages and writing purposes simply by varying the words you choose. For example, using words such as *angry*, *proud* or *surprise* trigger an emotional response in your writers. If you want to explore a particular inquiry theme, choose words that relate to your topic.

I have included a set of random words in the resources list at the end of this prompt to get you started, but build your list to suit your purposes. Include interesting sounding words, objects, particular parts of speech – I've even seen prepositions such as *between*, *under*, *over* and *around* inspire original pieces of writing. The possibilities are endless. Random words are pure writing inspiration.

How to use this prompt

1. Print a selection of random words, then cut them up and add them to a jar or container. (A downloadable print-ready grid of random words is available.)
2. Remind students of the many ways they can choose to respond to this word: personal narrative, persuasive argument, fictional scene, reflection, poetry, prose and so on.
3. Randomly choose a word or ask a class member to pick one.
4. Set the timer for five minutes of discovery writing in response to this random word.
5. Workshop responses.

Tips for working with this prompt

Here are a range of activities to extend this concept further.

Sticky-note sentences

1. Follow the initial instructions for this prompt up to and including Step 4.
2. After writing, ask students to read over their piece of writing and highlight their favourite sentence, phrase or line and write it on a sticky note.
3. Ask students to share their sticky-note sentence in the time allowed for workshopping. Sharing one sentence is a great way to build workshopping confidence.
4. Collect and display the sticky-note sentences. These sentences can also be used as future writing prompts, which is a good way to build your writing resources together as a class.

Threes

1. Choose three random words from your collection, lucky-dip style, but do not share them yet.
2. Explain to your students that they are going to write a story inspired by the words.
3. Read out the first word.
4. Set your timer for two to three minutes and ask students to use that first word somewhere in their story.
5. When the time has expired, read out the next word.
6. Set your timer for two to three minutes and ask writers to weave this second word into their story.
7. Repeat this process with the third word.

Random word mind-mapping

1. Choose a random word and place it in the centre of a mind map.

2. Set the timer for five minutes and instruct students to explore as many ideas as possible inspired by this single word in this mind map.

3. When the timer goes off, ask students to circle the ideas that feel most alive to them. This is a good way of giving your students the opportunity to recognise which writing ideas feel exciting and expansive.

4. Ask students to choose one or more of their circled ideas to inspire a piece of writing, then set your timer for five minutes.

5. Workshop responses. Consider asking students to break into pairs or small groups and share their writing topics mind maps.

Teaching focus

- Think creatively and make meaningful links between random ideas.
- Learn a range of techniques for generating original writing ideas.
- Write collaboratively using strategies.

Resources

Random words

Download a print-ready grid of random words to use with this prompt and all three variations.

4. It's all in the name

If you can visualise a character in your imagination, you have a much better chance of catching their voice and personality on the page. I'm always on the search for ways to help students develop three-dimensional characters.

If your writers have worked with 'The story of my name' (page 176), and I recommend that they do before moving on to this exercise, they will already understand how names carry personal stories and self-identity. It's possible to reverse-engineer this concept and use a name to inspire a fictional character and their backstory. In revealing the origin of your character's name, backstory details such as personality, family culture, feelings and experiences will rise to the surface. When writers workshop these stories, they often use accents and intonations – a perfect example of writer and character voice in action.

How to use this prompt

There are two ways to approach this prompt: students can create a character sketch and then name that character or they can start with a name and let their character develop from there.

Start with a sketch

1. The first time you use this prompt, provide a simple body or face outline that will allow writers to fill in the details. Although this restricts the style of character writers can create, it provides some scaffolding and reduces the decision-making load.
2. Set your timer for five minutes and instruct students to create a visual representation of their character. Prompt them, as they draw, to include details such as facial features, clothing, accessories, hairstyle and so on.

3. Return to your list of what your class knows about names, which you will have built together in 'The story of my name' (page 176). Students can use the many categories and ideas in this resource to choose a name for their character.

4. Now for the fun part. Set the timer for five minutes and invite students to tell the story of how their character got their name. They are free to write in first person or third person, blending fact (what they already know about names) and fiction to spin their tale.

5. Invite students to introduce their character and share their character's backstory. You can do this as a class or break into pairs. Sharing in pairs is a great way to develop workshopping skills.

Start with a name

1. Download the list of ten character names to use with this prompt (see also page 208).

2. Either print this numbered selection of names on poster paper or have it ready to share on your smartboard. Do not show this list to your writers yet.

3. Ask writers to select a number between one and ten.

4. Once they have chosen their number, reveal the list of names and invite students to work with the name that matches their number. (Alternatively, let writers read through the list and choose the name that inspires them.) Students will use this name to inspire their character.

5. First, ask students to imagine what type of character might have this name. Is their character a person, a mermaid, an animal? Writing up a quick list of categories as a class will help spark imaginations.

6. Once your students have a name and a character type, ask them to imagine where their character might live.

7. Set your timer and allow students to tell the story of how their character got their name. Does the selected name suit their character? Who gave this character their name and why? Does the character's name link them to where they live? Using a character name as a prompt in this way allows important details about the character to naturally rise to the surface.

Tips for working with this prompt

- Here's a tip for creating more character names to use for the 'Start with a name' variation of this prompt. You may have seen name games on social media like 'Find your pirate name' or 'Find your mermaid name'. (My personal favourite is 'Find your chicken name'.) Head to Pinterest to find all sorts of variations on this theme, with results like Clover Mac Rainbow (fairy name) and Captain Stinky Breath (pirate name).
- These activities combine well with other prompts in this book. For example, once writers have created a backstory for their character using this prompt, they can use mind-mapping to create a character profile (see page 170 to revisit the basics of mind-mapping).

Teaching focus

- Use simple techniques to generate ideas for characters and plotlines.
- Develop characters using visualisation.
- Use personal stories and experience to develop fictional pieces of writing.
- Play with writer's voice to reveal a character's personality and backstory.
- Understand the link between character development and strong narrative plots.

Resources

Character names

Here is a numbered list of ten character names you can use when running the 'Start with a name' variation of this prompt (page 206):

1. Twinkle Toes
2. Ginger Snaps
3. Vantablack
4. Peppermint May
5. Sky
6. Silver Shine
7. Tucker
8. Serenity
9. Plum Dandy
10. Pigeon Gray

Download a reproducible version of this list.

5. Object writing

One of my most popular writing resources is a collection of objects in a small, decorated case. There was little to no cost involved in setting up this resource (find more information about this in 'Resources' at the end of the prompt), but it's a fail-safe way to inspire original storytelling.

Objects have the power to unlock original and extraordinary tales. All abstract ideas are derived from concrete objects. Objects ground and anchor us in our everyday lives. When we use an image as a writing prompt, there's usually a foreground and a background. There's often a range of objects or characters with implied relationships and connections. There are feelings and emotions to consider. For many young writers, especially those with busy minds, such a starting point can be overwhelming. But using a single object narrows the focus and has the power to trigger memories, associations, experiences, feelings and sensory perception. The writer is in full control, creating ideas rather than working with imagery that has been given to them. Objects are often used by writers to disrupt the plot in some way. Think about the ruby-red shoes in *The Wizard of Oz* and Lucy's cordial in *The Lion, the Witch and the Wardrobe*.

If you have a student who always writes about the same topic, objects can disrupt their pattern and encourage them to write outside of their comfort zone. For example, I once encountered a student who always wrote about netball, a sport she played and loved. When challenged to include a small, felt turtle in her story, she had to consider a whole new set of possibilities for plot, character traits and more – or at least imagine the game from a new, turtley perspective.

How to use this prompt

In this prompt we use an object to inspire plot with the support of 'The perhaps game' (page 15). As we covered in Chapter 1, *perhaps* is a word that invites curiosity and an openness to new ideas. It also carries a sense of playfulness. This makes it a great place to start working with objects.

1. Choose an object and play 'The perhaps game' (page 15) to generate a range of plot possibilities together as a class.
2. Keep a record of these on the whiteboard to help visual learners remember them.
3. Set the timer for five minutes and invite writers to choose one of the options to inspire a scene or a story. You'll be amazed at what can be inspired by a single object.
4. Workshop and discuss the resulting writing.

Tips for working with this prompt

Here are three more ways to use objects to inspire writing in your class.

Story bags

1. Decide whether your writers will work independently or in small groups.
2. Organise a collection of three random objects in story bags – enough so that each group has access to a story bag. I use regular paper bags.
3. Explain to writers that they will work together to develop one story outline (orientation, complication, resolution) that links all three objects in their bag in some way. Writers will do this task orally and collect their basic ideas in bullet points.
4. Set your timer and give the group time to create their story.
5. Workshop the resulting bullet-point stories. This could include one or more groups sharing their work.

Zoom in

This variation encourages writers to look at objects carefully, to uncover the precious details that are sometimes overlooked.

1. Invite each student to take a single object from your class collection.
2. Instruct students to note as many details as they can about this object, from small cracks to fading colour. Sensory perception is all important here. Note textures, smell, sounds and so on. Relying on their senses encourages writers to pay attention.
3. Set your timer for students to observe their object and write (as a list or in prose) about the details they notice.

Crazy connections

'Crazy connections' is one of my favourite writing activities. Many writers find the random nature of this exercise frees up their mind.

This variation needs more time than a five-minute discovery writing session because writers will complete three three-minute writing bursts. Alternatively, you could choose a new object each day and allow writers to add to their story over the course of the week.

1. Choose an item from your collection.
2. Set your timer for three minutes and invite writers to use this object to inspire the start of a story.
3. Allow time for two or three students to share and workshop the start of their story.
4. Next select the second object and explain that this second object is to be incorporated into the original story.
5. Set your timer for a further three minutes of discovery writing.
6. Give time to workshop again, this time with writers sharing their story or the strategy they used to weave the object into their story. For example, 'I used the object as a portal.'
7. Select a third item for writers to incorporate into their existing story.
8. Set your timer for the final three minutes.
9. Allow time to workshop story endings. Reading one story from the start is always interesting.

Teaching focus

- Connect random ideas to unlock creative thinking.
- Use simple everyday objects to create original stories.
- Draw on sensory perception and personal experience to generate ideas for writing.

Resources

Object writing collection

It is handy to be able to draw from a collection of objects when running this activity. Here are my instructions for setting up your own collection:

1. Choose a basket, box, briefcase or other container to store your objects. It doesn't need to be too big – I'd opt for something about the size of a large shoebox.

2. Raid your junk drawer, watching for interesting colours, shapes or textures. Are there any leftover party favours, odd bits of decorations or even stacks of everyday items like cable-ties or rubber bands? Add anything that catches your eye to your collection.

3. Now check out your wardrobe. Look for those things you never wear or use but keep around anyway because they're eye-catching or special – think lairy sunglasses, funky socks, an old-timey brooch or perhaps even a beret. Those sorts of items have a story to tell.

4. Venture outside now to add some natural elements to your collection. Consider objects that activate different senses, like sprigs of lavender, powdery cuttlefish, interesting seed pods, colourful sea glass and so on.

5. Pilfer from any collections you may have. Postcards and polaroids, old keys, teaspoons and stamps from around the world, teacups fit for a queen and trinkets picked up in your travels can all inspire terrific stories. Add them to your collection.

6. Have a look around for magical items, such as crystals or containers of glitter that could become fairy dust to the right writer, and for objects that are attached to memories, like a childhood trophy or a soft toy.

7. Keep an eye out for garage sales and charity shops too. These are often full of odd and inspiring – and cheap! – objects. I've found all sorts of things, from copper teapots and delicate figurines to dress-up items like fancy gloves and even a pirate sword.

6. Flip the switch

Often writers recycle their bank of favourite words, characters and plots over and over in their stories. They may also recycle plots and characters from their favourite movies and books. It's time to flip the switch and inject some fresh ideas and language in the mix. This activity stretches your students' vocabulary and gets them trying something new!

The storm / no e
Rain drops fall.
Coat flaps fly.
Jolts of light
across a dark, dark sky.
Air is still.
Clouds push past.
Wind howls.
Run fast.

How to use this prompt

1. Choose a title from the list provided in 'Resources', such as 'The storm'. You will also need a set of five vowel cards (see 'Tips for working with this prompt').
2. Together on the board, build a word bank of vocabulary related to the chosen title to ignite imaginations.
3. Explain to your students that imposing limitations sparks creative thinking, so we are going to remove one of the five vowels from our writing during this prompt.
4. Now shuffle your five vowels and randomly choose one that writers must exclude from their writing. For example, the letter *e*.
5. Ask students to respond to the title without using any words that contain this chosen vowel. In this example, this means writing about 'The storm' without using the letter *e*.
6. Set the timer for five minutes of writing and encourage your students to use a lead pencil so they can keep reworking their piece.

7. Workshop the responses, encouraging students to collaborate and to copy down words (without the letter in focus) that could work in their own piece of writing.

Tips for working with this prompt

- To prepare for this activity you will need a set of vowel cards to choose from. You can download a grid of the five vowels, then print and cut them out ahead of Step 4. Alternatively, you can make these yourself by simply writing a vowel each on five sticky notes or index cards.
- Be prepared for students to need more time to work on this activity. This piece of writing almost becomes a puzzle to solve and students often want to keep working to get their piece to a point where they feel it is finished.

Teaching focus

- Experiment with language and extend vocabulary.
- Bypass the inner critic and be playful.
- Think creatively.
- Develop and consolidate word choice, spelling and editing skills.
- Collaborate and communicate with peers.

Resources

'Flip the switch' titles

Here are some suggestions of titles to use when running 'Flip the switch':

- 'The storm'
- 'My neighbourhood'
- 'The birthday party'
- 'School lunches'
- 'Inside the castle'
- 'At the beach'
- 'Home alone'

Time to Write

- 'Dinner time'
- 'Family holiday'
- 'In between'.

7. Show, don't tell

We experience the world through our senses, so to engage our readers' imaginations and make it easier for them to visualise our story we need to activate their sensory perception. Our senses are the gatekeepers to our imaginations. Activating the senses is the difference between showing and telling.

This simple writing prompt packs a punch in terms of skill development. Writers must rely on sensory clues and tighten their descriptive language and work choice. Instead of saying your character is on a boat in the ocean at midnight, writers can describe the black waves lapping against the boat as stars fill the inky sky.

How to use this prompt

1. Choose a setting and a time from the lists on page 219. For example: a boat; midnight.
2. Write these details on the whiteboard.
3. Ask writers to describe the scene in writing at this specific time without using the words on the cards. Their task is to provide all the clues the reader needs to imagine the scene.
4. Build a quick vocabulary list if required.
5. Set your timer for five minutes of writing.
6. Workshop responses, highlighting sensory details and figurative language so writers have clear examples about the sensory clues that activate a reader's imagination. Did the short visual pieces of writing ignite your students' imaginations? Could they see the scene in their mind's eye?

Tips for working with this prompt

- When students are first developing the skills associated with 'Show, don't tell', it may be helpful to allow them to first work with one half of the prompt. For example, writers could state

they are on a boat and then focus on how to show the reader that it is midnight.
- You can also extend your use of this prompt:
    - Try selecting from a set of characters (such as teacher, mother, father, toddler) and character traits (shy, creative, talkative) instead of settings and times. In this variation, ask writers to provide clues that tell us about their character and their central trait without using the words on the card. For example, if you were working with the combination of 'greedy' and 'chef', how could you show that your character is a chef who is greedy without using the words *chef* and *greedy*?
    - You could also try pairing settings and environmental conditions. For example, working with 'beach' and 'winter', how could you make it clear to your reader that you are at the beach on a winter's day without stating this fact? What sensory clues would you need to include?

Teaching focus

- Extend vocabulary and figurative language.
- Develop writing technique and the use of sensory details.
- Tighten descriptive writing skills.
- Practise editing and revising skills.

Resources

Settings and times

Here are lists of some settings and times to get you started. As you work with this 'Show, don't tell', ask your class to contribute to these lists. Building the resource together in this way will allow you to represent your students' lives and experiences.

Imaginative writing

Settings:
- boat
- school
- shopping centre
- movie theatre
- the park
- the farm
- forest
- in a cave
- amusement park
- jungle.

Times:
- midnight
- summer solstice
- daybreak
- the witching hour
- autumn, summer, winter or spring
- twilight
- noon
- dusk
- lunchtime
- bedtime.

8. Playing with poetry

Poetry combines imagery, language and emotion which makes it a powerful source of writing inspiration. In this prompt, writers innovate on an original structure and style of a poem to create something new.

> **After 'The red wheelbarrow' by William Carlos Williams**
>
> *Year 5 class*
>
> so much depends
> upon
>
> a golden key
>
> rusted over time
>
> in the middle of the
> busy road.

Due to its strong scaffolding nature, this prompt works especially well for less confident writers. 'The red wheelbarrow' by William Carlos Williams (1923) is a poem I have used with writers from Year 4 upwards with great success, and it is here I suggest you start with your students.

How to use this prompt

1. Before your class gets ready to write, analyse the structure of the poem together. You are going to work together as a group to innovate on the original structure of the poem to create a new version of the poem, as I did with a class of Year 5 students to create the example given at the start of this prompt. (Download a document that breaks down the structure used in the sample poem.)

2. Before you get started, ask students to list colours and objects they could use to build their class poem. You could also select objects from your object writing collection to spark ideas (see 'Object writing' on page 209). For example, William Carlos Williams's poem features a red wheelbarrow, but the students who produced the sample chose a golden key when creating their own poem.

3. Then ask your students what words they could use to describe the selected object – in this case, a golden key. Ask students where they may have seen keys before. How did the key look? Choose one of the examples for your next line. In the sample poem, this is 'rusted over time'.

4. Now place your object somewhere. Where will the key be found? List prepositions together so students can start to imagine the possibilities. This class chose to place the golden key in the middle of the road. Taking this one step further to complete the poem, they added an adjective to describe the road as busy.

5. Once your students have a framework for innovating on this structure, set the timer for five minutes and invite them to create their own version of this poem. They may choose from the list of objects and colours you created in Step 3 to inspire them or work with their own objects and colours.

Tips for working with this prompt

- Poems with a solid structure work best for this activity. We've started with 'The red wheelbarrow' by William Carlos Williams, but you might also consider working with other structures. Haiku poetry, made up of three lines and seventeen syllables in total (five in the first line, seven in the second and five again in the last), is particularly effective as a base for this prompt.
- Your choice of poem determines the skills your students will focus on. For example, if you choose a rhyming poem your students will play with rhyming words, rhythm and pace.
- Innovating on a poetic structure, such as that of 'The red wheelbarrow', can also provide a springboard for developing fiction because it evokes so many curious questions. For example:
  - Who does the key belong to?
  - Why is it rusted? Where has it been?
  - Who dropped it on the road?
  - What does the key unlock?

  Once your writers have innovated on the original poetic structure, ask them to write a list of questions that naturally arise. These questions can form the seeds of an interesting story.

Teaching focus

- Explore the importance of word choice; well-chosen adjectives create powerful images.
- Understand parts of speech, for example nouns, adjectives, prepositions and how the placement of words effectively builds an image.
- Engage sensory perception and visualisation skills.
- Use a known structure to help generate writing ideas.

Resources

'Playing with poetry: Structure' template

Download a document that breaks down how the structure of 'The red wheelbarrow' was used to create the sample poem, scaffolding the process for your class.

More inspiration

Many of the poems featured in *Love That Dog* and the sequel *Hate That Cat* by Sharon Creech (2001, 2009) can also be used as a starting point for this prompt.

9. Shape a story

I'm not exactly sure where the original inspiration for 'Shape a story' arose, but I've used it successfully with students and teachers alike. This prompt combines writing and drawing, forging interesting links between objects to create an original story idea. Drawing frees up time to incubate ideas before moving into writing. This activity encourages whole-brain thinking and I've found it supports reluctant writers.

How to use this prompt

1. Download the 'Shape a story' templates and print a copy of the appropriate template (featuring four, six or eight shapes) for each student. Which template you choose will depend on the age and stage of your writers. Younger writers may find it easier to work with four or six shapes, while more experienced writers can work with eight shapes.

2. Set your timer for five minutes and ask students to turn each shape on their page into an object. For example, a circle might become a watch; a triangle, the roof of a house; a square, a birthday present. If writers have more time, invite them to add interesting details to their objects.

3. Allow some time to share and workshop pictures in pairs or small groups. The aim of this time is to use the shapes to create a story. For example, the watch is inside the box and it's a birthday present for the girl who lives in the house. Writers are free to connect all or just some of the pictures.

4. With the pictures and any notes about connections they've made in view, set the timer for a further five minutes and instruct writers to begin writing their story.

5. Workshop responses so students have a chance to share their stories. It's always fascinating for teachers and writers alike to see the range of ideas sparked by a set of simple shapes.

Tips for working with this prompt
- Be sure to stress that the focus for this activity is on forming creative links rather than producing high-quality artwork.
- Experiment with using a different number of shapes or with multiple copies of the same shape in different sizes.

Teaching focus
- Engage in whole-brain thinking to stimulate creativity.
- Connect drawn objects to generate new and original story ideas.

Resources

'Shape a story' templates

Download the print-ready templates of four, six and eight shapes to use with this prompt.

10. What a place!

The setting of any story has three main aspects: location, environment and time. For example, as I write this sentence:

- I'm sitting at a desk in a small room (location).
- The room is bare and white; I hear the rhythmic snoring of Mac, my dog; I see birds sunning themselves in the top branches of the tree opposite my window (environment).
- It's 5.30 pm; the sky is clear blue, but the long afternoon shadows of my house fall across my neighbour's yard (time).

In this prompt, writers explore how to combine these elements to develop a sense of place in their writing so their reader can visualise the setting clearly.

How to use this prompt

1. Draw a triangle on the whiteboard, marking the points with 'location', 'environment' and 'time' as in figure 7. This is an effective symbol for the three elements of setting.

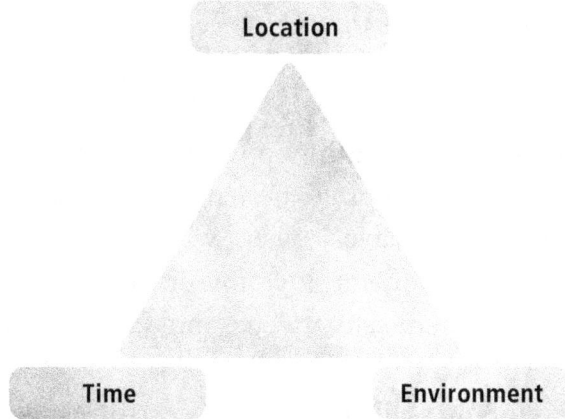

Figure 7: The three elements of setting
A free reproducible version of this figure is available

2. Choose a setting from the list on page 227 and write this in the middle of the triangle.
3. Ask writers to then choose the time of day, the location and the environmental details of this particular setting. For example, if the setting is 'bedroom', writers might choose to describe a bedroom in the country at midnight: the room is cold and dark, moonlight shining through the large window. Capture these details in bullet points at the points of the triangle before discovery writing begins.
4. Ask students to close their eyes and visualise this setting, noting any objects they see, the weather, the light, the sensory details. Capture these details too.
5. Explain to writers that their challenge now is to create a scene that combines all three aspects – location, environment and time – so their reader can imagine the setting clearly. Remember the reader will experience the setting through their senses, so sensory clues and details are important.
6. Set your timer for five minutes of writing.
7. Workshops responses, highlighting the sensory details that evoke a sense of place in each piece of writing.

Tips for working with this prompt

- This prompt can be built upon with elements of 'Show, don't tell' (page 217). For more experienced writers, for example, you could impose a caveat where writers cannot explicitly mention the environment, location or time of day. They will then need to drop in sensory cues and language to help their reader see the scene clearly.
- When developing skills to evoke a sense of place, it's easier for writers to start with settings they know well, full of details they can easily recall. Good settings to start with could be the classroom, their bedroom or the playground.

Teaching focus

- Explore the three elements of setting and how it relates to storytelling.
- Develop a plotline generated by a sense of place.
- Use descriptive language and sensory details to bring the setting to life.
- Cultivate atmospheric and mood writing skills.

Resources

Setting suggestions

Here are some settings to use with this prompt:

- classroom
- bedroom
- playground
- canteen
- football oval
- park
- jungle
- beach
- the snow
- library.

'The three elements of setting' template

Download a reproducible copy of the 'The three elements of setting' template to use when running 'What a place!'

Reflective writing
Hello writer

Writing is dynamic discipline. Many authors have written instructional books packed full of their writing experiences and tips, but you can't discover the secrets of writing by *reading* about writing. Believe me, I've tried! A new member once joined The Writer's Club late in the year. On this particular day we started the session with a 'Hello writer' prompt. The young writer looked confused. 'Are we writing about writing? That's weird.' But writing about writing is anything but weird. It is a deeply valuable process that connects your students to their creative agency.

I appreciate that teachers have their hands full teaching writing skills, without making time for students to reflect on their experience of writing. It might feel counterproductive in terms of our use of time, but when we engage in conversations about writing we demystify the creative process and allow writers to recognise and appreciate their own processes. Sharing our similarities and differences helps us understand that there is not one right way to approach the writing process. We begin to have faith in our unique differences and styles. Our writing experiences often mirror each other. This makes us feel less alone, less vulnerable. These discussions build trust and a strong sense of community, which we know is so important for supporting young writers. Inviting your students to actively see themselves as writers, rather than simply students of writing, strengthens their writing identity in ways that build self-confidence and self-belief. These valuable discussions are also powerful teaching tools. Workshopping gives students an opportunity to connect with one another and share their experiences, which offers teachers meaningful data about the way their students approach writing tasks. It's a window into the minds – and hearts – of your students and helps reveal strengths, weaknesses, challenges and *aha* moments that may otherwise go unnoticed.

Some of these activities are pick-up-and-go exercises and some require some prior understanding. If you typically work on a fifteen-minute time frame for your writing practice, you may need to allow more time to complete these exercises or schedule these discussions prior to your writing time.

These are the ten different reflective writing activities in this section:

1. Untangling the creative process
2. Working with images
3. Writing spaces
4. Writing symbols
5. Choosing a writing mentor
6. Letter-writing
7. Planning styles
8. Mind freeze
9. Creative flow
10. Writing inspiration

1. Untangling the creative process

Reflecting on our experiences of creativity demystifies the creative process and helps writers explore their personal actions and reactions. The more aware we are of our behaviour and mindset, the better equipped we are to understand and regulate our thinking. If we want to help move writers through this process smoothly, we need to give them research, knowledge and tools to recognise their creative strengths and manage the many challenges they will face along the journey.

How to use this prompt

The stages of creativity

1. Introduce Graham Wallas's (1926) model of the four stages of creativity – preparation, incubation, illumination and verification – and the key goals of each stage in relation to writing. Encourage students to directly link and compare their experience with Wallas's theory. Here's a recap of the four stages and key aims:

   Preparation – writers focus their attention on a particular problem, gather materials and begin planning.

   Incubation – your unconscious mind intersects your experience with your knowledge; you soak up sensory and intuitive information and begin to see patterns and connect ideas.

   Illumination – writers are actively organising and structuring ideas into a cohesive piece of work; you may experience the thrill of creative flow and lose sense of time and space.

   Verification – there is a sense of letting go, be that through sharing your work with an audience or achieving some other form of closure to the cycle.

2. Allow time for active and open discussion about the creative process, emphasising that the model is not always sequential; everyone will experience this process differently.

3. You'll find a selection of prompts on page 236 to encourage your students to explore the creative process. Choose a prompt from the list and invite your students to respond. Set a timer for five minutes.

4. Workshop responses, recording any ideas that surface so they can be displayed and shared in an ongoing way. For example, you might make a list of activities that help with incubating ideas as a resource for your writers.

Navigating self-talk

One of the biggest creative breakthroughs I experienced as a writing teacher occurred on a wet, winter's afternoon at The Writer's Club. After being cooped up in classrooms all day, students were wired and noisy when they arrived at our afternoon class. To contain their restless energy, I decided on a whim to try walking meditation. We walked in a giant circle around the outskirts of the room, breathing in time with each step. The room eventually fell silent, apart from the occasional giggle. Finally, when we gathered on the floor, the energy was calm and receptive.

Students had previously discussed and written about their experience of the stages of the creative process, but I was keen to know how aware they were of their self-talk. I drew a simple flow chart on the whiteboard, showing the stages of the creative process and common responses writers experience as they cycle through the process (figure 8).

I then talked about my own writing experience and how I love starting projects but often stall between 'This is rubbish.' and 'I am rubbish.' And I often start looking for a new project to begin so I can experience the thrill of gathering ideas. I saw one writer's eyes open wide.

'That's me!' she yelled out. 'That's what happens to me!'

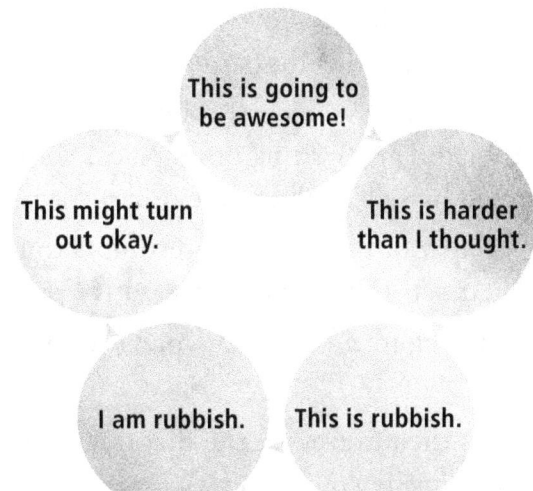

Figure 8: Self-talk and the creative process
A free reproducible version of this figure is available

The floodgates opened. Voices chimed in from everywhere, wanting to share their experiences. Surprisingly enough, the self-talk all sounded vaguely familiar in our stories. The concept of fear loomed large. Some of us feared the blank page or running out of ideas mid-story. Some of us worried about making the wrong decisions and locking ourselves into plots that didn't work. All of us felt the pressure to get it right the first time, especially in assessment tasks. We talked about our strengths too. Some of us were great at generating ideas, while others struggled. It was one of those magic, teachable moments that builds trust and community.

We headed back to our tables to write about our experience of the creative process. The writing was intimate and funny. It didn't matter that we were different ages and at different stages of our writing journey. That afternoon, we were a community of writers untangling something extraordinarily complex.

1. Download figure 8, which follows the self-talk that often accompanies the creative process and share copies with your students.

2. Come prepared to share your own experiences to build trust and lead writers into this discussion.
3. Allow time for writers to digest, compare and share their experiences before any writing takes place. Some writers may not be plagued by self-doubt, while others may be gripped by it.
4. Talk through any of the following prompts to invite writers to reflect on their self-talk during the creative process:
    - What thoughts go through your head when writing a story?
    - How do the phrases on the diagram match up to what happens inside your mind?
    - Are there any activities which trigger negative self-talk?
    - Think about your latest creative project, from writing a story to baking a cake. Can you write a monologue of your self-talk? What was going through your mind as you were creating?
    - Do you have any tips for managing self-talk?
5. Set your timer for five minutes and invite writers to respond in any way they wish to your discussion or follow their own thoughts on the creative process.
6. Allow plenty of time to workshop and discuss ideas.

Switching mindsets
1. Revisit the stages of the creative process and the self-talk depicted in figure 8 (page 233).
2. This time ask students to lean into a growth mindset and write an encouraging response to each phrase. For example, 'This is harder than I thought' could become 'Be curious – inspiration is everywhere!'
3. Allow time to workshop these positive statements. Students could add positive statements to their copy of the model and paste this into their notebook for future reference.

Understanding how the creative process unfolds inside your students' minds in terms of self-talk provides valuable data that you can access immediately.

Tips for working with this prompt

- Teachers often benefit from doing some reflection prior to leading these discussions, so take some time to think about the prompts given in the instructions for this activity to think about your experience of the creative process. You might also find it helpful to return to the reflection questions at the end of Chapter 1 (page 36) before getting started.
- In Chapter 7 (page 129) we learned about the benefits of connecting with a wider literary community to support your students on their writing journey. Use Wallas's (1926) theory as an anchor point for discovering how your favourite writers interact with the writing process. Consider the following avenues:
    - Can you find an author interview online where the writer discusses their creative process?
    - Could you source an interesting and related podcast for students to listen to as a homework task?
    - Can you contact authors via their websites and ask them any of process-related questions?
    - Could you interview a local or visiting writer?

Teaching focus

- Explore and reflect on the stages of the creative process.
- Be mindful of self-talk and the impact this has on creative confidence.
- Understand and develop a personal process to support creativity.
- Develop a deep understanding of their creative strengths and weaknesses.

Resources

'The stages of creativity' variation prompts

Share one of the following prompts with students to get them thinking about their creative process:

- Choose a creative task you have completed, from writing a story to making something with Lego. Can you map your experience using the four stages of creativity? What key tasks were happening at each stage? It's helpful for teachers to model this process with a personal experience first.
- Write about a time when you moved through the creative process smoothly and experienced success.
- Write about a time when the creative process stalled and you found it challenging to keep going. What did you do?
- Write about your favourite stage of the creative process. Why is it your favourite?
- Write about the most challenging stage of the creative process for you. What trips you up?
- What stage of the creative process showcases your greatest strength?
- When and where do you get your best ideas?
- What activities help you incubate ideas? Are there any activities that activate this process, leading to you finding solutions and having those *aha* moments? (Lots of people report having their best ideas in the shower!)
- Focus on the preparation stage of the creative process. How do you prepare to write? Do you plan first in detail? What helps you feel ready to write?
- How do you keep track of your ideas? What tools do you use?
- How does it feel to finish a piece of writing?
- Verification is focused on closing out the creative process. In terms of writing, this could mean publishing. What forms of publishing do you like best and why?

'The creative process' diagram

Download a reproducible copy of the 'The creative process' to share with students.

2. Making metaphors

Imagery and metaphor ground abstract thinking in the real world. They provide a framework for working with complex ideas. When we build metaphors to help us understand complex ideas in ways that makes sense to us, learning suddenly becomes more real and engaging.

Developing metaphors to anchor complex concepts supports writers in two ways: imagery personalises understanding and engages creativity, but it also teaches your students a process for creating and playing with metaphors as part of their own writing.

Before we step through the instructions, I'd like to share how I used this prompt to explore the narrative arc with a group of young writers (8–12 years old). After a short introduction, students used playground equipment like slides and tunnels as well as their experiences with food to explain the concept of the narrative arc and plot structures. Part of this activity would need to be completed outside your writing practice time, but I have included discovery writing sessions so you can see how it can be incorporated.

At The Writer's Club we had been focusing on creating plots and complications for narratives. On this one afternoon, I drew a simple narrative arc on the whiteboard to illustrate the 'rule of three' plot (figure 9). In this narrative structure, the main character faces three escalating challenges, building to a climax and then ending in a resolution.

'What does this illustration remind you of?' I asked. 'What shapes can you see?'

'It's like a mountain,' one student observed.

The group then began drawing comparisons and playing with the mountain metaphor as a way of making sense of the narrative process.

'The climax is like the view from the top,' one writer observed.

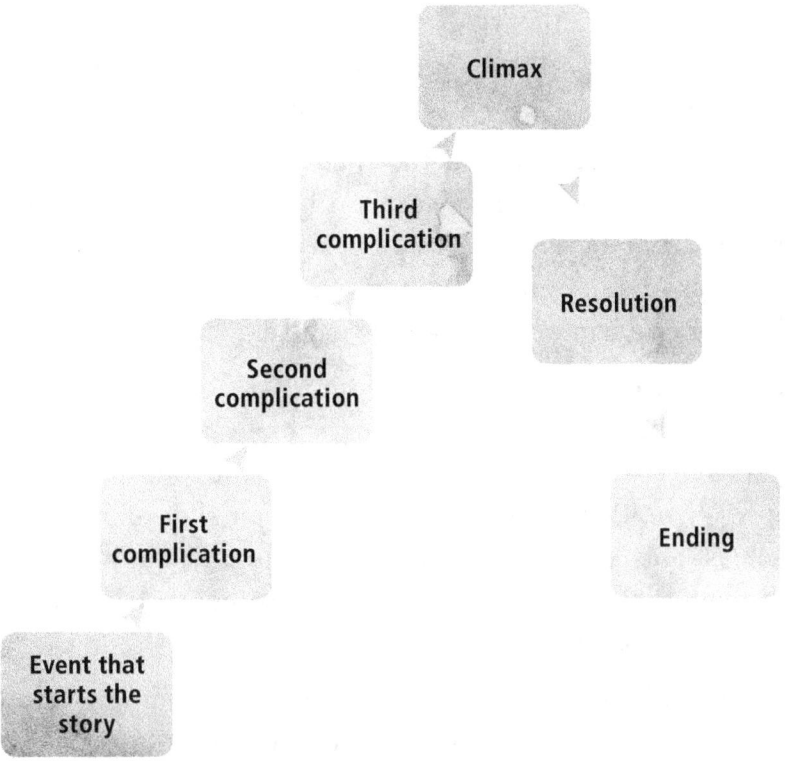

Figure 9: 'Rule of three' plot illustration

'Climbing the mountain gets harder and harder. You are tired and it gets steeper – just like when you get tired writing a story,' another replied.

'But the view from the top is the best!'

Then Jack jumped up to share his idea.

'It's like you light a stick of dynamite at the bottom of the mountain and it's slowly burning and then suddenly it explodes. That's the climax of your story.'

'It could be like a volcano!' someone else added.

The conversation (and the metaphors) naturally shifted along the plotline towards story endings, so we looked at the possibilities. We decided a happy ending means that your character achieved their goal, while a sad ending means your character didn't get what they wanted.

But our favourite was the ironic ending. In this ending, your character gets some of what they wanted, but perhaps not everything. For example, your character found the treasure, but lost their friend.

Many students shared books they had read that illustrated different types of endings. For some, it was as if the penny just dropped. They suddenly understood the connection between their characters' motivations and how a story ends. Endings are not random events; they are linked to the problem or the character's goal.

One member of our group called out, 'I've got it! It's like there's a tunnel down the right side of the story mountain. When it's a happy ending, the character slides down the tunnel and lands in a pile of soft cushions. When it's a sad ending, the character slides down the tunnel and the cushions are gone. It's a hard landing. When it's ironic, they slide through, but the writer has removed some of the cushions. The landing is a bit rough.'

Everyone had their own version of the tunnel analogy. Happy endings meant jelly and ice cream at the end of the tunnel. Sad endings equalled broccoli. Ironic? That was fish and chips without tomato sauce. The energy was high as we headed back to our seats to write about and illustrate our narrative arc metaphor.

How to work with this prompt

Preparation

1. Choose an idea or concept to explore together. For example, the narrative arc.
2. Prepare some form of sketch or visual cue to capture the idea. In the example provided I chose a triangular mountain shape (see figure 9 on page 239). Your visual cue can be a basic outline; its purpose is to invite students to see the concept in another form and open the door to your writers' imaginations. If you google story arc images, you will find a range of

examples that allow you to vary your image outline. If your writers need some scaffolding for this activity, use a more detailed image that assists them to build the metaphor together first, such as a rollercoaster.

3. Label your chosen visual cue to help your writers explore the concept further. When describing the narrative arc, for example, labels such as 'beginning', 'escalating obstacles', 'rising action', 'conflict/complication (problem)', 'climax', 'resolution' and 'ending' help students visualise how the parts of a story fit together.

In class

1. As a class, work with the image you have selected for your concept. Students will use this image to craft and shape a metaphor. Ask students to see if the shape or basic outline reminds them of anything – perhaps a mountain, a volcano or a rollercoaster. If you elected for a more detailed shape in the preparation stage, you might choose to talk through its features in this step.

2. Once you have chosen the overall theme for your metaphor (let's say a story arc rollercoaster), explore some related vocabulary that might be associated with this metaphor. Rollercoaster-related vocabulary could include *frame, route, engineer, launch, brakes, peaks, loops, circuits, seatbelts, relief, fear* and so on.

3. A metaphor gives your students a sense of the feelings and emotions characters encounter during a story. For example, the beginning of a story holds the thrill of what's to come, just like the feeling you get as you board the rollercoaster.

4. Now that you are ready to start building your metaphor together, ask students to compare the chosen concept and metaphor. What similarities can they find? For example, in

comparing the narrative arc of a story to riding a rollercoaster, students might suggest the following:

- In the beginning of a story readers and writers are buckling themselves in for adventure.
- The escalating obstacles may relate to the size and peaks of the ride, starting small and getting bigger each time.
- The climax could be a loop, the most exciting part of your story.
- A rollercoaster ending usually provides time for the excitement and fear to settle, much like a story ending.

5. Record all these ideas on your whiteboard outline so students can refer to them.
6. Now that you have your metaphor in place, ask students to copy the basic outline onto a page of their notebook and label key elements. You could also or provide each student with a copy of the basic outline.
7. Set your timer for five minutes to allow students to capture their version of the metaphor on their page. They can modify, extend and illustrate ideas.
8. Workshop responses, ideally in pairs so writers can talk through their ideas.
9. If time permits, you can set the timer again or plan to come back and work on the metaphor the following day so they can continue to refine and clarify their thinking.
10. Allow metaphors to be displayed so writers can publish and share their thinking.

Tips for working with this prompt

- If you choose to explore narrative arcs with this prompt, the resulting metaphor diagram can be turned into a story-planning graphic organiser and will hold considerable meaning for your students as they continue their writing practice.

- Consider using this approach to explore more unusual narrative structures, such as circular stories. A circular story starts and finishes in the same place. Two great examples are:
    - 'Learn to read with Andy' in *Just Crazy* by Andy Griffiths (2000)
    - *Jeremy's Tail* by Duncan Ball (1990).
- Whenever you have a rule or writing tip you want your students to remember, try creating a metaphor.

Teaching focus

- Explore and clarify key elements of writing, such as narrative structure, as a way of understanding the writing process.
- Engage both their creative and logical thinking to illustrate the writing process.
- Create a template for developing stories.
- Explore the concept of imagery and metaphor as a writing and thinking tool.

3. Writing spaces

Our writing space can impact our sense of safety, focus and creative flow. Writers can be very particular about their writing space.

I know I write best at my own desk. I like having a window opposite my desk. Voices and direct conversations are distracting to me; however, ambient noise (played through my noise-cancelling headphones) is a game changer in terms of my ability to concentrate. I've discovered that I write especially well when I write with others in community. I didn't learn any of this by reading about how other writers create their writing spaces. I know my preferences by trying lots of options and actively measuring the impact on my focus and productivity. I've had many discussions about writing spaces with young writers over the years and have compiled a list of conditions related to writing places which serves as an interesting starting point for your class discussions.

How to use this prompt

1. Choose a prompt from the list on page 246 to begin the process of inquiry and invite writers to reflect on where they like to write and where they write best. This list of prompts ranges from broad to specific so that writers can explore general themes and then zoom in on specifics.
2. Set your timer for five minutes and ask students to respond to the chosen prompt. Encourage students to write about or even draw designs of rooms or spaces.
3. Workshop ideas and discuss responses.
4. Come back to these prompts regularly so students can clarify and refine their ideas on this topic.

Tips for using this prompt

Try these variations to further explore how your writers experience and are affected by their writing spaces.

Writing-space binary opposites

Binary opposites encourage writers to place themselves somewhere on a continuum. Below is a list of binary opposites teachers can use to stimulate discussions about writing spaces and writing conditions. As students write daily, they will accumulate more and more information about the factors that support them on their writing journey.

1. Give your students a copy of the basic list of binary opposites shown in figure 10 (available to download) and ask them to mark the point on each continuum that best matches their preferences.

Figure 10: Binary opposites on continuums
A free reproducible version of this figure is available

2. Set the timer for five minutes and ask students to expand on their answers, providing reasons for their responses.
3. Allow time for workshopping so students can share their work.

Writing outside the classroom

When I started teaching, local excursions were a regular part of our programs. A heady mix of time constraints and public liability has curbed these outings, but I'm keen to see them make a comeback. Unleashing your writers into the great outdoors helps define the conditions that make writing easier and harder. Writing in different environments also stimulates imaginations and creative thinking.

First up head out of your classroom and into another part of the school. Try writing:

- outside in the school yard
- in the school library
- in another classroom
- in the principal's office.

Once you have tried writing in new places at school, consider taking your class to write in new and interesting places in your local community, such as a public library or park.

Teaching focus

- Consider how factors such as writing space impact focus and creative flow.
- Learn how to regulate their immediate environment to support creative thinking.
- Become aware of their personal writing preferences.

Resources

'Writing spaces' prompts

Share one of the following prompts with students to help them understand how their writing environments impacts them:

- Describe your ideal writing space.
- How does your writing space impact or affect your writing?
- Describe a writing space that wouldn't work for you at all and tell us why.
- If you could write anywhere in the world, where would you choose? Describe the exact location. Where are you? Why is this place so perfect for writing?
- Describe the best place you've ever opened your notebook to write. Do you remember what you were writing about?

- What are your writing-space deal-breakers? How can you match up some of these conditions with your writing space at school?
- Make a list of all the things you use in your writing space. Detail your preference for items like pens or pencils, paper (lined or plain, heavy or light), notebook and so on.
- What writing materials do you need in your writing space? What writing materials would you like to try?
- Focus on your immediate space within the classroom – your desk or table. How can this space be best organised to support your writing?

'Binary opposites on continuums' template

Download a print-ready list of binary opposites to use with this prompt.

4. Writing symbols

Asking students to choose a symbol or object to represent their writing practice allows your writers to reflect on the relationship they have with writing and creativity. In Chapter 3 (page 55) I discussed my writing symbols and how I use them as part of my writing routine.

A writing symbol mirrors the beliefs or philosophy you have about writing. It might represent how you feel about writing right now or how you would *like* to feel about writing. Whichever way you decide to approach writing symbols, the goal is to encourage your students to use concrete objects to represent their abstract, intangible relationship to writing and creativity.

As well as keeping an image of their writing symbol or object itself in their writing space, I often ask writers to draw, paint or otherwise attach their writing symbol to their notebooks or writing equipment such as bags or pencil cases to act as a conscious reminder of the importance of writing and creativity in their lives.

I have set this out as a four-part process. Feel free to modify the process to suit the maturity and skills of your writers.

How to use this prompt

Part 1: Reflection

This section helps writers explore how they feel about writing as a lead-in to understanding their writing identity and the relationship that exists between them and the craft of writing. I suggest planning to respond to three or four prompts over a week or so before you head into the process of thinking about writing symbols.

1. Introduce to your students a prompt from the list on page 252.
2. Set your timer for five minutes and invite students to respond to the chosen prompt. Only work with one prompt at a time and expect that some students will use their writing time to

think and mull over ideas. Ideas don't always land on time. Sometimes they need to incubate or bump up against each other.

3. Workshop responses and share ideas.

Part 2: Thinking about metaphors for writing

1. Invite your students to use objects as metaphors for their relationship with the writing process. Use images, videos, or actual objects so students have a context for how the object works. For each of the following prompts, ask writers to find meaningful links between the object and the craft of writing:

   - Writing is a bubble.
   - Writing is a hot air balloon.
   - Writing is a circus performer.
   - Writing is a mountain.
   - Writing is a doorway.
   - Writing is deep water.
   - Writing is a key.

   I reiterate that there are no right or wrong responses and the skill of crafting and developing metaphor requires practice. Some writers, depending on their personality, may have a greater affinity for imagery and symbolism, but that's why workshopping is so important. It helps writers build ideas and concepts in context.

2. Choose one of the statements above and, if possible, set the scene by directing attention to the physical object (for example, a doorway or key) or showing an image or video of the object in action (for example, a hot air balloon in flight).

3. Build a word bank of vocabulary on the whiteboard to scaffold the process. You might look at the function of the object, how it moves, what it is made of and so on.

4. Set your timer for five minutes, giving writers time and space to make connections between the object and the writing process so they can build their metaphor.
5. Allow time to workshop ideas together. As you are all working with the same metaphor in this prompt, this is a great opportunity to collaborate and combine responses to create a class metaphor.

Part 3: Playing with objects

1. Revisit the list of metaphors for writing discussed in Part 2 and ask your writers to come up with their own metaphors to add. Sentences should start: 'Writing is …'
2. If you feel your writers need some scaffolding for this activity, have a selection of objects available to spark their imaginations. Your object writing collection (page 212) can be helpful here.
3. Set your timer for three minutes and ask students to list their ideas for metaphors about what writing is (as covered in Step 1). Encourage students to suspend judgement and censorship, and to use a wide range of objects. Not every idea needs to be followed up on, but sometimes, once the obvious choices are covered off, some interesting and original responses appear.
4. Workshop responses and suggest students add any new ideas to their lists. This will come in handy for the next part: choosing a writing symbol.
5. Ask students to choose one of the 'writing is' statements from their list or your newly created class list and extend this metaphor. How is writing like this object? Encourage writers to find at least two and up to five connections or similarities.
6. Workshop responses and share ideas. This can be done in pairs or small groups so everyone has a chance to speak to their metaphor.

Part 4: Choosing my symbol

Now that your students have had some experience with working with objects and metaphors, it's time for them to choose a personal writing symbol to represent their relationship with writing.

1. Point writers towards your class list of objects and metaphors. Some of these may be options for personal writing symbols.
2. Ask writers to choose an object to work with for the next timed writing block.
3. Set your timer for five minutes and invite writers to find connections between how they feel about writing and the elements of the object they have chosen. For example, the colour of my writing symbol, the gold fountain pen, represents something precious, rare and valuable; ink from the pen flows across the page, but can also be messy. Writing can be that way too. A simple mind map may be a good way to capture these vital links and encourages radiant thinking.
4. Remind students that they are free to change their minds. They are not locked into this symbol and can keep experimenting and playing with ideas until a symbol feels right to them.
5. Workshop responses and keep adding possible writing symbols to your class list.
6. Once writers find a symbol that speaks to them, they can decide how to include their symbol into their writing ritual.

Tips for working with this prompt

- Students can add images of their chosen writing symbol to their writing notebook or writing materials so they can return to it as part of their writing practice.
- Images of and writing about the symbols could be collated into a class book.
- This activity is closely linked with 'Making metaphors' (page 238).

Teaching focus

- Reflect on students' relationship with writing.
- Use objects and imagery as aspirational goals.
- Engage higher order creative thinking skills to make interesting and meaningful connections between ideas.
- Practise using metaphors and similes to illustrate objects and ideas.

Resources

'Part 1: Reflection' prompts

Here is a selection of reflective writing prompts to for you to choose from when running the first part of this activity:

- How does writing make you feel? What do you like about it? What do you dislike about it?
- Who is you writing hero and why? What do you admire so much about them?
- How would you like to feel about writing?
- Make a list of facts about writing that are true for you. Start with: 'Writing is …'
- If your writing practice was a character, what sort of character would it be? A rabbit? An astronaut?
- If your writing practice was an object, what would it be? Why?
- If your writing practice was a colour, what colour would it be?
- If your writing practice was a texture, what would it be? Silky? Rough? Scrunched-up paper? Smooth as a pebble? Worn edges like sea glass?
- Have you ever had a lucky charm? Pretend you are going on a writing adventure. What lucky charm would you choose to take with you and why?

5. Choosing a writing mentor

In Chapter 7 (page 129) we explored the place of community in our writing practice. I love broadening this sense of community by welcoming in the wisdom of writers, both past and present. Encouraging your writers to choose a writing hero or mentor is one way to tap into the global literary brains trust and share this wealth of knowledge with your class. I have many writing mentors and keep their quotes and thoughts about writing together in a digital file. I often read their thoughts especially when I'm stuck or blocked, and it never fails to shift my perspective. I also keep a list of articles, podcasts and other resources that help me connect with my favourite writing mentors.

Albert Einstein is one of my writing mentors. His comments on the creative process are instructional. Here are three quotes, often attributed to Einstein, that I use to support my creative practice:

> *A person who has never made a mistake has not tried something new.*

> *It's not that I'm so smart, it's just that I stay with problems longer.*

> *Imagination is more important than knowledge. For knowledge is limited, whereas imagination embraces the entire world.*

With these quotes, Einstein inspires me to take risks and be prepared to make mistakes. He also reminds me that creativity takes time, grit and determination.

Discovery writing is a great way to think on paper about our writing mentors and their philosophies.

How to use this prompt

Discovering mentors

1. Choose and share a writing prompt from the list starting on page 255.
2. Set the timer for five minutes and invite students to respond to the chosen prompt.
3. Workshop responses.

Getting to know your mentor

In my experience, writers need some time to write and think about their literary heroes before choosing mentors.

After your class has had some time to consider writing mentors and their different philosophies, begin to narrow the focus. Your writers are on a mission to discover which writers' philosophy most resonates with them.

Once they have chosen their mentor, research and reflect on the following questions:

- What is the writer's process or system? Is there something in the way this writer approaches writing or creativity that inspires you?
- What does this writer say about the writing process?
- What does this writer say about creativity?
- What do you admire most about this writer?

Tips for working with this prompt

- Choosing a writing mentor makes a great project or topic for an oral presentation. Your whole class benefit from each other's information and discoveries.
- Students could create a brief A4 summary of their chosen writing mentor, including how this person influences and supports their writing practice. These summaries can be

collated into a class resource book or used for reading comprehension and other complementary literacy activities.

- Invite students to think about objects and symbols that are related to their writing mentor as a way of linking activities, building visualisation skills and practising higher order thinking.
- Quotes from writing mentors could also be collected on index cards for students to read when they need support and encouragement. Students could read their quote cards as part of their writing rituals (see also: 'Creative flow', page 269).

Teaching focus

- Reflect on beliefs about and personal experience of the writing process.
- Extend knowledge of the writing community, both past and present.
- Develop curiosity and research skills.
- Belong to a wider community of writers by identifying similarities and deep connections with favourite writers.

Resources

'Discovering mentors' prompts

Here are some prompts to for you to choose from to get students thinking:

- Who is a writer you most admire? Why?
- Imagine sitting with this writer. What do you think the writer might say to you?
- If you could meet any writer (past or present), who would you choose? Where would you go? What would you do? What would you talk about? What one question about writing would you like this person to answer?
- What book do you wish you had written? Why?

- Think about your favourite writer. What is this person's writing superpower? What is it about their writing that gets you every time?
- Write a letter to a favourite author. Tell them why you admire them as a writer.
- Choose one of your favourite authors. What do you have in common with this author? How are you most different?
- What writing tips (or even life lessons) have you learned from your favourite writers?

6. Letter-writing

In the last workshop of each term, I invite members of The Writer's Club to stop and reflect on the lessons we have learnt. In one of these discussions, one writer shared his experience of 'brain freeze', an apt description of that desperate sinking feeling of staring down a blank page.

> **A letter to my inner critic (AKA Mr Jim Frank)**
>
> *Ruby (12 years old)*
>
> Hello Mr Jim Frank,
>
> When I write I feel like I'm hurtling down a hill at full speed on a bicycle. But with you, I feel like I have the handbrakes on. You're my inner critic, giver of opinion but burner of hope. I think you might also be responsible for a few mind blanks here and there. When you're in my head, you don't stop, and my face looks as though I've eaten a handful of lemons with the skin on. You take over my mind and my bicycle. I'm happy with you walking on the path but I'd like the bicycle for myself.
>
> Signed, Ruby

It wasn't long before our conversation turned to the voice inside our heads that steps in and takes over: the inner critic. I was surprised at this group's level of understanding. We so often underestimate young writers.

'If you could speak to that voice,' I asked, 'what would you say?'

There were many animated responses. I suggested we each write a letter to our inner critics. I decided to write one too. Then we shared our letters. Some were poignant. Some were hilarious. Sharing our letters somehow shifted the balance of power. These letters to our inner critics gave voice to our fears and vulnerabilities. It reminded me that the stories we have about ourselves as writers are often a greater hurdle than our writing skills. Mindset directs our course in life and writing.

Since that day, I've used letter-writing in many ways and have found that it gives students an immediate audience and invites them to speak from their heart. It also appeals to reluctant writers. Some of the prompts below can be used with little introduction, but others, like the letter to our inner critic, need some prior class discussion. This activity builds on 'Untangling the creative process' (page 231).

How to use this prompt

1. Choose one of the following subjects to write a letter to:
    - your favourite literary character (What do you admire about this character? What questions would you ask them?)
    - a friend or family member that has supported your writing (Imagine you writing a thank-you letter to this person. How have they supported you? What practical things have they done? What are you grateful for?)
    - your writing mentor
    - a famous writer, like Shakespeare or Roald Dahl
    - a community leader (Are there local or global issues you would like to tell them about?)
    - your five-year-old self (What would you tell your five-year-old self about learning to write? How would you encourage them?)
    - your inner critic.
2. Set the timer for five minutes and invite students to write a short letter to their chosen recipient.
3. Workshop responses together. Often writers who are reluctant to share their stories will read parts of a letter out loud.

Tips for working with this prompt

- If the chosen prompt involves writing to a construct (for example, your inner critic) rather than a person, some students may find it easier to give the subject a name, just as Ruby did. It speeds up the personification process by humanising a more abstract concept.
- Depending on the ages and stages of your writers, you might like to scaffold the letter-writing process by creating some sentence starters before you begin.

- Letter-writing prompts can be developed into extended pieces of writing. For example, letters to literary characters can turn into excellent book reviews and reports, while letters to community leaders can be published in various media outlets.
- Using a more casual approach to letter-writing like this allows students to express their thoughts and feelings freely before they are required to construct a more formal piece of writing.

Teaching focus

- Use writing as a tool for critical thinking and self-reflection.
- Strengthen valuable personal skills such as self-awareness, empathy and self-compassion to support the creative journey.
- Develop the language and structure used in letter-writing.
- Cultivate writer's voice by allowing personality to shine through in writing.

7. Planning styles

Templates and graphic organisers are useful writing tools; however, expecting all students to find the same method useful fails to recognise differences in personality and writing styles. Not all students fit neatly inside the same planning framework – one size does not fit all.

> **Planning styles**
>
> *Choetzo (12 years old)*
>
> I'm a planner when I write non-fiction because I like to have all the information there in front of me. For example, if I'm writing about animals, I'll research habitat, food, living, appearance. But when I write fiction, I'm a pantser. I can make it all up in my head because there is no right or wrong.
>
> The good thing about planning is that you don't have so much editing. The bad thing about planning is that you might not get the story down, just the plan.

This exercise helps teachers understand why some students carefully work the plan, while others fill out the plan and then write an entirely different story. It also gives students valuable information about adapting planning styles to suit their personality and preferences. But most importantly, this prompt models a great truth about writing and creativity: there are many structures available to support us. Armed with this knowledge, students can take responsibility for how they approach the writing process.

As well as introducing a range of planning tools, encourage your students to reflect on their natural tendencies and preferred methods of planning a story. Although writers may prefer one planning style, it's important to be open and flexible to new and different ways of working to get the best results.

How to use this prompt

1. Start by reading out the following three broad planning descriptors to your students: *planner*, *pantser* and *ponderer*. I like to provide a hard copy so students can read along too. (A reproducible version of these descriptions is available.)

Planner:
If you are a planner you like to know exactly where you're going with a piece of writing before you begin. You especially want to know how your story will end. You breathe a sigh of relief when your teacher hands you a planning document. You like nothing better than filling it in, and then off you go. You also like to follow your plan to the letter. Sometimes new ideas bubble up as you're writing, but you don't let them float into your story. You follow your plan.

Pantser:
A pantser finds planning tight and restrictive. A pantser dives right in and starts writing. The word pantser *comes from the saying 'to fly by the seat of your pants'.*

(Many children have never heard this saying before, so expect lots of laughter!)

This saying dates to when pilots flew planes without navigational tools and complex computer systems. The pilot used their knowledge, experience and intuition to make judgements and decisions regarding the flight as it progressed. So, if you're a pantser, you rely on your intuition and write as you go, rather than being limited by a predetermined plan.

Ponderer:
A ponderer likes to think things through before writing their plan. In fact, a ponderer likes to think things through before writing anything at all. By the time they get their ideas down on paper, their story is often clear and detailed. Ponderers make interesting and creative connections between ideas because they have considered many options before picking up a pen. A ponderer might suffer from having too many ideas – or the opposite affliction, too few ideas. The pressure to work fast

makes a ponderer feel anxious and hot under the collar. A ponderer might also have a noisy and bossy inner critic; it's hard to stride out into the middle of your story when you have a voice in your ear questioning your every move. Perfectionists will often present as ponderers. They don't want to get ideas down unless they think they are right.

2. Ask students to think about and choose the descriptor or descriptors that best match their planning style. Descriptors help clarify our processes. Usually, we are a delicate mix of all three styles, depending on what we are writing and how we are feeling, but we often identify more strongly with one particular planning style.

3. Share the student sample given at the start of this prompt or my sample here:

   I am undoubtedly a ponderer. I like to think (and think). I like to explore and join all the dots in my head before I start writing. I don't like to miss anything. When I participate in writing workshops myself, I marvel at writers who write quickly and effortlessly.

4. Set your timer for five minutes and invite students to explore their planning processes. Which descriptor did they choose? Explain why and give details if possible.

5. Workshop responses and discuss ideas. Do some planning styles work better for different genres?

Tips for working with this prompt

Extension: The good, the bad and the curious

You may recall using 'The good, the bad and the curious' as a thinking tool for reviewing your writing practice in Chapter 5 (page 106). Here we use Chris Durham's (2003) structure to help students think more deeply about their own planning styles and extend their understanding of how their planning style influences their writing practice.

Reflective writing

Your students need to have completed one or more discovery writing sessions reflecting on their planning style before beginning this extension activity.

Part 1: Getting clear

1. Give your students three large sticky notes each and instruct them write their main planning style at the top of each, followed by 'Good' at the top of one, 'Bad' on the second and 'Curious' on the third.

2. Ask students to respond to the following three prompts on the relevant sticky note:

    a. Write one good or positive aspect of your particular planning style.

    b. Write one bad or negative point related to your specific planning style.

    c. Write one curious question that you would like to explore further.

    Here are examples of responses I might give as a ponderer:

    Good:
    I include lots of details/ideas in my writing because I've thought about the topic in some depth.

    Bad:
    I overthink a topic, which makes me a slow writer. It takes me much longer to get my writing projects finished. Trying to include all the information holds me back. So does perfectionism.

    Curious:
    How do I know when it's time to stop thinking and start writing? What sort of planning template works best for me? Why am I worried about what people think?

3. As a class, collate your answers. For each of the three planning styles you'll now have a list of positives and negatives, plus a host of interesting questions to explore further.

Part 2: Building on curiosity

Your curious questions make excellent student-centred discovery writing prompts. The second part of this extension activity provides inspiration for building on what was learnt in Part 1 to take students' understanding of the planning process to the next level.

Work your questions:

1. Choose one question collected at the end of Part 1, ideally one that is relevant to all planning styles. For example: 'How do I know when it's time to stop thinking and start writing?'
2. Set the timer for five minutes of discovery writing and encourage students write everything they can on that topic.
3. Workshop and discuss responses.

Writing tips and tricks:

1. Choose one of the negative points collected in Part 1. For example:

    I overthink a topic, which makes me a slow writer. It takes me much longer to get my writing projects finished. Trying to include all the information holds me back. So does perfectionism.

2. Flip this response to create a list of writing tips and hacks to address the problem.
3. As a class, list all the actions a ponderer could take to stop overthinking and start writing. Now students can use this class list to produce an instructional piece of writing, such as 'Five ways to stop overthinking and start writing!' In my experience, these pieces of writing are often comical and light-hearted as well as informative.

Letter-writing:

1. Using the structure set out in 'Letter-writing' (page 257), ask students to write a letter to themselves about their dominant planning style.

2. Set the timer for five minutes and prompt students with the question, 'What advice can you give yourself about planning?' Here's my sample:

    Dear Ponderer,

    I know you like to think about all the variables and get ideas sorted in your head, but this sometimes makes it almost impossible to get started. Why don't you try writing in pencil so you can rub things out if you need to add ideas? Also, just jump in sometimes and see what happens. Nothing is set in concrete. You can change your mind, revise and edit.

3. Allow time to workshop and discuss responses.

Teaching focus

- Understand the planning process in greater detail.
- Identify personality and planning style.
- Cultivate being open and flexible to different ways of planning writing.
- Develop problem-solving skills to manage the planning processes.
- Take responsibility for personal processes.

Resources

Planner, pantser or ponderer

Download a free reproducible version of the three broad planning types: planner, pantser and ponderer.

8. Mind freeze

All writers at one time or another have experienced a mental block – or 'mind freeze', as one writer aptly described it to me. It's a fear recognised by writers everywhere, especially during assessment tasks.

> **Untitled**
> *Anonymous*
>
> When I have no ideas, I usually just sit still and stare into space, trying to open my mind, but all I see is blackness. Thinking as hard as possible but nothing.
>
> When this happens, I think of other stories that I've read: what were the elements?
>
> Suddenly something pops into my head and then I think, 'No, but wait. What if I put it with this like that and then I start writing as fast as possible?'

Giving voice to fears instead of glossing over them helps writers unpack their assumptions and personal stories.

A mental block can feel like an assault on our intelligence, but it can also be seen as a regular creative obstacle to overcome. I'm always amazed at the wisdom and experience young writers have to offer each other. Sometimes by normalising mind freeze, a pocket of fresh air opens in our minds – and an open mind is the very thing we need when we are stuck for ideas. 'Mind freeze' is a unique opportunity to tune in to how writers work and encourage them to support each other. This activity is best approached after writers have had a chance to explore the creative process.

How to use this prompt

1. Allow time before you start writing to introduce the topic. The sample given at the start of this prompt helps writers tune in to their thoughts and feelings about the topic.
2. Introduce one prompt from this list to get your writers talking and writing about mind freeze:
   - Can you think of a time when you experienced a mental block and simply had no ideas to get started?
   - Describe in detail how your body feels when you experience mind freeze?

- Write a script that captures the words or conversation that might be taking place inside your head? What conversations are happening inside your head when you experience mind freeze?
- Write a list of ways you overcome mental blocks. Write down everything you can think of that has helped in the past.

3. Set your timer for five minutes of discovery writing about the chosen prompt.
4. Workshop responses, recording any helpful tips for overcoming mind freeze.

Tips for working with this prompt

- Having recorded helpful tips while workshopping, consider collating these ideas to create a class resource. 'What to do when you run out of ideas' is a list of tips collected from writers in Years 4–6, and was printed and distributed to be stapled into their notebooks for future reference.
- If you choose the third prompt, your students will create a brief script to give voice to the internal conversations happening during a mind freeze. These scripts can be transformed into monologues and even comic strips.

What to do when you run out of ideas
Years 4–6

Clear away all distractions from your desk.

Look out the window. Does anything out there trigger an idea?

Take a break – go for a walk out of the room.

Get off your screen. Try handwriting.

Study your plan: what's your character's No 1 goal?

Don't overthink it. Keep it simple.

Ask for advice.

Read what you have written so far. Connect with your story.

Break it down. Focus only on the next paragraph.

Be kind to yourself – positive self-talk.

Read a book in the same genre that you are writing to stimulate new ideas. Or read a book in a completely different genre to spark creative connections.

Teaching focus

- Recognise and normalise the fear associated with mental blocks.
- Troubleshoot common writing obstacles and share ideas and resources.
- Reflect on behaviour and approaches to writing.
- Troubleshoot solutions to common issues and develop problem-solving skills.

9. Creative flow

Creative flow is the mental state of being completely present and fully absorbed in a task. Flow is an ideal state, and it is not achievable every time you sit down to write; however, the more I teach writing, the more I believe that planning for creative flow is the cornerstone of any writing program.

When students experience the magic of creative flow, they see the importance of setting boundaries and managing group behaviour. Your students' experiences of creative flow may relate to a range of creative activities. Encourage your students to start paying attention to what creative flow feels like and how they can get more of it in their lives.

How to use this prompt

Describing creative flow

1. Ask your students to pay attention to how flow feels in their minds and physical bodies.
2. Make one or more of the following three prompts available to start with:
    - What does creative flow feel like to you?
    - Describe what creative flow feels like in your body and in your mind.
    - Can you compare creative flow to other activities? (For example, creative flow feels to me like gliding – weightless, directed but loose, rhythmic.)
3. Set your timer for five minutes of discovery writing and invite students to write about their own flow experiences regarding writing and other creative pursuits.
4. Workshop and compare responses, looking for commonalities.

Maintaining flow

Exploring a selection of binary-opposite working conditions helps writers respond instinctively to a range of personal factors that relate to assisting and maintaining flow.

1. To allow your writers to choose the element that interests them as their prompt, give your writers a hard copy of the pairs shown in figure 11 (available to download and reproduce) and ask them to circle the conditions work best for them. You could instead select a set as a class-wide writing prompt if you prefer.

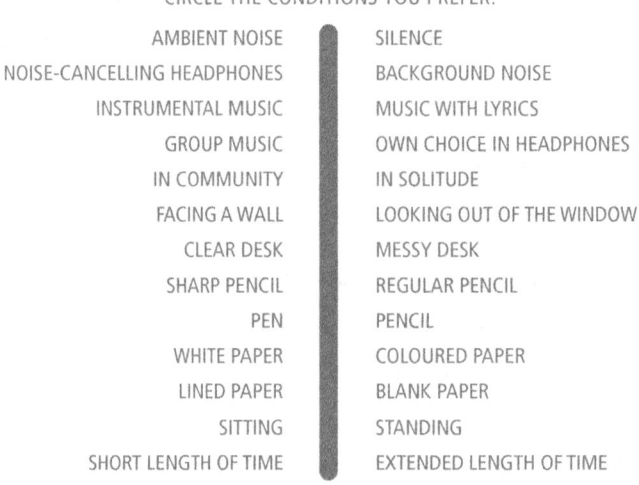

Figure 11: Binary opposites
A free reproducible version of this figure is available

2. Once writers have circled their preferences, set your timer for five minutes and invite writers to expand on any pair that interests them.

3. Workshop and share responses.

Finding flow

Even though discovery writing sessions are limited in time, our writing routines and rituals assist us to find focus and flow.

Reflective writing

1. Prompt writers to reflect on and discuss their writing routines at school and at home. Here are some reflection questions to get you started:
   - How does your writing space impact your ability to be in flow?
   - What distractions break your sense of flow?
   - What parts of the class writing routine really help you access creative flow?
   - What personal routines helps you focus?
2. Set your timer for five minutes and ask students to use this discussion to focus on the specifics of finding flow in their writing.
3. Workshop and share responses.

Tips for working with this prompt

Experiment with ambient noise

It's important to give your students many opportunities to collect valuable data about their creative process. Ambient background noise can improve concentration and flow, so this is a great starting point.

I can recommend trying out *A Soft Murmur* (asoftmurmur.com) in your writing classes. *A Soft Murmur* has an easy interface that can be easily used by writers of all ages, and hosts a range of calming sound clips from wind and fire to white noise. You can play the audio clips at different volumes and on top of one another. The combinations are endless. Best of all, it's free! You can also search YouTube for interesting soundscapes to share with your class, but be careful of distraction-causing ads.

Try bringing some ambient noise to your writing practice and allow time for your class to reflect on the experience.

Teaching focus
- Explore the environmental elements that affect how writers access creative flow.
- Reflect on personal preferences.
- Develop routines and ritual to support creative flow.

Resources

'Binary opposites' template

Download a print-ready list of binary opposites to use with this prompt and extend thinking about writing space.

10. Writing inspiration

What influences and experiences inspire us to write? The process of writing a story doesn't always start when you pick up your pen. Sometimes, an idea is silently planted in your imagination and starts to send out hopeful little shoots and leaves long before the story begins on paper.

If you feed your imagination a good diet of curiosity and inspiring ideas, you'll always be ready to write. If you want to be a better writer, you not only have to pay close attention to the world around you; you also need to find a way to seek out inspiration and store your ideas. If your writers don't record and use their ideas, they are like gardeners who work hard in a vegetable patch but never get to enjoy the luscious bounty.

How to use this prompt

1. Choose and share one of the following prompts designed to help your writers explore inspiration:

    - What places have you visited (virtually or in real life) that have inspired you to pick up a pen and write?

    - Often strong emotions or feelings trigger ideas for writing. Can you think of any times of high emotion or particular personal experiences that have filtered into your writing?

    - How do other writers inspire you to write?

    - How do you collect and record your writing ideas and inspiration? What methods do you use? Digital tools or notebooks? Do you know any methods used by authors and writers for collecting and organising writing ideas?

2. Set your timer for five minutes and invite students to respond to the chosen prompt.

3. Workshop and share responses.

Tips for working with this prompt

Extension: Inspiration maps

To extend this idea further, have students build on the 'Mind maps' activity on page 170 to create an inspiration map. Writers will need a piece of fictional writing and a highlighter for this activity. The fictional writing could be one of the scenes previously created in their notebook. This is an interesting way to show writers the importance of paying attention to what inspires them.

1. Instruct students to read through their story to see if they can trace the inspiration for different elements within their writing. Is anything based on a personal experience? Had they heard it before? Read it? Seen it?
2. Use a highlighter to highlight any parts of the story where writers can map their inspiration.
3. Rather than workshop as a group, break into writing buddies and allow students time to share their writing and any links they recognise.

Teaching focus

- Pay attention to the environment and experiences as sources of inspiration for writing.
- Understand that creative ideas are everywhere and open to everybody.
- Explore simple ways to collect and store ideas for writing.
- Follow curiosity and interests.

Editing games

Editing is a challenging part of the writing process for both teachers and young writers. It's much more than 'cleaning up' a piece of writing at the end of the writing process. Students need relevant, 'on-the-job' training to learn these essential skills.

Editing feels time-consuming and dull compared to the thrill of generating ideas and developing interesting characters. It requires young writers to understand a range of language conventions and to also know how (and when) to apply these rules and concepts to their writing. Immediately we can see the challenges posed by peer editing.

I often see worksheets used to teach grammar and language conventions, but students don't always transfer these skills to their writing. I've found it's more effective to teach skills in context using real writing.

A note on prewriting

Scaffolding the writing process lightens the editing load considerably. When young writers have the opportunity to generate ideas, develop characters, write scenes and map out a story structure before they start writing, the end result requires less editing. In an overcrowded timetable, the effort that goes into prewriting can feel counterproductive, but if you can't find time to build stories with your students, then be prepared to devote (your) time at the end of the writing process to correct, edit, conference and help your writers restructure their writing. Either way, the writing process takes time. It's far less frustrating to put the work in during the creative phase when energy levels are high.

The importance of games

So much time and energy go into writing a story. Young writers are firmly attached to their words on the page. They're also attached to how many words are on the page and how many pages they have written. We praise them for their focus and effort, but in the next breath we suggest they start deleting this or changing that. Reframing this process makes all the difference here. It helps to get playful and turn editing into a game.

Just because you put the word *game* after the word *editing* doesn't mean you'll immediately have your class on board, but once you start to play, watch out. I've seen even reluctant writers willingly – and enthusiastically – participate in these editing games.

Points to consider

Editing games, with their fast pace and edit–share structure, provide a rich source of teachable moments. While you may be holding the space for your class and facilitating the process, it's your writers who have control over their writing. They are actively making decisions about the changes they want to make. These games encourage writers to read their work and take responsibility for maintaining punctuation, spelling and other conventions. This is powerful.

Editing games require teachers to be on the ball, ready to catch the conversation on the whiteboard and be open to any teachable moments that naturally arise. Try scheduling editing games for times when you feel fresh and energetic.

Editing games

Once your writers can play the games confidently, it's possible to get them working together in pairs or small groups. This style of peer editing has real potential, so harness the collective energy.

Set boundaries. Noise levels, available time frame and length of the piece to be edited are all within your control and can have a real impact. The key is to keep it quick. Most writers can edit enthusiastically for short periods of time, so choose just one or two paragraphs to focus on at a time and give your students a deadline to keep the process fast and dynamic. Don't aim for editing a whole story unless it's a particularly short one.

This section contains four different editing games for you to play with your writers:

1. Dumper
2. Scale up
3. The writer's hot seat
4. Turn on your senses

1. Dumper

I've used this simple, fast-paced game over the years to help writers make their writing stronger and more powerful by deleting unnecessary words. In 'Dumper', writers dump (delete) a given number of words in a set period, helping them to clarify their message and make their writing more compelling. After all, editing a piece of writing isn't specifically about pleasing your teacher. It's about being true to your piece of writing and giving it a chance to shine.

To explain the concept of 'Dumper' I use the metaphor of making cordial. When you add less water, the brew is more concentrated; the colour and the taste is stronger and more satisfying. Too many unnecessary words water down our writing. For some writers getting the words down on the page is such an achievement that they do not want to edit or delete a single word. Turning this process into a fun game helps students loosen their grip a little while also teaching writers to read their own work carefully.

How to play this game

Warm-up round: Starting sentences

This warm-up round allows teachers to scaffold learning and build confidence.

1. Ask students to select one or two paragraphs of writing in their notebooks and outline these with a highlighter. This highlighted section of writing will be their game board.

2. Select and explain the time frame and the target number of words to be 'dumped' per round. I usually set two three-minute rounds (including the warm-up round) and aim to dump two or three words in each. The target number will depend on your writers and the length of their pieces of writing.

3. Rather than cross out words completely, instruct students to put a line under the words they choose to delete. This allows writers to track changes.
4. Ask students to put a mark down for every word they delete so they know when they have reached their target.
5. For your warm-up round, ask students to look at how they have started their sentences. Words like *as, so, now* and *because*, for example, are often superfluous and can be deleted.
6. Write these words on the whiteboard so writers can refer to them.
7. Set your timer for three minutes and invite writers to get dumping.
8. Allow time for workshopping and teaching after each round. Students benefit greatly from listening to each other's decisions and reasoning.
9. Choose two or three students to share any of the words they deleted, reading both original sentences and edited versions.
10. Record interesting points of discussion as you go.

Round 1: Intensifiers and adjective strings
1. Working with the same outlined paragraph (or paragraphs) as in the warm-up round, ask students to focus on intensifying words like *very* and *really*. If words like this appear, are they needed? Do they add to the sentence? How does the sentence sound if they are removed? For example, students may have written 'It was very big!' which could simply be 'It was big!'
2. Suggest that students also look for strings of adjectives in this round. Do they all mean the same thing? Would one well-chosen adjective work more effectively?
3. Set the timer for three minutes and get started.
4. As in the warm-up round, allow time to workshop, choosing two or three students to share any of the words they deleted, reading both original sentences and edited versions.

Playing two rounds is usually enough for most writers. It is always best to finish with energy to spare so your students are willing to come back to the activity on another day.

Round 2: Wild card

By now your writers understand how the game works. They are learning to read their own work, make deletions and compare notes with their peers. They are ready to go deeper.

1. Introduce this round as being free choice. Writers are free to choose their own deletions and should aim for at least one or two changes in their pieces of writing.
2. Set the timer for three minutes.
3. As in the first two rounds, allow time for two or three students to share original and edited versions of their work.
4. Maximise the teachable moments in this activity and highlight the impact of word choice, readability and sentence structure.

Teaching focus

- Learn that less is more when it comes to writing.
- Understand that words are powerful and they shouldn't be overcrowded.
- Listen to the rhythm and feel of words as writing is read aloud.
- See that word choice makes a real difference to writing and that it is important to choose the words that capture the exact image you want to convey.

2. Scale up

The mechanics of 'Scale up' work in a similar way to 'Dumper' (page 278), but the focus falls on language and word choice. Writers look for words that can be 'scaled up' to clarify meaning and imagery.

Think of vague descriptions like *big*, or even *very big*. Is there a single word that could work more efficiently? Are you looking for the word *tall*? Or perhaps *gigantic*? 'Scale up' teaches writers to be specific and to swap general overused nouns, verbs and adjectives for words that paint a clear picture in readers' minds.

How to play this game

Warm-up round: Adjectives

As in 'Dumper', this warm-up round allows teachers to scaffold the learning and build confidence.

1. Ask students to select one or two paragraphs of writing in their notebooks and outline these with a highlighter. This highlighted section of writing will be their game board.

2. Select the time frame and the target number of words to be scaled up per round. I usually set two three-minute rounds (including the warm-up round) and aim for two to five words in each.

3. Rather than cross out words completely, instruct students to put a line under the words they choose to change and write the scaled-up words just above them. This allows writers to track changes.

4. Ask students to put a mark down for every word they scale up so they know when they have reached the target.

5. For this warm-up round, ask students to read their writing for vague or general adjectives such as *nice, good, cool, awesome, old* and *young*.

6. Write a selection of these sorts of words on the board so writers can refer to them. Discuss what kind of words might better capture the meaning they want to convey, then underline the vague adjectives and add your substitutions on top to demonstrate what writers will do.
7. Set your timer for three minutes and invite students to start scaling up.
8. Allow time for workshopping and teaching after each round. Students benefit greatly from listening to each other's decisions and reasoning.
9. Choose two or three students to share any of the words they scaled up, reading both original sentences and edited versions.
10. Record interesting points of discussion as you go.

Round 1: Verbs

In this round, writers will identify and refine their verb usage. Identifying verbs is an interesting grammar lesson. We often rely on worksheets for this type of grammar work, but learning to identify parts of speech in their own writing can be more useful for students.

1. Working with the same outlined paragraph (or paragraphs) as in the warm-up round, direct students to read through their paragraph and underline at least three verbs.
2. Provide an example, such as 'The horse ran up the hill.' Is *ran* the word that best describes how this horse moves? How can we scale up this verb? Did the horse gallop?
3. Set the timer for three minutes and get started. If students need help refining their verbs, consider using a thesaurus.
4. As in the warm-up round, allow time for two or three students to share any of the words they scaled up, reading both original sentences and edited versions.

Playing two rounds may be enough for some writers. It is always best to finish with energy to spare so your students are willing to come back to the activity on another day.

Round 2: Wild card

By now your writers have built their confidence and understand the game. They will have compared notes with their peers and will be ready to go deeper.

1. Introduce this round as being free choice. Writers can choose any words they wish to scale up and should aim to make at least three changes.
2. Set the timer for three minutes.
3. As in the first two rounds, allow time for two or three students to share original and edited versions of their work.
4. Maximise the teachable moments in this activity and highlight the impact of word choice, readability and sentence structure.

Teaching focus

- Choose verbs that best describe the actions of nouns.
- Zoom in and be specific in conveying ideas.
- Read sentences aloud, taking notice of the rhythm and feel of words.
- Choose words that capture the exact image you want to convey.

3. The writer's hot seat

In a bid to motivate writers to pay attention to their writing I created a game called 'The writer's hot seat'. In this game, the writer in the 'hot seat' reads a piece of their writing to the class, while selected class members act out the scene or describe to the writer how they visualised the story. Sometimes, hot-seat writers are totally baffled or even annoyed by the feedback.

This activity gives writers real data about their writing. I've seen writers shift from 'I don't care how it reads and I like it the way it is!' to demanding their classmates listen to the revised version as they head out the door for recess.

How to play this game

1. Ask for a volunteer to read a short piece of writing – ideally just a paragraph or so.
2. Gather your class around the writer so the reading feels contained and focused.
3. Direct audience members to listen carefully, perhaps even closing their eyes to visualise the scene as the writer reads aloud.
4. Now ask the writer to read the piece a second time.
5. Set your timer for three minutes and ask audience members to list as many details about the scene as they can remember.
6. Workshop lists and share responses. Ask probing questions like 'What language helps details stand out in our imaginations?'
7. Record any interesting points of discussion.
8. Set your timer for a further three minutes and this time ask the audience to sketch some detail of the scene – the setting, a character, an object and so on.

9. Workshop these sketches and share with the writer. Is this how the writer imagined it?
10. If time allows, ask members of the class to act out the scene so the writer (and the class) can see it in action. Are there any missing details that need to be added?
11. Give the audience an opportunity to ask the writer any questions.
12. Allow the writer to respond to the feedback. What have they learnt through the process?

Teaching focus

- Observe why details are important.
- Experience testing writing on an audience.
- Receive critical, helpful feedback.
- Understand that the writer's job is to convey ideas to readers as simply and easily as they can.

4. Turn on your senses

We experience the world through our five senses. Sensory details and metaphor activate and engage readers' sensory perception and unlock imagination. Sensory words light up different parts of the brain and allow the reader to hear, see, taste, smell and experience the scene as if they are part of the writing.

Young writers often rely on a string of bland adjectives, opting for quantity over quality, but effective sensory cues point to subtle clues and information. They show rather than tell. The reader has an opportunity to bring the scene to life in their imagination. In this game writers are adding sensory clues to their writing to activate the readers' imagination.

How to play this game

1. Demonstrate the importance of sensory details by using a short excerpt of literature, such as the following three sentences from *Harry Potter and the Philosopher's Stone,* to highlight the impact of sensory details on the reader:

   The envelope was thick and heavy, made of yellowish parchment and the address was written in emerald-green ink. There was no stamp. Turning the envelope over, his hand trembling, Harry saw a purple wax seal bearing a coat of arms; a lion, an eagle, a badge and a snake surrounding a large letter H. (Rowling, 1997, p. 30)

2. Provide copies of your mentor text so writers can listen and see the details in action.

3. Identify and underline the sensory information contained in these three sentences. Consider these fields:
   - weight (heavy)
   - size (thick, large)

- colour (yellowish, emerald-green, purple)
- absence of detail (no stamp)
- texture (parchment, ink, wax)
- emotion (trembling).

4. Now ask students to select one or two paragraphs of writing in their notebook and outline these with a highlighter. This highlighted section of writing will be their game board.
5. Select the time frame and the target number of sensory details to be updated per round. I usually set two three-minute rounds and aim for two to five words.
6. Ask students to read their writing and make choices about where and what sensory details they could add to provide 'show don't tell' clues to engage their readers' senses. Could they give a clue about the size or weight of an object? Could they add a colour or texture? For example, leaves might crunch when a character walks over them. These subtle sensory clues bring a piece of writing to life. Use the fields listed in Step 3 to get started.
7. Set your timer for three minutes and ask students to put a mark down for every sensory detail they add or update so they know when they have reached their target.
8. Rather than cross out a word completely, instruct students to put a line under the word they choose to change or add a caret (^) to mark additions. This allows writers to track their changes.
9. Allow time for workshopping and teaching after each round. Students benefit greatly from listening to each other's decisions and reasoning.
10. Choose two or three students to share any of the words they updated or added, reading both the original sentence and edited version.

11. Record interesting points of discussion as you go.
12. Once you have workshopped and shared ideas, give students an opportunity to have another round as by now they will have additional ideas and sensory details to incorporate into their work.

Extension
1. Ask your writers to choose a sentence or two in the book they are reading, taking note of sensory details.
2. Collect these sentences, the title of the book, author and page number as a resource to draw on for future discussions on this topic.

Teaching focus
- Activate and engage sensory perception.
- Add description and details that bring writing to life.

Conclusion

Once, when my daughter Molly was a preschooler, we sat on a hill near Elwood Beach in Melbourne on a cold winter's evening, watching the sunset.

'If you had good eyes, you could see the whole world from up here. Couldn't you Mum?' she asked.

I shrugged, looking out toward the distant horizon. It had been a long, wet Sunday and I was feeling particularly uninspired.

'You could,' she nodded confidently. 'You just need the right kind of eyes.'

'The right kind of eyes?' I asked.

'Yep. If you have the right kind of eyes, you can see nearly everything!'

She skipped off, but I stayed looking out over the water for some time. That clear image of the right kind of eyes has kept me company for many years now, reminding me to stay open to ideas, to expand my horizons, to widen my perspective.

A new perspective on writing

This book is a personal invitation to teachers of writing to sit back and take in the view. When it comes to our writing programs, it's clear that front-loading curriculum standards and assessment outcomes isn't giving our students the best chance to appreciate writing as a life skill that deepens their creative capacity and enriches their understanding of themselves and the world. If we want to create lifelong independent engaged writers, we need a new way of perceiving the constant push and pull of structure and rigour versus creative freedom.

Your writing practice affords you this middle ground. Your writing practice is designed to help you cultivate creativity in the face of the many demands tugging at your sleeve. For a short period of time each day, you can stop bumping up against the constraints of the system and let your writing program come alive with possibility. You don't need to choose between skill development *or* creativity, between meeting assessment standards *or* acknowledging diversity. Now you have a safe container, a writing practice that promotes writing skills *and* creative processes, independence *and* community, curriculum standards *and* connection, processes *and* outcomes.

Just start

If you have always suspected that there is more to writing than meets the eye, let this book be your guide for the creative journey ahead. But don't just read and reflect – take the action plans offered at the end of each chapter and get started! Within these pages, you have everything you need to develop a daily writing practice in your classroom. Remember to rely on partial solutions and look for ways to get started with what you have, right where you are. Commit to finding out what works for you then modify and adapt your practice as you go to meet the needs of your students. Your daily writing practice is an organic dynamic system. It doesn't require additional materials or fancy resources, but it does require your full attention and intention.

Conclusion

There's room for you to grow here too. When you focus on developing your own relationship with writing, your teaching and facilitating skills will flourish alongside your students. In time, you will also begin to discover the easy flow between your writing practice and literacy program, you will see how they nurture and sustain each other's goals and purpose.

Try, try again

Creativity can feel like a fickle thing. A good piece of writing has me walking on air, whereas a bout of writer's block sees me dodging the often-nasty critique of my inner critic. For some reason, we try to save our students from discovering the simple reality of creativity: we can't create anything unless we are prepared to fail and pivot and try again. Writing more often, making mistakes and trying again is critical if writers are to learn to trust themselves. This is one of the greatest gifts a daily writing practice offers your students.

Growing independent writers takes time; you have to keep at it day after day, but the rewards are great. Your classroom practice sends a powerful and generous message to your students. It says, 'I see you and I hear you. I believe you can be discerning, make interesting connections, claim your creative processes and take responsibility for your writing development.'

When I first started yoga, I had a wonderful teacher called Rita. Once, she stopped us mid-pose and paused for dramatic effect before saying four words that have since become my mantra: 'Be your own guru.' Those four words call me to tune in to myself and rely on my intuition. And now I pass Rita's words on to you. Be your own guru.

The writing process itself is your finest teacher. May this book awaken your intuition, your creativity and your love of teaching and writing. In this age of experts, it's time to back yourself and let writing work its magic.

References

Ahlberg, A. (1991). *Heard It in the Playground*. Puffin.

Allen, K.-A., Kern, P., Waters, L., & Vella-Brodrick, D. (2018). Why don't Australian school kids feel a sense of belonging? *Pursuit*. https://pursuit.unimelb.edu.au/articles/why-don-t-australian-school-kids-feel-a-sense-of-belonging

Anderson, T. D. (2014). Making the 4Ps as important as the 4Rs. *Knowledge Quest*, 42(5), 42–48. https://link.gale.com/apps/doc/A371688428/AONE?u=anon~12c33d71&sid=googleScholar&xid=6908877f

Australian Curriculum, Assessment and Reporting Authority. (n.d.). *Critical and Creative Thinking (Version 8.4)*. www.australiancurriculum.edu.au/f-10-curriculum/general-capabilities/critical-and-creative-thinking/

Australian Primary Principals Association (APPA). (2013). *Primary Principals: Perspectives on NAPLAN Testing and Assessment* (Canvass report). Australian Primary Principals Association.

Ball, D. (1990). *Jeremy's Tail: A Story*. Scholastic.

Barnes, T. D., Kubota, Y., Hu, D., Jin, D. Z., & Graybiel, A. M. (2005). Activity of striatal neurons reflects dynamic encoding and recoding of procedural memories. *Nature, 437*, 1158–1161. doi.org/10.1038/nature04053

Baumeister, R. F., & Leary, M. R. (1995). The need to belong: Desire for interpersonal attachments as a fundamental human motivation. *Psychological Bulletin, 117*(3), 497–529.

Bickford, D. J., & Wright, D. J. (2006). Community: The hidden context for learning. In D. G. Oblinger (Ed.), *Learning Spaces* (pp. 4.1–4.22). Educause.

Brookfield, S. D. (2015). *The Skillful Teacher: On Technique, Trust, and Responsiveness in the Classroom* (3rd ed.). Jossey-Bass.

Buckner, A. (2005). *Notebook Know-How: Strategies for the Writer's Notebook*. Stenhouse Publishers.

Burningham, J. (1994). *Would You Rather?*. Penguin Random House

Buzan, T. (2002). *How to Mind Map: The Thinking Tool That Will Change Your Life*. HarperCollins.

Cameron, J. (1992). *The Artist's Way*. Tarcher.

Claxton, G. (1998). *Hare Brain, Tortoise Mind: Why Intelligence Increases When You Think Less*. HarperCollins.

Clear, J. (2018). *Atomic Habits: An Easy and Proven Way to Build Good Habits and Break Bad Ones*. Random House.

Cleese, J. (2020). *Creativity: A Short and Cheerful Guide*. Random House.

Crabtree, J. R., & Crabtree, J. (2011). *Living With a Creative Mind*. Zebra Collective.

Creech, S. (2001). *Love That Dog*. HarperCollins.

Creech, S. (2009). *Hate That Cat*. Bloomsbury Publishing.

Cregan, B. (2020, August 6). Host a reading. *Write Away With Me*. www.writeawaywithme.com/blog/host-a-reading

References

De Bortoli, L. (2018). *PISA Australia in Focus Number 1: Sense of Belonging at School.* Australian Council for Educational Research (ACER). https://research.acer.edu.au/ozpisa/30

Dirksen, D. J. (2013). *Student Assessment: Fast, Frequent, and Formative.* R & L Education.

Duhigg, C. (2012). *The Power of Habit: Why We Do What We Do and How to Change.* Random House.

Durham, C. (2003). *Chasing Ideas: The Fun of Freeing Your Child's Imagination.* Finch Publishing.

Education Services Australia. (2019). *The Alice Springs (Mparntwe) Education Declaration.* www.educationcouncil.edu.au/site/DefaultSite/filesystem/documents/Reports%20and%20publications/Alice%20Springs%20(Mparntwe)%20Education%20Declaration.pdf

Elbow, P. (1998). *Writing Without Teachers* (2nd ed.). Oxford University Press.

Fletcher, R. (2003). *A Writer's Notebook: Unlocking the Writer Within You.* HarperCollins.

Fox, M. (2013, August 12). The Donald Graves memorial speech for ALEA 2012. *Mem Fox.* https://memfox.com/for-teachers/for-teachers-the-donald-graves-memorial-speech-for-alea-2012/

Fritz, R. (1989). *The Path of Least Resistance: Learning to Become the Creative Force in Your Own Life.* Fawcett Columbine.

Fryer, M. (1996). *Creative Teaching and Learning.* Paul Chapman Publishing Ltd.

Gardner, P. (2011). *The Reluctant Writer in the Primary Classroom: An Investigation of Mind Mapping and Other Pre-Writing Strategies to Overcome Reluctance* (Final Report of the Queens Park Lower School – University of Bedfordshire Partnership: Funded by the Bedford Charity). University of Bedfordshire Repository. https://uobrep.openrepository.com/bitstream/handle/10547/225302/The+Reluctant+Writer+in+the+Primary+Classroom.pdf?sequence=1

Gear, A. (2016). *Writing Power: Engaging Thinking Through Writing*. Hawker Brownlow Education.

Goldberg, N. (1990). *Wild Mind: Living the Writer's Life*. Open Road Media.

Goldberg, N. (2005). *Writing Down the Bones: Freeing the Writer within* (2nd ed.). Shambhala Publications.

Graves, D. H. (1985). All children can write. *Learning Disabilities Focus*, *1*(1), 36–43.

Gregoire, C., & Kaufman, S. B. (2016, January 6). Are the brains of creative people different? *World Economic Forum.* www.weforum.org/agenda/2016/01/are-the-brains-of-creative-people-different/

Griffiths, A. (2000). *Just Crazy!*. Pan Macmillan.

Heick, T. (n.d.). What are the kinds of questions that help students see themselves as learners? *TeachThought.* www.teachthought.com/critical-thinking/student-should-be-able-to/

Janzer, A. H. (2016). *The Writer's Process: Getting Your Brain in Gear*. Cuesta Park Consulting.

Jeffrey, B., & Craft, A. (2010). Teaching creatively and teaching for creativity: Distinctions and relationships. *Educational Studies*, *30*(1), 77–87. doi.org/10.1080/0305569032000159750

Kaufman, J. C., & Beghetto, R. A. (2009). Beyond big and little: The Four C Model of Creativity. *Review of General Psychology*, *13*(1), 1–12. doi.org/10.1037/a0013688

Kirmizi, F. S. (2009). The relationship between writing achievement and the use of reading comprehension strategies in the 4th and 5th grades of primary schools. *Procedia – Social and Behavioral Sciences*, *1*(1), 230–234. doi.org/10.1016/j.sbspro.2009.01.042

Kuh, G. D., Kinzie, J., Schuh, J. H., & Whitt, E. J. (2005). Never let it rest: Lessons about student success from high-performing colleges and universities. *Change: The Magazine of Higher Learning*, *37*(4), 44–51.

Laminack, L. (2017). Mentors and mentor texts: What, why and how? *The Reading Teacher*, 70(6), 753–755. doi.org/10.1002/trtr.1578

Longmuir, F., Allen, K.-A., & Grove, C. (2020, October 5). Begin with belonging: Why schools in Victoria need to focus on connection and wellbeing for term four. *Lens*. https://lens.monash.edu/2020/10/05/1381438/begin-with-belonging-why-schools-in-victoria-need-to-focus-on-connection-and-wellbeing-for-term-four

Macquarie Dictionary Publishers. (n.d.). Create. In *Macquarie Dictionary*. Retrieved May 4, 2022, from www.macquariedictionary.com.au/features/word/search/?search_word_type=Dictionary&word=create

Maisel, E. (2000). *The Creativity Book: A Year's Worth of Inspiration and Guidance*. Penguin.

Ministerial Council on Education, Employment, Training and Youth Affairs. (2008). *Melbourne Declaration on Educational Goals for Young Australians*. www.curriculum.edu.au/verve/_resources/national_declaration_on_the_educational_goals_for_young_australians.pdf

National Advisory Committee on Creative and Cultural Education (NACCCE). (1999). *All Our Futures: Creativity, Culture and Education*. https://sirkenrobinson.com/pdf/allourfutures.pdf

Puccio, G. J. (2017). From the dawn of humanity to the 21st century: Creativity as an enduring survival skill. *Journal of Creative Behavior*, 51(4), 330–334. doi.org/10.1002/jocb.203

Quate, S., & McDermott, J. (2009). *Clock Watchers: Six Steps to Motivating and Engaging Disengaged Students Across Content Areas*. Heinemann.

Robinson, K. (2009). *The Element: How Finding Your Passion Changes Everything*. Penguin.

Robinson, K. (2011). *Out of Our minds: Learning to Be Creative* (2nd ed.). Capstone.

Rowling, J. K. (1997). *Harry Potter and the Philosopher's Stone.* Bloomsbury.

Seban, D., & Tavşanlı, Ö. F. (2015). Children's sense of being a writer: Identity construction in second grade writers workshop. *International Electronic Journal of Elementary Education*, 7(2), 217–234.

Uncapher, M. R. & Wagner, A. D. (2018). Minds and brains of media multitaskers: Current findings and future directions. *Proceedings of the National Academy of Sciences*, 115(40), 9889–9896. doi.org/10.1073/pnas.1611612115

Wagner, R. (2016, February 16). Plummeting sheep and the tortoise mind: John Cleese on 'liberating' creativity. *Forbes.* www.forbes.com/sites/roddwagner/2016/02/16/plummeting-sheep-and-the-tortoise-mind-john-cleese-on-liberating-creativity/?sh=552fa3a83fb4

Wallas, G. (1926). *The Art of Thought.* Harcourt, Brace.

Williams, M. C. (1923). *Spring and All.* Contact Publishing Co

Yagelski, R. P. (2011). *Writing as a Way of Being: Writing Instruction, Nonduality, and the Crisis of Sustainability.* Hampton Press.

Index

A

adjectives
   for atmosphere and mood, 198
   editing, 121, 279–280, 281–282
   responding to prompts, 162, 221
   review, 165, 222
   sensory details, 286

Ahlberg (1991), 161

Alice Springs (Mparntwe) Education Declaration, 27–29, 35, 44

Allen et al. (2018), 132

Anderson (2014), 23–24, 26

assessment
   collegial discussions, 87, 105, 127
   formal and informal, 12–13, 92, 100, 105, 127
   impact of, 6, 7, 17
   as learning activities, 6
   single or multiple phase approaches, 91
   tools, 100

auditory tools
   ambient noise, 271
   for atmosphere and mood, 198
   examples of, 72, 74, 200–201
   to inspire genres, 103
   soundtracks, 200

Australian Curriculum, 27, 29, 34–35

author visits. *see* literary connections

B

Ball (1990), 243

Bickford and Wright (2006), 131

binary opposites
   and continuums, 247
   for persuasive writing, 190
   as prompts, 247, 272
   and writing flow, 270
   writing spaces, 245

Brookfield (2015), 23, 50, 84

Buckner's (2005), 176

Burningham (1994), 180

Buzan (2002), 170

C

Cameron (1992), 136

characters
    collaborating and sharing, 206
    in the conclusion, 239–240
    developing, 32, 37, 46, 98, 103, 155, 157, 168, 205–208, 287
    examples of, 37, 157
    journals, 157
    from literature, 258
    in plot development, 31, 238
    visual prompts, 195, 207
    voice development, 191

Claxton (1998), 48, 55, 70

Clear (2018), 57, 60

Cleese, John (2020), 55, 70

codes of conduct, 74, 86, 107, 150–151

collaborating and sharing
    benefits of, 44
    codes of conduct, 150–151
    and feedback, 93
    metaphors, 250
    parents and guardians, 138, 143
    in workshopping, 48
    writing environment, 73

collegial discussions
    classroom observations, 87
    creativity and environments, 70
    'everyone is creative', 36
    informal and formal assessment, 105, 127
    routines, 70
    suspending judgement, 87
    workshopping writing, 87
    writing conventions, 88
    writing programs, 36

community and belonging, sense of
    Australian education goals, 27–29
    in Australian students, 131–132
    benefits of, 132, 150
    classroom, 39, 113
    developing, 132
    human connectors, 131
    and mentors, 253
    Organisation for Economic Co-Operation and Development (OECD) on, 131
    workshopping, 48, 66
    writing community, 11, 51, 129, 131–132, 146
    and writing practice, 113, 131
    writing practice, 230

confidence building
    in editing process, 278–279, 283
    parent and guardian connections, 142–143
    risk-taking, 74, 175
    sense of security and safety, 58
    using feedback, 50, 84

Crabtree and Crabtree (2011), 24

creative flow, 107–108, 269, 270, 271, 273, 274

creativity
    choices and decisions, 32–33
    collaborating and sharing, 16, 29, 33
    collegial discussions, 36
    and connections, 202, 252
    feedback, 22–23
    Gregoire and Kaufman (2016), 22

and imagination, 20
impacts on, 23–24, 30
Kaufman and Beghetto (2009), 20–21, 23
myths about, 19–26
National Advisory Committee on Creative and Cultural Education, 20
planning and preparing for, 231–233
processes, 20–21, 236
prompts, 33
risk-taking and trial and error, 31
science of, 21–22
tools, 237
and visual perception, 289
Wallas (1926), 22–23

Creech (2001, 2009), 222

Cregan (2020), 142

critical thinking skills, 97, 147, 189

curriculum
and creativity, 290
cross-curriculum, 27, 44, 97, 147
guidelines, 85, 99
Melbourne Declaration of Educations Goals for Young Australians (2008), 26–27
national. *see* Australian Curriculum
and NAPLAN, 5
standardised, 17, 83, 91–92, 101

D

De Bortoli (2018), 131

Duhigg (2012), 57

Durham (2003), 106, 262

E

editing
and classroom management, 277
collaborating and sharing, 284–285
intensifiers and adjectives, 279–280, 281–282
paragraph starters, 278–279
self-editing, 103
sensory words, 286–288
skill development, 103
for succinct writing, 278–279
with thesaurus, 282
verbs, 283
vocabulary choices, 281
and writing process, 275–276

Education Services Australia (2019), 27–28, 44

Elbow (1998), 43–44

emotional intelligence, 113, 179

environment, 41, 43

environments for writing
classroom, 60
collegial discussions, 70
distractions, 62–63
at home, 138–139
silence or sounds, 73
workshop ideas, 244–247

F

feedback
and assessment, 92–93
to build confidence, 50–51, 151
builds confidence, 84
encourages writing, 84
examples of, 84, 88–89
loop, 49–50, 93

    student centred, 92, 97, 115, 117–118
Fletcher (2003), 166
flow of writing
    in creative writing, 25–26, 269–271
    distractions, 271
    guidelines, 63–64
    questions of, 107–108
    and routines, 10, 43
    sensory cues, 59
    stream-of-consciousness, 45
    writing practice, 155, 248, 269–270
    writing spaces, 244, 270
Fox (2013), 135–136, 140
Fritz (1989), 32, 33

G

Gardner (2011), 111–113, 126, 128, 137
Gear (2016), 155
genres and structures, 196
Goldberg (1990), 47, 48, 163–164
Goldberg (2005), 63–64
Graves (1985), 3, 42, 135–136
Griffiths (2000), 243

H

handwriting, 68

I

icebreakers, 176, 186
imagery
    developing, 46
    and ideas, 61, 75
    imaginative writing, 46
    and metaphors, 238
    and parts of speech, 222
    in poetry, 119, 193
    and visualisation, 193–195
    word choice, 281
    workshopping, 75
imaginative writing
    auditory prompts, 199–201
    character development, 205–208
    poetry, 221
    sensory details, 211
    settings and times, 219, 225, 227
    visual prompts, 195, 212–213, 223

J

Janzer (2016), 34
Jeffrey and Craft (2004), 23–24, 134
journalling
    benefits of, 13, 179–181
    Cameron (1992), 136
    home writing tasks, 138
    prompts, 180–181

K

Kaufman and Beghetto (2009), 20–21

L

Laminack (2017), 147
letter-writing, 257–258
literary connections, 145–146, 235

M

Melbourne Declaration of Education Goals for Young Australians (2008), 26–27
mental blocks, 146, 266, 267
mentors, 147, 148, 253–255

metaphors
  benefits of, 241
  collaborating and sharing, 250
  developing, 238, 243
  and imagery, 238
  and word banks, 249
  of writing, 249
mind-mapping
  benefits of, 172
  building connections, 204, 251
  for character development, 207
  examples of, 171–172
  planning writing, 170
mood and atmosphere, 195, 198–200

N

NAPLAN, 5–7
National Advisory Committee on Creative and Cultural Education, 20, 23

O

objects
  to develop ideas, 250
  examples of, 212–213
  and mentors, 255
  as personal symbols, 251
  prompting connections, 209, 211–212
  as prompts, 209–213
  and vocabulary development, 220, 249

P

parents and guardians
  building connections, 134, 137–138, 140–142, 143–144, 176
  expectations, 112, 137

personal writing, 46, 157–159, 183–184
plots
  development, 46, 239, 241
  endings, 240
  visual cues for outlines, 240
poetry
  analysing, 160–161
  collaborating and sharing, 220
  haiku, 120, 123, 221
  list poetry, 119, 121, 159–162
  prompts, 162
  samples, 169
  storyboarding, 120
  structure analysis, 220
  tools, 222
  verbs in, 159
  Williams (1923) 'The red wheelbarrow', 220–221
  workshopping, 160–161
prompts
  auditory, 198–199
  collaborating and sharing, 154, 180
  for creative thoughts, 15
  debate-centred, 190–192
  examples of, 158, 162, 236, 252
  icebreakers as, 187–188
  for journals, 154, 180–181
  for mental blocks, 266
  for mentors, 255
  for personal writing, 158
  perspectives on, 191
  for poetry, 162
  and questions, 167, 174
  reflective writing, 252
  revisiting, 154
  sketching as, 120

and topics, 165
visual, 195–197, 209–213, 223
psychology of creativity, 21–22

Q

questions
    developing, 166–167, 169
    examples of, 115
    for personal writing, 183–184
    and prompts, 167, 174
    for teacher data collection, 115–116
    techniques, 83

R

reading aloud, 39, 47
reflective writing, 47, 252
reluctant writers
    causal models, 111–113
    and editing, 276
    engagement of, 122–124
    letter-writing, 257
    visual prompts, 223
    workshopping, 82, 118
Robinson, (2009), 3–4
Robinson, (2011), 20
routines
    adaption of, 67, 95
    auditory cues, 72
    benefits of, 56–59, 66, 68, 70–71, 74
    collaborative planning, 67, 71
    collegial discussions, 70
    distractions, 73
    examples of, 66, 71
    impact on students, 58
    and neurological pathways, 57
    in writing programs, 45

Rowling (1997), 286

S

self-evaluation, 101–103
self-perception, 132, 259
self-talk, 120, 232–235
sensory tools
    and classroom management, 60
    cues, 57, 59–60, 72
    examples of, 59–60, 165
    objects, 209, 211–212
    perception, 22, 67, 83–84, 217
    in writing, 80, 157, 163, 164, 286–288
settings and times, 37, 198, 217, 219, 225–226, 227
spaces for writing. *see* environments for writing
storyboarding, 120
stream-of-consciousness writing, 45
students
    authorship examples, 161, 198, 200, 257, 260, 267
    collaborating and sharing, 44, 106–107
    confidence, 27–28, 44
    home writing tasks, 138
    impact of routines, 58
    impacts on engagement, 6
    individual voice and style, 29–30
    inner critic, 44
    learning, 27, 28, 29, 34
    notebooks, 52–53
    ownership of processes, 8, 25, 71, 82
    question lists, 166–167
    self-evaluation, 101–102

self-knowledge, 263
self-perception, 132, 178–179
self-talk, 232–235
sense of belonging and community, 28–29
skill identification, 120–121
suspend judgement, 250
and writing conventions, 276
writing identity, 132–133

T

teachers
    aims and goals, 116, 154
    building trust, 234
    collaborating and sharing, 14, 137
    and creativity, 77
    expectations of, 6
    flexibility, 25, 154
    impact of, 23–24, 79, 112, 134
    observations and data collection, 78–79, 81–83, 87, 93, 97–101, 113–114, 116–117, 120
    planning and preparing, 235
    positive feedback, 79–80, 83
    pressures on, 26
    question techniques, 83
    and reluctant writers, 112, 118
    workshopping, 49, 76, 104–105
    as writers, 134–137, 175, 177
thesaurus, 282
time
    impact of shortages, 4, 17
    positives of restraints, 26
tools
    formulas, graphic organisers and templates, 25, 31
    mind-mapping, 170–172
    for personal writing, 184
    poetry analysis, 220, 222
    productive or counterproductive, 25
    quote cards, 255
    timers, 62
    verb lists, 103
    vocabulary lists, 204, 215
    writing practice, 94
trust, building, 175, 234

V

verbs
    editing, 283
    'ing' verbs, 159
    lists, 103
    workshopping, 103–104, 159–160, 282
visual prompts
    for character development, 207
    objects, 130, 209–210, 212–213, 220–221, 248, 250–251, 255
    and questions, 195–196
    shapes, 223
voice
    characters, 191, 205
    and discovery writing, 45
    in letter-writing, 259
    literary voices, 145
    in poetry, 159
    reading aloud, 48, 140

W

Wagner (2016), 62
Wallas (1926), 22–23, 24, 32, 231, 235
Williams (1923), 220, 221

workshopping
    benefits of, 47, 74, 76, 140
    collaborating and sharing, 48
    collegial discussions, 87
    hearing language patterns, 48, 75
    mindful pauses, 66
    preparation, 84, 105–106
    for skill development, 85
    teacher reservations, 76
    verbs, 103–104, 159–160, 282
    voice, 48

writing conventions
    collegial discussions, 88
    role of, 147
    spelling, 30, 155
    students take responsibility, 276

writing practice
    aims and goal-setting, 65, 116
    audience, 257
    codes of conduct, 74, 86, 107, 150–151
    and emotional intelligence, 113
    individual approaches, 44
    inner critic, 257
    language of, 3
    linear process, 31–32
    metaphors for, 61, 104
    reflection on, 114–115, 203
    routine, 40–43
    self-talk, 120
    time constraints, 43
    valued, 133

writing processes and programs
    author visits, 145
    collegial discussions, 36
    goal-setting, 125
    linear, 3
    single period productions, 3
    timed writing, 64–65

writing spaces. *see* environments for writing

Y

Yagelski (2011), 130

www.ingramcontent.com/pod-product-compliance
Lightning Source LLC
Chambersburg PA
CBHW081718100526
44591CB00016B/2416